# THE BEST BUSINESS SCHOOLS' ADMISSIONS SECRETS

## A Former Harvard Business School Admissions Board Member Reveals the Insider Keys to Getting In

## CHIOMA ISIADINSO, M.ED.

SOURCEBOOKS, INC.®
NAPERVILLE, ILLINOIS

Published by Sourcebooks, Inc.
PO Box 4410, Naperville, Illinois 60567-4410
(630) 961-3900
Fax: (630) 961-2168
www.sourcebooks.com

Library of Congress Cataloging-in-Publication Data
Isiadinso, Chioma.
  The best business schools' admissions secrets : a former Harvard Business School Admissions Board member reveals the insider keys to getting in / Chioma Isiadinso.
    p. cm.
  Includes bibliographical references and index.
  1. Business schools--Admission. 2. Master of business administration degree. 3. Business education. I. Title.
  HF1111.I85 2008
  650.071'1--dc22
                                    2008015091

Printed and bound in the United States of America.
VP 10 9 8 7 6 5 4 3 2 1

*To Ari for bringing me constant sunshine*

# CONTENTS

# ACKNOWLEDGMENTS

THERE WERE COUNTLESS INDIVIDUALS who were instrumental in making this book a reality.

I'd like to thank my husband, Obinna, for your entrepreneurial spirit which has somehow rubbed off on me. Your ability to envision possibilities and your unwavering support has enabled me to write this book.

I happen to believe in fate and faith and I have to thank Rita Rosenkranz, my agent, for believing in me and taking a step of faith with me on this journey. I extend a heartfelt thanks to Fern Reiss who provided me with the opportunity to meet my wonderful agent. I would like to also thank the publishing team at Sourcebooks for their professionalism and commitment to this book. A special thanks to my editor, Peter Lynch, for his encouragement, patience, and incisive ability to help me tell this story in the best way possible.

I am grateful to the many talented clients I have had the fortune to work with through my consulting practice, EXPARTUS. Your stories continue to inspire me and I am thrilled for your successes. I want to also thank all the business school alumni and students who volunteered to share their essays for this book. Thank you for opening up your lives and essays. Your stories will help many future applicants glean insights on how to tell their stories in a compelling way. Many thanks to everyone who participated in interviews for this book: Fred Chima, Selena and Khary Cuffe, Fernando D'Alessio, Recy Dunn, Jevelyn Bonner-Reed, Chris Ryan, Andrew Yang, and Rachel Zlotoff.

I would also like to thank Michael and Bonnie Carter, Nadja Fidelia, and Dr. Gloria Hill, for your mentorship and continued support. This book talks about the importance of having brand champions and you have been a major blessing! Mariela Dabbah, your editorial help was truly remarkable. Thank you for believing in this book from its inception.

I would be remiss not to thank the amazing individuals I have had the fortune to work with both at Harvard and Carnegie Mellon. Particularly, Kirsten Moss, Eileen Chang, Patty Dowden, Dee Leopold, (Prof) James Cash, Brenda Peyser, (Dean) Mark Wessel, Ty Walton, Barbara Brewton, Elizabeth Casale, Carol Young, (Prof) Janusz Szczypula, and (Provost) Mark Kamlet. My amazing team at EXPARTUS, thank you for being a joy to work with.

A special thanks to all my family and friends for their patience and for putting up with me while I raced through completing my manuscript during the busiest application season. Drs. Emmanuel and Maria Obiechina, you remain amazing role models. I am blessed to have you as parents and you continue to motivate me to do the best I can. I will be forever thankful to my beloved mother-in-law, Mrs. Rose Isiadinso, for her calm spirit and help as I balanced managing a business, writing a book, and being a new mom.

I am grateful for the opportunity to live my passion of helping people access the best education possible. For this, I am blessed and thankful to God.

# FOREWORD

I HAD ONLY APPLIED TO one MBA program, Harvard Business School. At the time, applying to an MBA had been a last minute idea. I had originally planned to pursue a Law degree and a legal career in the footsteps of one of my heroes, Reginald Lewis. However, a mentor of mine challenged me to really take inventory of the type of career to which I aspired and to reconsider what was truly the best environment in which to build the necessary skill set to ultimately reach my goals. After a painful reassessment of what I was really seeking as a career, I came to the determination that an MBA was the ideal preparation. I scrambled to apply and mailed it the day of the final deadline. Fortunately, I was admitted. This was 18 years ago.

The MBA application process has become increasingly more competitive in recent years, with schools admitting only a fraction of applicants. Yet the MBA remains a powerful education in preparing individuals to accelerate their career growth as well as make significant career change. In reflecting on my own business school application, I know that I was quite fortunate to be admitted. I recognize that the odds of pulling off a stunt like that today is nearly impossible and certainly not advisable.

Why should anyone applying to business school read this book? If you want to have a guide that can give you a road map to navigate what can be a difficult and treacherous road, and you want to increase your odds of success, then this is precisely the book for you. *The Best Business Schools' Admissions Secrets* removes the guess work out of the application process and lays out necessary steps to help you shore-up your weaknesses and play to your strengths. This book is written by an admissions expert who has worked for top institutions and has actually sat on the admissions board evaluating candidates. Chioma understands the subtle and not so subtle positioning that differentiates those who are admitted and those who are rejected. The insights covered in this book will arm you with a game plan that increases your likelihood of success.

Admissions people are looking to understand what makes each candidate tick and they seek to understand what each candidate will bring to the class. At the end of the day, all you have are the sum of the activities, experiences, and impressions that you have left in your wake. And when I think about what has really influenced the trajectory of my current career, it has been about developing and maintaining a reputation of courage, integrity, and leadership. You want to leave that type of impression with every client, colleague, and employer you encounter. A commitment to excellence should be the key "leave behind" for everyone interested in providing a memorable profile, especially for the Admissions staff who will evaluate your application. However, building your brand does not end with enrollment in business school; one must continuously manage his/her brand while in school and throughout one's career. After all, the classmates you meet in business school are forming their impressions of your brand and may over your career be positioned to act upon those impressions in the capacity of a competitor, partner, and in some cases employer. In summary, your brand and reputation are really all you have at the end of the day—so manage them well.

*Michael Carter, Managing Director, Lehman Brothers Inc.*

# INTRODUCTION

I HAD BEEN IN THE admissions business for three years (Carnegie Mellon) when I moved to Cambridge to take on an assistant director role at Harvard Business School. From the open houses to information sessions to the countless phone calls that barraged the admissions offices every day, one thing was clear: applicants to business school were stressed out about their applications. Business schools, sensitive to the stress that surrounds the application, have made strides to create more admissions transparency and provide applicants with more opportunity to "connect" with the Admissions Board. But it is safe to say that with rejection numbers still in the 80 to 90 percent range, applicants recognize that they are up against significant odds to earn an admission spot at their top MBA program. Application numbers are not slowing down either; the Graduate Management Admission Council (GMAC) reported that two thirds of member MBA programs indicated an increase in the number of applications in 2006. The GMAT current trend indicates a 13.70 percent increase in worldwide test volume in January 2008 compared to the same time in 2007. The numbers are growing as well outside of the United States. GMAC reports that registration volume outside the U.S. grew by 27.58 percent in January of this year compared to the same time last year.

It is this sheer competition that drives applicant sentiment to a frenzied crescendo. In this high-stakes world, many intelligent individuals discard common sense for myths and hearsay. The folklore surrounding admissions to elite business schools is legendary and endless. Some of them include bets that applying in particular rounds can guarantee a favorable admissions outcome; others focus on the belief that recommendations from alumni are a shoo-in versus those from recommenders who do not have a brand name degree; others center around jumping on bandwagons that applicants believe are popular. The social enterprise bandwagon is one such example. While on the Admissions Board at Harvard Business School, I saw my fair share of the awkward social enterprise tack-on that was simply an attempt on the part of the applicant to say, "Look, I have my quota of social-conscious contributions." Admissions Boards see right through such gimmicks quickly.

Of course one can't talk about the misconceptions of business school admissions without encountering the issue of legacy. Unlike undergraduate admission, where children of alumni get a slight bump, at the top MBA programs, legacy does not have much bearing in the admissions process. It is important for candidates to know ahead of time that they cannot count on having a parent who attended Stanford or Wharton to be enough to get them admitted.

One of the most popular myths surrounding MBA admissions is the perception that there is a certain profile or formula that leads to a coveted offer. I often hear candidates lament over the fact that they don't come from blue chip firms like Goldman, TPG, McKinsey, and Schlumberger. Others focus on the fact that they attended South Dakota State University and worry that they can't compete with the Ivy-educated applicants who saturate the admissions pool. This perspective could not be further from the truth. The reality is that there isn't a hidden formula that guarantees acceptance to a top business school. Certainly, you will find a good number of Ivy-educated candidates from name brand firms in the applicant pool. But you will also find a sizeable number of non-Ivy-educated candidates from firms that do not fall in the "usual suspect" category. The diverse backgrounds of admitted students show that there isn't a cookie cutter profile to the selection process.

But the process of selecting who gets admitted and who doesn't is a combination of science (the numbers) and art (the branding). The MBA Boards evaluate candidates on limited information (a few pages in an application and a thirty-minute conversation) to decide which candidates are a fit and have the most compelling stories. This is why it is very common to see two applicants with nearly identical backgrounds (as far as raw numbers and work experience) apply to the same business school but one receives a rejection letter while the other is admitted.

The difference in outcome is usually a result of how each candidate marketed himself or herself. We have all heard of the 750 GMAT, 3.7 GPA, Ivy-educated Wall Street superstar analyst who received interview invitations from Harvard, Stanford, Wharton, and Columbia, only to be rejected by all four schools. Clearly this candidate had the numbers, but having the numbers isn't enough to guarantee admission. It's how you position the data and what that information reveals about you that can make or break the application outcome. Successful applicants present a profile that is differentiated from others with similar backgrounds. It is this differentiation that tips the scale on who gets a congratulatory phone call and who doesn't.

These differentiated candidates often have one thing in common: they were memorable. I pondered what these candidates had that gave them an edge in the application process. It wasn't until after I left Harvard and launched my consultancy firm EXPARTUS that it dawned on me that the successful applicants to business school had figured out what many consumer goods companies know too well: the importance of selling one's value proposition to the customer. The 20 percent of applicants who are admitted to top business schools understood that the application process is a marketing exercise. These successful candidates have a strong sense of their personal brand (what sets them apart from their competition) and have been effective in communicating their uniqueness to the Admissions Boards.

## PERSONAL BRANDING AS A POWERFUL TOOL IN THE ADMISSIONS PROCESS

I focus *The Best Business Schools' Admissions Secrets* on personal branding as it relates to the admissions process. After many years in the admissions business, I am convinced that the greatest mistake applicants to business schools make is that their applications lack a compelling brand. Most applicants pay way too much attention trying to "game" the system and figure out what the Admissions Boards want to hear instead of taking a step back to assess their own stories and to present them in an authentic, powerful way.

Developing one's personal brand requires significant introspection, something that is a make or break in the application process. Also, being extremely smart, with an 800 GMAT score and near-perfect GPA, isn't enough to guarantee admission to your dream business school. The applicant pool is teeming with candidates with precisely the same academic backgrounds. Being brainy can be a necessary but not sufficient prerequisite in the application process. Conversely, there are enough instances of successful candidates with academic data that are below the school's admission range. An interesting and compelling brand can land candidates into their dream schools, even when their academic numbers are not exceptional. Nonetheless, this is not an excuse to ignore the academic components of the application.

*The Best Business Schools' Admissions Secrets* will examine how applicants can use branding techniques to achieve admission success. I will begin by discussing why a candidate would even consider an MBA in the first place. I will also discuss the three main admissions criteria that candidates are evaluated on (academic ability, leadership track record, and uniqueness) and will provide specific insights on how to address each of them. I will provide anecdotes to convey the nuanced differences that lead to successful brand positioning. I will also devote a chapter to each of the application components (essays, resume, recommendations, and interviews). Wherever applicable, I will present a case to illustrate how an applicant navigated the application process.

*The Best Business Schools' Admissions Secrets* will also examine the common admissions mistakes candidates make as well as offer practical tips to help you avoid making the same application errors. I'll examine admissions outcomes and how to effectively manage each of them.

I often hear applicants raise the issue of financing the MBA, so I have also devoted a chapter to discussing financing resources and how to go about planning to fund the business education. I have also interviewed alumni of top business schools as well as a GMAT test provider and former Admissions Board member to present additional insights to help you navigate the challenging admissions terrain.

The idea of individuals as personal brands is a relatively new way of thinking made popular by personal brand guru Tom Peters. Personal branding is based on tried-and-true principles of traditional marketing. Robin Fisher Roffer, author of *Make a Name for Yourself*, describes the power of personal branding when she says, "Branding makes you an active partner in fulfilling your destiny in business and life."

I have written *The Best Business Schools' Admissions Secrets* not only to help candidates gain admission to top business schools but also to help them develop a clearer sense of "who they are" and "what matters to them"—their brand. Books that have been the most meaningful to me often have every other page marked up, highlighted, or overrun with a lot of notes. I encourage you to write down your thoughts as you read this book. It should be a good reference even after you have read it once, and you should go back and revisit sections that are relevant when you begin working on your application.

While I don't expect that this book will answer every single question you have about the application process, I anticipate that it will answer the majority of the burning ones. I have written this book for anyone who is seriously considering an MBA and wants to maximize his or her chance of gaining admission to a top business school. I have focused the examples primarily on top business schools that are based in the United States. Many of the lessons learned here can be applied to any business school, however. This book will give you an inside perspective of how the nation's top MBA Admissions Boards think and how they evaluate candidates.

*The Best Business Schools' Admissions Secrets* is also designed to empower you to reach for your dreams and to begin to take the necessary steps to live a passion-filled life. It is more than simply getting into the school of your dreams. It is about finding fulfillment in your life, tapping into what matters most to you, and charting a plan to achieve those things that bring you meaning.

I believe that every individual has a God-given set of talents and passion and when you pursue your dream, you have no choice but to succeed. I ultimately believe that if you spend most of your time doing what you truly enjoy, you will become brilliant at it and will achieve success in other areas of your life. Getting into your dream MBA program is one of the steps along the journey of living a passion-driven life. I wish you great success along the way.

# CHAPTER ONE

## Deciding on the MBA

WANTING AN MBA IS a good thing. It suggests that you are ambitious and willing to push yourself to achieve a goal. But before starting on your application, you should examine what an MBA means to you. Be clear of your motivations and goals before embarking on the extremely challenging and expensive application process.

All top business schools will expect you to address why you want an MBA. They each will word this question differently, but what they want to understand is what your career goal is and whether an MBA is necessary to help you achieve it. Equally important to the MBA Board is understanding whether your career aspirations reflect your true passion or whether they are simply the way for you to get your ticket punched. The issue of fit is also a very important one to business school Admissions Boards. They want to ensure that their program is right for you and that you are right for their program.

The justification for an MBA will vary from one applicant to the next. The important thing is to remain true to who you are when presenting your rationale for pursuing an MBA. In this chapter, I will examine the four most popular reasons applicants cite for wanting to attend business school and how the

Admissions Boards view these reasons. I will also review the benefits of obtaining an MBA and the different variables that candidates use in selecting a business program.

Applying to business school will cost you a fair chunk of money. The average application fee is $200, and given the acceptance rate of 10 to 20 percent, most applicants apply to four or more schools. In addition to the cost of the application fee, there is the Graduate Management Admission Test (GMAT) to think of. With average GMAT prep programs charging about $1100 to $1500 (not including one-on-one tutoring), you should expect to shell out at least $2000 just to apply to business schools. If you decide to hire an admissions consultant to guide you along the way, this figure can increase significantly. The MBA itself is a very expensive investment, with costs north of $140,000. And I haven't even touched on the opportunity cost of leaving a lucrative job and forfeiting a salary and bonus for two years. If you include the lost income, the MBA price tag can easily be more than $200,000. So before you take the application plunge, make sure the MBA is necessary to achieve your career goals.

The good news is that although the MBA costs a considerable amount of money, the payoff can be substantial, with many graduates from top programs earning twice what they used to earn prior to receiving an MBA. But the payoff isn't only monetary. Many MBAs receive other perks, such as greater career exposure, contacts, skills, and so on. Before delving deeper into the benefits of the MBA, which I will further examine in this chapter, let's take a look at two major admissions traps that applicants fall into: jumping on MBA bandwagons and applying because they are unemployed.

## AVOID MBA BANDWAGONS

The MBA Board will be checking to make sure you are not simply getting on the MBA bandwagon because all of your friends are applying to business school. The MBA Board also wants to ensure that you are not applying simply because your firm has a structure where employees complete a two-or three-year analyst program and then have to leave. Analysts and consultants in investment banking and strategy consulting face this issue the most. It is understood that a majority of analysts and consultants will "move on" after two to three years and a significant number will end up pursuing their MBA degree. But this expectation of going for your MBA is not a strong enough reason to convince the MBA Board that you are serious about the degree. Candidates in these categories need to make a clear pitch for what their specific MBA goals are and how the particular program is best positioned to help them achieve their future success.

Be wary of jumping on career bandwagons. Someone once asked me whether I thought she should join a private equity (PE) shop after working two years in consulting in order to get a PE stamp. My answer was that it depends on what you wish to do in the long term. If your passion is to start or lead a PE company, then making the leap now is fine. On the other hand, if it is simply to get a stamp, then it isn't the right path to take.

MBA Boards can also see through someone's ploy of leaving a consulting or engineering job to join a nonprofit organization right before applying to business school specifically to get a social enterprise stamp of approval. On the other hand, if social philanthropy is a genuine interest, then make sure you connect the dots to other evidence in your professional and personal life to show that social enterprise isn't just a passing fancy.

Quite frankly, there is no set profile or work experience that guarantees admission to a top business school. So, at best, simply jumping on trendy bandwagons will signal to the MBA Board that you are not authentic about your career goals. Because each candidate's story varies, it is important to embrace your unique circumstance and articulate how the MBA fits with your goal and how it will transform your career.

## GAIN ADMISSION DESPITE A PINK SLIP

Another potentially flag-raising reason applicants give for applying to business school is that they lost their job and have nothing better to do. Obviously this situation is likely to yield an unfavorable outcome. Many casualties of the dot-com disaster contributed to the unprecedented application volumes seen at many leading business schools in 2001. Not surprisingly, many of the applicants did not gain admission to business school.

From 2002 to 2004, many individuals received pink slips as a result of a slow economy. The 2007-2008 sub prime problems have led to job cutbacks in positions in mortgage backed securities. Many financial services companies have announced layoffs and some have shut down entire mortgage business units. Not surprisingly, some of those receiving pink slips will view business school as a viable option.

Should you find yourself in the unfortunate situation of being unemployed, avoid saying that you are pursuing the MBA as a way to get back into the job market. I know, it sounds very obvious, but I have come across this rationale enough times to know that the obvious isn't always "obvious." Even if you don't explicitly state this reason for why you want an MBA, if you receive a pink slip and do not find alternative employment, the MBA Board will still likely conclude that you are seeking the degree because you do not have anything better to do.

However, unemployed candidates are not necessarily doomed to rejection. I have worked with several unemployed candidates through my consultancy, EXPARTUS, and despite receiving pink slips, each was able to gain admission to elite schools. If you are unemployed, the important thing you should keep in mind is to use the time wisely to reassess your plans and to engage in activities that reinforce your brand. Using the time to learn a new language, to develop real skills that you truly care about, or to engage in activities that affect people's lives, through focused and committed volunteerism, can be justifiable reasons for how you have spent your time.

For instance, if you were a varsity squash player and have always been interested in community involvement, now that you are not working a one-hundred-hour workweek, you can join an organization like StreetSquash to lend your skills to empower inner-city kids through athletics. Better yet, if you are trying to make a switch from finance to marketing, you can lead marketing initiatives to help this organization secure funding. The brief marketing experience you gain can provide insightful material for your essays and reinforce your justification for the career change.

## TOP FOUR POPULAR REASONS FOR PURSUING AN MBA

Jumping on an MBA bandwagon will only hurt your admissions chance. The same goes for applying simply because you have lost your job. So what are the common rationales that are acceptable for desiring an MBA? In this section, I will go over the four most common reasons that drive MBA applicants' decision for business school as well as how the MBA Board feels about each of them.

Responses to why you want an MBA often fall into four categories: financial reward, intellectual challenge, personal development, and professional advancement. Let's examine each and discuss how Admissions Boards view them.

### Financial Reward

There is no doubt that the return on investment of an MBA (especially for top MBA programs) is very high. A glance at career brochures or websites of leading MBA programs reveals that after graduating from business school the average starting salary for the newly minted MBA is about $100K. And these data do not include the bonuses that can often be in the tens of thousands of dollars, depending on the industry. You don't have to be a math whiz to recognize that the MBA offers significant financial reward that pays for itself. If this is your main reason for pursuing an MBA, that's fine—but I recommend keeping it to yourself. The MBA Board already recognizes that financial reward is one of the key reasons people choose to study for an MBA. Stating this reason as your main driver for an MBA communicates a superficiality that doesn't help your candidacy. You are better off focusing on a deeper reason like personal or professional fulfillment. We will get to those shortly.

## Intellectual Challenge

For many candidates, the draw of the MBA is the intellectual stimulation and challenge that they will experience in the classroom. Without a doubt, the MBA builds skills and equips students with new insights to business issues. The joy of learning new material and concepts makes the MBA attractive to candidates who welcome the intellectual and invigorating conversations inside and outside the classroom. Stretching yourself intellectually is a fine rationale for why you want an MBA. However, this rationale can raise flags for the MBA Board if you have multiple graduate degrees but no work experience; candidates with this background can be seen as "degree collectors" or "perpetual students." Your comfort level operating in the real world may be called into question. So, regardless of what your background is, it is important to balance your quest for knowledge with practical experience.

## Personal Development

The personal development justification for the MBA is often tied to professional benefits as well. The draw for many people who chose to pursue the MBA is the personal confidence and credentials that an MBA gives them. As an MBA alumna phrased it, "My MBA gave me the courage to think bigger, step farther, and pursue my lifelong dream…" The one thing that most MBAs have in common is an ambitious spirit and a desire to achieve something significant—the teacher who wants to create charter schools across the nation, the cellist who plans to transform her national music conservatory in Bulgaria, or the business analyst who wants to run an emerging market hedge fund. What all these individuals have in common is a desire to have greater impact beyond where they are in their lives. The confidence that an MBA provides allows many individuals to achieve significant goals, and this remains a major driver for many who seek a graduate business education. One can't talk about the personal development impact of the MBA without addressing the incredible social network that surrounds the MBA experience. Through lifelong friendship and diverse networks, many MBAs are able to achieve their goals. It is no surprise that personal development is a popular rationale given by many applicants for why they want an MBA. This rationale makes complete sense to the Admissions Boards.

## Professional Advancement

The majority of applicants indicate that they are seeking an MBA for the career development benefits. More specifically, they say that they want the MBA to increase their understanding of the business world. This is a popular and compelling reason to give for why you want an MBA.

For some candidates, an MBA is a necessary next step to jump-start a stalled career. For others, they have been bypassed on promotions because they lack the degree. And then there are those applicants who are ready for a significant management role but who lack some fundamental skills that would be necessary to succeed in the new position. Entrepreneurs also find the MBA environment to be a great value in building their skill set and helping them refine their business model, reposition their product, and learn more successful ways to scale an already successful enterprise.

And of course, there are the career changers—I can't talk about the professional development benefit of the MBA without discussing career changers. Many MBA candidates can be characterized as career changers. In fact, more than 70 percent of MBA students change their industry or function after attending business school. If you are a career changer, you probably see the MBA as a bridge to enable you to transition into a new industry or function. And indeed, that is one of the major benefits of the MBA.

However, it is not enough to say you plan to use the MBA to change your job. You must be able to show that you have made a significant impact in your current career. It is also important that you present strong evidence based on your brand that you have what it takes to make a career switch. Regardless of whether you will change careers or remain in your current industry, it is acceptable to use professional development as your justification for why you seek an MBA.

I will discuss career changers and branding in greater detail in the chapter on building and selling your brand.

## THE VALUE OF THE MBA

The MBA is an expensive investment. Harvard Business School (HBS), for example, has a price tag of about $140,000. Add to that the financial impact of not earning an income for two years and it is clear why many individuals shy away from pursuing the MBA in the first place. Yet, ask anyone applying to business school, and you are likely to hear that they believe that the return on their investment can be significant. The numbers from graduates of top business schools support this: 86 percent of women and 89 percent of men surveyed in a Catalyst study reported that they were very satisfied with their MBA career after attending business school.

Often, the value of the MBA can be characterized as falling within one of these eight benefits:

1. Expanded network
2. Strategic skills
3. Analytical skills
4. Quantitative skills
5. Soft skills (leadership, communication, negotiation, agility in thinking on your feet, team management, etc.)
6. Increased knowledge
7. Significant salary bump
8. Access to new career

The Graduate Management Admission Council (GMAC) conducts a biannual survey of MBA alumni. Seventy-nine percent of the alumni polled in the 2006 alumni survey indicated that they are positive about their decision to pursue an MBA (Source: MBA Alumni Perspective Survey, September 2006).

So if you have decided that the MBA is for you and you are clear on why you want to pursue this degree and what it will offer you in the long term, let's examine the specific influences that shape which MBA program a candidate chooses.

## DIFFERENT TYPES OF MBA PROGRAMS

MBA programs have evolved over the years and now have available various versions to meet the different needs of students. The most prevalent MBA options are as follows: full-time two-year MBA, accelerated one-year to eighteen-month MBA, part-time MBA, and executive MBA. Although this book focuses primarily on the full-time two-year MBA program in the United States, I will discuss some other options in this section to give you a sense of what each program offers and the type of student for whom it is a good fit. MBA programs tend to have strict transfer policies, so do not count on being able to switch from a part-time MBA program to a full-time MBA program at a top business school. To avoid disappointment, you should do your research early to ascertain the program that is the best fit before enrolling in business school.

## Two-Year MBA Program

The two-year MBA program is extremely popular in the United States. The full-time MBA program is ideal for career changers for two reasons: (1) It offers greater opportunity to step back and reflect on their experiences and goals, and (2) It provides them with greater flexibility to take many classes in the new career they are pursuing. This option also offers students the opportunity to pursue an internship the summer after their first year to assess whether the new career is a good fit.

The curriculum of two-year MBA programs provides students with the opportunity to gain a broad exposure to the different business areas as well as a chance to develop a specialization. The MBA programs vary in how much curriculum flexibility they offer to the students. A program like Chicago Graduate School of Business (GSB) is one of the most flexible, allowing students the greatest freedom to opt out of classes and to design their own schedules. HBS, on the other hand, has one of the more rigid curricula, requiring students to take a core set of classes their first year.

Applicants who pursue the full-time two-year MBA program find that it is the most expensive MBA option given the price tag and the lack of income for two years. Some firms offer sponsorship for their star employees to pursue a full-time MBA program. Find out what your company's policy is for sponsorship by speaking with your manager and by talking to individuals you know who have gone to business school and returned to the firm. The expectation is usually that you would return to your firm if you receive financial support from your firm. For some individuals, this golden handcuff may be too high a price to pay, and they may pass on the employee sponsorship if they already know that they prefer to work at a different firm or industry.

If you are a career changer who plans to work in strategy consulting or in investment banking, then you should definitely pursue a full-time two-year MBA program. The availability of a summer internship will provide you with entrée into banking or consulting, which will make you more marketable to the banks and consulting companies.

## Accelerated MBA Program

The accelerated MBA program typically lasts for one full year or eighteen months and can start in the summer or winter. This type of program usually does not offer an opportunity to work in the summer because students take a full load of courses then. This program is usually a fit for someone who is already in his or her industry of choice but who needs to build up specific business skills. Also, entrepreneurs who plan to return to a family business will find this option attractive because of its shortened length.

## Part-Time MBA Program

The part-time MBA program is a popular choice for individuals who want to remain in their job while developing their business skills. Many firms are supportive of employees who wish to pursue a part-time business degree because they are able to retain them. Some even offer the option to sponsor the applicant with some stipulation on the number of years the employee must remain at the firm. Each firm varies in terms of their policy on eligibility and sponsorship. You may even have to take the GMAT and score at a certain level for your employer to sponsor your application. It is important to find out if your firm offers tuition reimbursement and the terms associated with it.

The part-time MBA option is not convenient for career changers for different reasons. The most prominent is the inability to "test out" a new career during the summer internship.

The part-time MBA curriculum is similar to the two-year MBA program, but the difference is that the students take fewer classes at a given time and classes are taught in the evenings and weekends. Companies looking to aggressively retain their best talent are forming formal relationships with business schools for their top employees. Lehman is one such example. It has established a formal part-time MBA program with New York University (NYU) for its star employees. This customized program has been designed to fit the employees' schedule and ensures that little disruption takes place while they pursue the MBA.

## Executive MBA Program

Of all the MBA program types, the executive MBA has the most variation available (a combination of weekends, evenings, onsite engagements where students congregate on campus, and online study). Many top institutions offer an Executive MBA program while others offer certifications and other short-term executive education training. An example of the latter is Harvard Business School's executive programs that last for a few days to several weeks that focus on developing the managerial skills of seasoned professionals.

Executive MBAs often provide exceptional employees with sponsorship. Even if your firm does not have a formal sponsorship policy, it is worth speaking to your manager to explore whether your firm would be able to sponsor you. Besides the financial sponsorship, it is also important to get your firm's support because most executive MBA programs require students to leave their jobs to be on campus for periods of time.

Deciding whether an Executive MBA (EMBA) is the right option for you will depend on where you are in your career and why you want the MBA. If you are relatively early in your career, the EMBA is not typically a good fit since it is designed for individuals who are further along in their career and have professional responsibilities and management experience that is substantive. It is no surprise then that the majority of students in the Executive MBA programs are over thirty and have a decade of professional experience. The EMBA is also ideal if you are looking for credentials, deepened industry knowledge, and expanded skill sets as opposed to making a major career change. Career changers are better served in a two-year, full-time MBA program.

## SELECTING THE RIGHT MBA PROGRAM

Having discussed the different variations of the MBA program, I would like to more closely examine the variables that applicants consider when selecting an MBA program. Here are the top ones that influence applicants' selection decisions.

### Length of the Program

As I discussed earlier, a number of variables affect your decision of whether to pursue a full-time two-year MBA program or a part-time or executive MBA program. Is time a factor for you? Are you trying to complete the MBA in as short a time as possible? Is the high cost of an MBA prohibitive? Are you already in the industry you want to be in? Can you bypass the summer internship? If you answered yes to these questions, it may be worth exploring MBA programs that are less than two years. Many of the top MBA programs in the United States have one-year or accelerated MBA programs. Chicago, Kellogg, and Columbia are just a few examples that come to mind. The MBA programs outside of the United States are also good options if time is a major factor for you or if you are open to an international career. INSEAD and IMD are popular programs in Europe that offer a full-time MBA program in less than two years.

## Geographic Location

Is geography of critical importance to you? Some candidates cannot imagine themselves in an urban environment; hence schools like Haas, Chicago, Columbia, and HBS will not make sense for them. On the other hand, there are applicants for whom the small town community of schools like Darden, Tuck, and the Johnson School at Cornell University is ideal. Individuals seeking international exposure must take the geographic location into account. Candidates planning to pursue a career in Europe may want to consider programs like IMD (Switzerland), INSEAD (France), Bocconi (Italy), and London Business School.

## Size of the Program

The size of the class can also play a significant role in where an applicant chooses to apply. The small program size of Haas (University of California, Berkeley), Tuck, Yale School of Management, and Stanford Graduate School of Business (GSB) could be a major draw for some applicants and a turn-off for others. So decide whether you are someone who will thrive in a large environment or a smaller, more intimate one. Having clarity on the environments you enjoy will save you the hassle of going through two years of misery in a place you hate.

## Teaching Method

We can't discuss variables affecting school selection without addressing the teaching methodology of the programs. Darden and HBS may be appealing to some applicants for their emphasis on the case study method (90 percent of the teaching is done via the case method), whereas this idea can be terrifying for other applicants. Also, some candidates believe you cannot teach finance effectively through the case method and would be loathe to attend a program that is primarily case focused.

## Flexibility of the Program

MBA programs differ in the range of flexibility they offer their students. MBA programs like Chicago GSB are among the top programs with significant curriculum flexibility. This level of curriculum option is ideal for candidates who are seeking a program where they can exempt out of classes they have taken before in order to create space to take new materials. Stanford GSB's recently transformed curriculum now offers greater flexibility to customize the MBA program for each student.

## International Business Exposure

Some applicants are attracted to international business. So although these students may opt for an American MBA, it is important to them to attend a program that offers the opportunity to either study abroad or tackle an international project that allows them to live abroad.

The Ross MBA at Michigan, Johnson MBA at Cornell, Wharton, and Kellogg are some of the programs that offer significant international experience and exposure. At Ross, for instance, you can take a semester exchange at one of the finest MBA programs in Europe, Australia, or Asia. Stanford GSB can be added to the list of MBA programs that have a strong international exposure since it has overhauled its curriculum. Stanford addresses their goals to "globalize the experience of their students" by stating: "The School will continue to globalize its cases and course materials, and a global experience will be required of each student during his or her two years at the School. This can be fulfilled by a study trip, an international internship, an overseas service-learning trip, or a student exchange, such as the School's new program with Tsinghua University's School of Economics and Management in China" (Source: Stanford Admissions website).

## Brand of the Program

Last but not the least is the overall brand of the MBA program. There is a certain feel and culture that permeates each MBA program. By visiting the programs and attending classes, you will be in a better position to ascertain whether a program is right for you. The MBA programs also have areas that they are brilliant at and are known for. I encourage all applicants to take the time to thoroughly research each MBA program to ensure that they select the ones that are a fit with their brand and goals. We address the topic of MBA programs as brands in the next chapter.

---

By now, I anticipate that you have a clearer sense of whether the MBA is worth it for you. You also have a practical sense of admission traps to avoid when making the decision to apply. Furthermore, you should be aware that whatever rationale you give to the Admissions Board for why you wish to pursue an MBA will be scrutinized. Assess your own circumstance carefully before deciding on your particular reason(s) for an MBA. But equally important, you will need to select the right type of MBA program given different variables that are important to you. I have covered the main variables that influence MBA program selection and I hope this information has helped you to decide whether a two-year, part-time, or executive MBA program is ideal for you. Taking the time to assess what you need from an MBA program and knowing yourself well will help you make the appropriate decision in the long run. A $140,000 misstep is too costly a mistake to make and I'm glad you are investing in the research and assessment early in the process.

# CHAPTER TWO

## Personal Branding and the
## MBA Application Process

S O WHAT EXACTLY DOES personal branding have to do with the admissions process? Everything! Applicants with strong and compelling brands distinguish themselves from the pack and capture the attention of the Admissions Boards. But applicants are not the only ones who have to think of themselves as brands. MBA programs are also brands and the MBA Board is charged with identifying the best candidates who are a fit with the brand of each of their programs.

In my ten years in the admissions industry and from my experience running EXPARTUS, I have come to recognize that there is a special chemistry that admitted candidates bring to the table: a strong and clear sense of who they are, what matters most to them, and where they are heading in the future. What comes to mind when a board member thinks about the candidate he or she just read about? What unique characteristics emerge that sets that candidate apart from all the other individuals within the same category? It is the salient attributes and unique perspective and experience that the candidate has that sets him or her apart in the application pool. Making sure that your unique brand stands out is critical to achieving admissions success.

A brand is what differentiates a product (or person in the case of MBA applicants) from the pack. Let's look at a few strong brand examples. Who do you think of when you hear the phrase "Motivational Talk Show Maven"? If you guessed Oprah, you're dead on. How about "International Rock Star Activist"? Bono should immediately come to mind. OK, you might be thinking, "Bono and Oprah have one thing in common; they are famous people with tons of money." The point is taken. However, not all famous people have brands or a strong characterization that accompanies their names.

Make no mistake about it—business school application is an exercise in marketing; it requires you to be able to sell the value you will offer to an MBA program. Successfully marketing your story to an Admissions Board requires a clear understanding of your personal brand.

## WHAT EXACTLY IS A BRAND?

A brand can be a product, a company, or even a person. The personal branding guru, Peter Montoya, puts it this way: "Strong brands instantly communicate simple, clear feeling or ideas to us about a product, company, or person" (*The Personal Branding Phenomenon*, 2002, p. 5).

What attributes come to mind when you think about a product, person, or company? Do you have a positive or negative reaction? Or worse, are you indifferent, which can suggest the absence of a brand?

What type of feeling or idea does your brand communicate to the MBA Admissions Board? What image does the Admissions Board have of you after reading your application? Does it match with the message that you set out to convey? Understanding the elements of successful brands will help you begin to think of yourself as a brand as you present your story to the Admissions Board.

I will discuss four fundamental brand rules that help MBA applicants differentiate themselves. I will also use case examples of individuals and companies that apply these branding principles to illustrate how you can do the same to make your application stand out.

# THE FUNDAMENTAL RULES OF PERSONAL BRANDING

| | |
|---|---|
| Rule #1: | Be focused. |
| Rule #2: | Be an expert. |
| Rule #3: | Be a leader. |
| Rule #4: | Excel and deliver results. |

## Rule #1: Be Focused (Companies as Brands)

Let's look at the case of two companies and the effect the rule of focus has had on them.

Branded companies know a secret: branding requires focus. Take the Volvo Group. Although it is a company that special-izes in commercial transportation, it has successfully positioned its car in the marketplace. Today, one can't think of a Volvo without thinking of security and safety. You won't associate "the ultimate driving machine" with a Volvo. Someone who is looking for speed or the flashiness of a sports car will opt for the BMW over a Volvo any day. But Volvo has done a great job of developing a car that consumers expect will not only last but will protect their greatest possession, their family. It is no surprise that Volvo's 2005 annual report shows a 37 percent increase in earnings per share.

Now let's look at General Motors (GM). If I asked you to tell me what type of car GM specializes in, you may be hard pressed to come up with a quick phrase that captures its essence. If you said "sporty, all-terrain, average all-American car" you would be right—this statement describes the Corvette, Hummer (H2 SUT), and Saturn, all GM cars. But one of GM's biggest problems is that it doesn't own a message in the consumer's mind. By diversifying so much and offering products that appeal to the widest customer base, the brand of the company has been diluted in the process. It is no wonder GM reported a third quarter earnings loss in 2006 of $115 million. Companies that try to be all things to all people are very quick to lose the attention of the consumer.

The rule of focus applies to applicants to business school in a similar way. You should identify one or two things that you are brilliant at and focus on using them to create value at your firm. By focusing on these core elements, you will be able to build a reputation and develop a track record that establishes your brand. Avoid spreading yourself too thin because it only creates confusion about what you stand for. Applicants who try to be different things at the same time (innovator, change manager, operations guru, accounting whiz, and human capital champion) run the risk of creating confusion about their brand and ultimately raise red flags for the Admissions Board. Pick the few themes that are core to your value, skill, and goals and build your brand on them. As an MBA applicant, you will increase your chances of success if you can identify key attributes or brand elements that differentiate you from your competition. I go into more detail on brand attributes in the chapter on building and selling your personal brand.

## Rule #2: Be an Expert (Companies as Brands)

Microsoft is a company that has leveraged its expertise—software—to become a multibillion-dollar company. With few exceptions, one can't turn on any personal computer worldwide without having to rely on a Microsoft Office product to perform basic functions. Microsoft's expertise developing "easier, faster, smarter" software has enabled it to capture significant market share, which translates to billions of dollars in revenue.

More recently, YouTube, a company started by three young, former PayPal employees has revolutionized the way information is transmitted around the world. Their tagline, "Broadcast Yourself," is at the heart of their brand, providing a vehicle for anyone to get their message out to a global audience. In the space of a few years they have transformed the way video files are shared. The recent purchase of YouTube by Google for more than $1 billion is evidence of the power a brand can have when it focuses on its expertise and uses it to meet a need in the marketplace.

Applicants to business school must identify an area that they are brilliant at and use it to create value for their firm, team, or clients. What is a need that is not being met at your firm? Is there a new product that can improve the revenue stream at your company? Do you have knowledge that can help facilitate that? Are you an athlete who has special understanding of the sports product business? For instance, you may be a marketing associate at Nike and can draw from your experiences as an athlete to shape the development of the latest sneakers design that is being introduced in the market. As a minority, you may be able to offer unique insights into how your company should position itself when marketing to minority communities. A Chinese national with experience working on the mainland can help her company navigate its expansion into China given her geo-political awareness of the region.

Even personal experiences can influence the development of a candidate's expertise. For example, you may develop an interest in pharmaceutical products because of health issues. Your own self-study and research can position you as a resident expert in the area of health care and pharmaceutical topics at your firm. Your knowledge could become valuable to help your firm expand its knowledge base in health care/drug industry deals.

International experience can also be an option. European applicants have an edge in language ability compared with their U.S. counterparts. Leveraging strong language ability, many candidates opt for international deals where they are able to use their linguistic expertise when working with clients. This is the case for a Turkish woman who works in M&A in London and because she speaks fluent German is able to work on many prominent German deals at her firm. The insights she gleaned working in the United Kingdom and Germany, combined with her awareness of her home country, Turkey, bring meaningful understanding of what is required to work in international settings. Regardless of your specific experience, as an applicant, it is important to figure out where you have unique, value-added expertise, which you should begin to use immediately to differentiate yourself from your peers.

## Rule #3: Be a Leader (People as Brands)

Branding requires a commitment to step up and stand for what you believe. Taking action and leading is another key to branding. The power of branding goes beyond companies and products and applies to people as well. Two great examples of individuals who demonstrate the rule of leadership in cultivating their brands are Bono and Wangari Maathai.

Bono of the rock group U2 has been a leader in addressing humanitarian problems and alleviating poverty, disease, and hunger in the poorest areas of the world. His steadfast commitment to social justice has led to his brand as an activist rocker. By raising funds, investing his own resources and money, and bringing to the attention of the world many of the issues plaguing Africa, his brand as an activist was born. Bono clearly represents an example of someone with an authentic brand who is living his passion and creating change and impact in the lives of millions. Today, Bono is viewed as the preeminent leader in advocating for the poor.

Wangari Maathai is another great example of an individual with a powerful brand built upon the rule of leadership. Known as the "Tree Lady," Wangari Maathai has had a distinct brand as a fearless conservationist who has refused to be cowed by Kenya's former dictatorial government despite death threats and imprisonments. To the majority of the world, she is known as Africa's first female Nobel Peace Prize Laureate. She founded a grassroots environmental organization called The Green Belt Movement, which introduced a vision of empowerment for women and conservation through the planting of trees. Maathai is clearly living her passion of improving the environment. Pursuing this vision has led to an environmental revolution the likes of which had never been seen in Africa. In 2004, she received a Nobel Prize, but before this honor was bestowed on her, she had already established an enduring brand as an eco-activist.

I'm not suggesting that all applicants to business school should become activists tomorrow. Leadership does not always require activism. Rather, it requires commitment and a willingness to take a risk to pursue your passion.

You may be passionate about education and may want to consider taking on leadership roles in a nonprofit educational organization. Denise is an applicant who had the guts to pursue her passion by changing her career before business school. An analyst in a Wall Street firm who was doing very well, Denise chose to turn down her third-year analyst offer to join a relatively young educational organization. Her two years at this organization enabled her to build credibility as an education advocate and future leader and gave her ample opportunity to tackle significant leadership challenges. Shortly after, she was admitted to a top business school, where she plans to establish a strong network and broaden her skill set before running charter schools.

Many of you may not be interested in changing your career as Denise did. You can still demonstrate leadership in a practical and tangible way within your firm. For instance, parlaying your analytics expertise to overhaul and lead the new training program at your firm may be the exact leadership role that works for your brand. Some of you may be like Fred, a pharmaceutical engineer from an emerging market country whose leadership impact is shown through working within the established system in his firm. Fred's impact was to seize the opportunity to partner with his firm to distribute pharmaceutical drugs that his firm did not want to use in hospitals and clinics in his home country. Or you may be like John, who started a small tutoring program in New York to empower inner-city kids whose grades suffered as a result of the dismal education they were exposed to in their public schools. What is important is that whatever leadership role you choose to cultivate, pick one that reinforces your brand and make sure you deliver impact with it. Authenticity is critical to the branding process, so focus only on the things that you are truly committed to.

## Rule #4: Excel and Deliver Results (People/Company as Brands)

Like her or not, Martha Stewart has established a brand as the great dame of home improvement. She is known for scrutinizing every item or product associated with her brand before putting her seal of approval on it. Some may see this as overkill; the reality, however, is that because she has been this closely involved with her products and has maintained a judicious vigilance in the quality associated with her brand, she has been able to build a multimillion-dollar business.

Although the majority of the applicants to business school have not started multimillion-dollar companies, adopting a Martha Stewart-like scrutiny to the product or service you deliver can pay dividends in the application process. Delivering excellence in everything you do—including the services you provide to clients, the products you develop, or the teams you manage—will ensure that you have a track record that will stand out when you apply to business school.

Although Martha Stewart has been successful in building a strong firm, she also represents a cautionary story of what happens when your personal actions are negative. Because Martha Stewart, the person, is intimately connected to her eponymous company, her conviction of perjury during her insider trading trial had an enormous impact on her company, with stock prices plummeting. Martha Stewart's example shows how one negative action can unravel years of establishing an excellent reputation. Applicants to business school must be careful not to make a mistake that can derail the reputation they have earned at their jobs. Consistently delivering quality results will enable you to firmly own a positive reputation/brand among your colleagues, superiors, and clients. After all, it is precisely this track record of excellence that your brand champions will rely on to support your application.

Applicants who show commitment to excellence and high-caliber work have an edge over their competition. Let's look at an example.

---

*John was a second-year analyst and was extremely committed to producing quality work. His work ethics of being the first in and the last to leave the office enabled him to manage his work effectively. His sharp intellect and the high quality of work that he became known to produce made him very popular among managing directors at his firm, many of whom would specifically request for him to be staffed on their deals. This reputation soon allowed John to work on many of the high-profile deals at his firm and gave him unusual access to senior leadership beyond what his peers were exposed to. Before long, John became known as a leader among his peers, as many analysts would also seek him out to get his perspective since he had worked on more complicated deals and could provide information on analytics and how to "manage up." You can imagine the type of recommendation an applicant like John would receive.*

---

If your work isn't at the level of individuals like John, it is never too late to begin to establish a reputation of excellence. Make the commitment today to begin operating beyond your job responsibility by looking for ways to fill an existing void at your firm as well as raising the bar in the quality of work you produce.

Individuals who understand the power of personal branding recognize the importance of consistent commitment to excellence and results. Producing a track record of excellence on a regular basis is one clear way to differentiate yourself from your peers who just do a "good job." Doing your job well is not enough. Going beyond what is expected of you and delivering excellent results regularly is one sure way to stand apart from your competition.

Even the physical application needs to demonstrate this brand of excellence. The mistake that some applicants make is to underestimate the importance of each aspect of the application. An unpolished and mistake-ridden resume can tip the scale to a rejection. That means that every aspect of the application, from GMAT score to essays, recommendations to transcript, and everything in between, should be of high quality. Never cut corners. It is the fastest way to earn a negative brand reputation.

But applicants to business school are not the only ones for whom branding matters. MBA programs are also seen as brands and applicants often apply to them based on how they view their brand.

## MBA PROGRAMS AS BRANDS

Each business school is distinctive and has a different culture or feel to it. As such, it is critical to understand the brand of each program in order to select the ones that best fit with your personal brand.

MBA candidates are not the only ones who use marketing to differentiate themselves. Even the MBA Boards are not impervious to marketing. They too do their fair share of marketing to ensure that their programs' brands are adequately communicated to their target applicants. It is no surprise that each year, dozens of members of MBA Admissions Boards embark on a grueling recruitment schedule across the nation and the world to "market" their unique MBA program and convince diverse and talented prospective candidates to apply. Whether the Admissions Boards are marketing their program through their annual fall open house events or through other means, including dynamic websites, glossy brochures, and on-campus events, their pressing goal is to attract the most talented, diverse, and accomplished individuals who are a fit with their program's brand.

Some MBA programs have done a brilliant job defining and marketing their brands. By contrast, there are those whose brands are quite ambiguous to the customer, making it difficult for people to articulate what the program stands for. MBA programs that attempt to be all things to all people without having a key component that they master face the possibility of owning zero percent of the customer's mindshare. (Similarly, MBA candidates who do not have a clearly articulated and compelling brand capture zero market share in the mind of the MBA Board.) It is therefore quite usual to see MBA programs and universities as a whole invest a lot of money to conduct a brand study to refine and revamp their brand. This exercise often involves extensive communication with alumni, current students, recruiters, and other stakeholders who are familiar with the program.

Make no mistake about it, business schools are not trying to simply admit a prototype applicant. That is, although Columbia has a fantastic brand as a finance program, it isn't looking to admit all its students from finance backgrounds. Neither is Kellogg trying to admit an entire class of marketing people. That would be extremely limiting and would defeat the overall purpose of a top business school: students from diverse backgrounds (both professionally and personally) interacting with each other and learning from the different perspectives covered in the classroom. The brand of an MBA program goes beyond the career area it specializes in, although this is important in shaping the brand of the school. Kellogg, for instance, has a strong reputation as a marketing program but is also known for its extremely collaborative culture and emphasis on teamwork. Does that mean you can't find teamwork at Columbia? Of course teamwork is a part of Columbia's culture (and of most top business schools). But Kellogg's emphasis and devotion to the collaborative community will always make it one of the premier team-oriented business schools in America. Tuck is another program that has a similar brand focus on teamwork and collaborative community.

Understanding and deciphering the brand of MBA programs isn't a simple, cut-and-dried process. It requires in-depth research. Applicants need to:

- Speak with products of the business school, in particular, alumni, current students, MBA Boards, and faculty.
- Visit the schools to get a firsthand experience of the program, its culture, and teaching style, not to mention the people who might someday become classmates.
- Talk to people in the industry to understand how the program is perceived to better understand the program's brand.

Top MBA programs have a lot in common. They all have high-caliber faculty, smart students, adept Admissions Boards, dedicated career services, and active alumni. They are similar in their value of diversity. Diversity is defined not simply by gender and ethnicity alone but includes socioeconomic backgrounds, geographic upbringing, career experiences, and unique perspectives. Despite these similarities, however, many top business schools have unique and differentiated brands. Here are a few examples.

## Stanford Graduate School of Business

Stanford Graduate School of Business (GSB) enjoys a strong reputation of honing and developing entrepreneurship. Partly a result of Stanford's proximity to Silicon Valley, the world's entre-preneurial capital, or perhaps the long history of innovation from Stanford alumni and faculty alike, Stanford's brand as the preem-inent entrepreneur MBA program is long established. That said, Stanford GSB is more than an entrepreneurial MBA program. It has many diverse offerings, including the Center for Global Busi-ness and the Economy, as well as a strong culture of social enter-prise, as seen in its dedicated Center for Social Innovation, Certificate in Public Management, and sizeable alumni base engaged in socially responsible businesses.

The reality is that if you are looking for an MBA program that would stretch you intellectually as well as creatively to explore new ventures and start your own business, Stanford GSB may be the ideal program for you. A large number of entrepreneurs (or aspiring entrepreneurs) are likely to be attracted to Stanford GSB. However, given Stanford GSB's commitment to diversity, you will find students who have not started a business and sold it for millions. However, what these admitted students have in common is an entrepreneurial mind-set, affinity for innovation, out-of-the-box thinking, and disparate experiences where they took a risk to try something new within an old guard company. It is for these reasons that Stanford students are often described as eclectic and "free spirits."

With that said, if you are looking to enter a career in general management, you will find Stanford to be a great environment where you can develop general management skills across different business areas.

## Columbia Graduate School of Business

Columbia Business School is another great example of an MBA program with a powerful brand. It is known as one of the leading finance business schools in the country. Its location in New York City, the financial capital of the world; the sizeable number of alumni who pursue finance-related careers; and the phenomenal faculty with excellent track records in finance and accounting all contribute to Columbia Business School's finance brand. I would be remiss if I stopped here, particularly given Dean Glenn Hubbard's innovative changes that are pushing entrepreneurship at Columbia.

Although Columbia Business School can likely succeed in attracting more entrepreneurs into its program and creating an overall stronger perception in the marketplace of being a place of entrepreneurship and innovation, it is unlikely that Columbia will fundamentally shift to become an entrepreneur-only program at the expense of its brand as one of the leading finance MBA programs in the nation.

## Kellogg

Another example of a school with a strong brand is Kellogg. Kellogg's brand is significantly tied to marketing and team-based learning. It is rare that you hear someone talk about a marketing MBA program in the United States without Kellogg being at the center of the conversation. Even the name, Kellogg, is tied to the multibillion-dollar consumer products company. Although Kellogg has a dominant brand as a marketing MBA program, it offers much more than marketing to its "customers." In fact, Kellogg offers an extremely flexible curriculum that allows students to specialize in a variety of functional business areas, with finance and strategy as the first and second most popular areas of study, respectively.

Despite this reality, the foremost thought on the minds of most prospective students when thinking of Kellogg is marketing. Even as Kellogg endeavors to educate applicants about its other areas of expertise, the program will likely face the challenge of how far to deviate from its core brand. Expanding its marketing brand to include other areas of strength, such as strategy, will continue to present a tough challenge to Kellogg.

## Ross Business School (Michigan)

Putting one's arms around the Ross brand is somewhat challenging because it is an MBA program that isn't necessarily known for one particular area. It is accurate to describe Ross as a "well-rounded" MBA program. However, I think the better way to categorize the Ross brand beyond being "well-rounded" is that it is truly action-oriented and has a culture of constant improvement. I think these two elements have enabled Ross to get top rankings in recent years. Even its motto of "Leading in Thought and Action" speaks to the brand of the program: it offers extensive opportunities to infuse the business education with real-life experience. The Multidisciplinary Action Project (MAP), a required first-year course offered the second half of the second semester, gives Ross students an opportunity to "test" many of the business ideas and theories they learned their first semester in a real-life environment. The students work on a consulting engagement to resolve a business challenge a real company faces. So candidates looking for a well-rounded program and hands-on experience for their MBA will be attracted to Ross Business School.

## Harvard Business School

One can't talk about an MBA program that builds its brand fundamentally on leadership without thinking of Harvard Business School (HBS). Does that mean that HBS is the only place where leaders can be found? Of course not! One can find a ton of leaders across the nation's top MBA programs. In fact, all of the top schools highlight leadership as a core aspect of their programs. However, Harvard's mission of "developing leaders who care about the well-being of society" strikes at the heart of what the program stands for.

Leadership permeates the HBS experience and is not only about formal roles (student leadership in organizations or career titles) but includes situational leadership where candidates seize opportunities to make a difference regardless of their role. The structure of the curriculum, the teaching methodology (case-based learning), and the projects outside of the classroom are all designed to challenge students to refine, rethink, confirm, and establish their perception of leadership and transform their own unique way of leading.

The previous examples are a snapshot of some of the MBA programs that proactively manage their brands. Of course there are other solid MBA programs not covered and I encourage each applicant to use the research steps described earlier in this chapter to further investigate the programs they are interested in.

Now, let's focus on the MBA Board to get a better understanding of who they are and how they operate in the convoluted application process.

## THE MBA ADMISSIONS BOARD

The MBA Board's role can be likened to that of a portfolio manager. Their job is to pick the right stock that will yield the greatest level of return to the program. Just as portfolio managers assemble diverse stocks, MBA Boards admit applicants with backgrounds and experiences that are unique and that will enrich the overall community. Applicants who have strong brands that are a fit with the MBA program will have a higher chance of being selected. Ultimately, the expectation is that these admitted students will graduate to become brand extensions of their program and will continue to strengthen their alma mater's brand.

Understanding the MBA Board should at the very least make them more approachable and increase your comfort level when interacting with them. Also, understanding where they are coming from and precisely what their role is will give you a clearer perspective of how to present your application as a whole.

First and foremost, the MBA Board members are human and compassionate. They are single and married, mothers and fathers, young and old. They are passionate about their job. They are not in it for the money and often consider their role a true labor of love. Some of them are alumni of the MBA program; many of them have an MBA or a graduate degree (although not everyone). The preceding description captures many Admissions Boards, but some programs also include students as members of the Admissions Board. Chicago GSB, the Johnson School at Cornell University, and Wharton are a few examples of MBA programs where second-year students serve on the Admissions Board. Typically, these students would do the first read and assess the candidate; then the application is evaluated a second time by an assistant or associate director of admissions before a final outcome is determined. (Admissions policy variations may exist from school to school.)

Each year, these talented and dedicated board members embark on a grueling recruiting schedule (from August to November) after receiving marching orders to identify smart, talented candidates with excellent leadership potential and track records. They're forced to admit only a limited number of applicants, which is further complicated by an application pool that is full of talented individuals who have achieved significant levels of success in different arenas. Because there is no formula to weed out weak applicants, the MBA Board invests in carefully evaluating each candidate. Admitting a diverse class made up of different perspectives (for example, industry, country of origin, talents, gender, ethnicity, and personal and professional experiences) while maintaining a balance presents a significant challenge.

Typically, each application is evaluated by at least two board members. If both board members' votes are in agreement, then the application often will move forward in the process. Of course, sometimes the two board members are in disagreement. In such situations, the application may be evaluated by a third board member. Another option may be to bring the application to the Admissions Committee, where the merits of the candidate will be discussed and a decision rendered. These meetings can be quite spirited as board members argue passionately about the candidate in question. Ultimately, the MBA Admissions Director has the final say in the fate of a candidate if there is dissension among the board members. If you want your application to stand out, you must make sure that your essays are engaging and differentiated, allowing the Admissions Board to quickly see the value your application brings to the overall class.

The admission season is long and strenuous. The MBA Board works extremely long hours during the busy season, which lasts from the end of August to the end of May. Each week, board members pick up bins filled with applications that need to be evaluated and returned within a small time window. Many board members work very late into the night, and it is easy for many essays to begin to blur into the next when they lack originality. MBA Board members love to read applications where they can really see who the candidate is and the rationale driving the choices that person made both personally and professionally. (This is why applicants should pay attention to the PGII Factor—passion, guts, impact, and insight—which I will further discuss in the chapter on essay fundamentals.)

Board members are not spared during holidays either. November is the heart of the application season for round one, and applications often are reviewed even during holidays like Thanksgiving. Most people take vacation to spend time with their family during the holidays. Given a compressed admission season where decisions have to be made by a certain deadline, board members do not necessarily take time off during special holidays. So board members have to carve out time during their holiday to review applications. You want to write interesting and captivating essays that are worth reading, especially if someone is giving up family time to evaluate your candidacy.

Successful applications are usually the ones that have a clear and strong brand message. After reading a well-branded application, the typical response from the MBA Board should be something like, "This is the visionary engineer who solves business problems creatively" or "I just read the application of a smart, unconventional banker who consistently focuses on developing junior talent." They can't come to these conclusions if the stories you have recounted in your applications are generic and lack focus.

I've often heard applicants say, "I'm not good at marketing and promoting myself." And my answer is, "Start practicing!" If you are not comfortable selling yourself to the MBA Board, you will likely leave out compelling aspects of your story in your application. Yes, you may find the idea of marketing yourself artificial and contrived, but it is a necessary process to ensure that your application is vibrant and distinctive.

Although I am a big promoter of self-marketing and branding, I don't endorse false marketing. Not only is it unethical, it will likely come back to haunt you. This book does not promote falsifying your story or presenting a brand that does not authentically reflect your personal and professional life.

The reason I am so bullish about developing your personal brand is so that you have a realistic and up-to-date awareness of who you are and what you have done in your life. Your grades and GMAT score are not going to be enough to communicate why you should be admitted to a particular MBA program. Writing essays that convey your brand's distinction will help your application stand out to the MBA Board. It will also enable the board member who evaluates your application to become an advocate on your behalf. The clearer and more impressive your brand is, the more likely he or she will be able to argue for your application when your candidacy is discussed in an admission meeting.

Ultimately, your goal is to turn the Admissions Board member reading your file into a brand champion. The board member has to "buy" your story in order to "sell" it to colleagues or the Admissions Committee. And just as with traditional marketing, where only products with powerful and compelling brands stand out, MBA applicants must have distinctive brands that capture the mindshare of the MBA Board. Self-aware candidates who can clearly articulate who they are (their brand) and their rationale for their choices and action will more likely capture the attention of the MBA Board. At the end of the day, the candidate's job is to get the MBA Board to say, "Wow! I'd love to meet this person."

Finally, applicants have to be careful in deciding how much face time they need to have with the Admissions Board. The MBA programs vary drastically on their preference for face time with candidates. Tuck, for example, has one of the most liberal policies on this and encourages candidates to visit Hanover and interact with the Admissions Board. Other programs may find it to be a nuisance if a candidate requests to meet with board members during a (noninterview) visit. Also, sending lengthy emails and making multiple phone calls to the Admissions Board can annoy the board members. It is important to follow instructions regarding sending additional materials to the MBA Board after the deadline. Some MBA programs (for example, Wharton and HBS) explicitly request that applicants not send additional materials even if they are wait-listed. On the other hand, a program like Chicago has been open to receiving additional information if it reflects a new update that isn't covered in the existing application. Typically, most programs are open to a short and polite thank you card after an interview. However, a two-page letter to the MBA Board where you wax eloquent about your achievements is unlikely to have the desired results. I have been approached multiple times by desperate candidates who have not heard back from the MBA programs and in their panic plan to have an alumnus of the program contact the school to find out what is holding up the interview invitation. I always advise the distraught candidate to resist having an alumnus call and "harass" the MBA Board. Calling the MBA Board will likely backfire and hurt the candidate's chance of admission. Exercising patience is the best strategy in this case. At the very least, candidates should find out what each program's policy is and adhere to it. Remember that the MBA Board is short on time and is already burdened with a very challenging workload. Annoying them ensures that they will not become advocates for your candidacy.

As long as the business school admission process remains competitive, applicants will continue to face significant pressure to communicate why they are unique and worthy of a coveted admission spot. Candidates who recognize the differentiating power of branding will maintain an edge over their competitors. I'll go into more details in the next chapter on personal branding and how applicants can use it to stand apart.

# CHAPTER THREE

## Building and Selling Your Brand

A PERSONAL BRAND IS IMPORTANT to helping you live a life that is passion-driven and grounded in your values. By having a clear sense of your personal brand you can actively engage in the things that matter to you, deliver results that you can be proud of, add value to those around you (both personally and professionally), and live a life that has meaning and impact. Building your brand will help you chart a clear path to achieve your goals and live your passion. Beyond these benefits, however, having a powerful and clear personal brand before you embark on the application process can be extremely effective in bringing about the admission outcome you seek. Applicants who have a clear sense of their personal brand often emerge the most successful from the application process. Let's look at how to build your brand.

One of the first things necessary to develop your personal brand is to identify your passion.

## WHAT IS YOUR PASSION?

Are you living your passion both personally and professionally? Is what you do bringing you fulfillment? Is there a major disconnect between how you see yourself and how others see you? Will getting an MBA enable you to achieve your vision for your life? It is important to take the time to address these questions; the answers will help you gauge whether you are living a life driven by passion.

The word "passion" is thrown around and used in various contexts in our everyday communication. But phrases like "I'm passionate about baseball" or "My passion is doing the rumba" do not quite capture the essence of what I mean by passion. Passion is not a hobby or simply what you like to do for fun. I have a slightly different perception of passion as it relates to business school application. I define passion as what gives meaning to our life.

A recent conversation I had at my favorite neighborhood coffee shop best illustrates the elements of a passion-filled life. I had posed this simple question, "What is your passion?" to Kim, a fellow latte-indulging customer. Her face immediately lit up, and she quipped, "Teaching and affecting the lives of my students." Kim has been teaching for several years in New York City elementary schools, and she is successful at what she does. She chose a teaching profession because it fit with her values to help kids succeed. As she described her work with her kids, it was impossible to miss the pure joy and fulfillment in her voice. The excitement that accompanied her description of what she does cannot be faked. When you are living your passion, your life will reflect the energy and joy that accompanies a passion-filled life.

So is what you are doing currently reflective of your passion? Stop for a minute to reflect on your passion. The important thing is to proactively assess whether what you do brings meaning to you, whether it reflects your values, skills, and interests. If that's not the case, then it may be time for self-exploration to determine what matters to you and time to begin to integrate that into your professional and personal life. A simple way to assess whether you are living a passion-filled life is to ask yourself whether you would do your job if you were not paid for it.

I encourage you to take a few minutes to complete the passion survey to see how aligned your passion is to what you do currently.

---

## EXPARTUS PASSION SURVEY

(For each question, rate your response from 1–3: 1 = not really, 2 = somewhat, 3 = absolutely. After completing each question, tally your scores.)

Are you aware of what your greatest passion is?

Is your passion connected to your personal brand?

Are you living your passion outside of your job?

Are you living your passion in your job?

Do you enjoy your job?

Do you have the right skills to live your passion?

Would you keep working in your industry if you weren't paid for your job?

Are you still being challenged by the work you do?

Does what you do have an impact on the lives of others?

Are you proud of your accomplishments?

Scores that range from 22–30 indicate that your job is in sync with your passion. Scores that range from 12–21 suggest that some changes are in order; this may not require a career change, but more active investment in aligning your passion with your career. Scores of less than 12 call for a major over-haul. Consider a thorough brand audit to assess what matters most to you and begin incorporating it in your life. Be open to a career change.

---

After completing the passion survey and determining whether your life is aligned with your passion, you can go a step further to assess and develop your personal brand. This process requires that you undergo a personal brand audit to identify your key brand themes and ultimately to distill your story into a personal brand statement. Let's get started first with an audit of your personal brand.

# HOW TO BUILD A COMPELLING PERSONAL BRAND

## Personal Brand Audit

The first step in building a powerful brand is undergoing a personal brand audit (PBA). The PBA is a candid assessment of who you are. It includes your values, goals, skills, and passion. Included in this assessment is a review of your strengths and weaknesses, your past achievements and failures, your track record, your perception of yourself, and how other people perceive you. After completing this audit, the next step is to distill it down to the core of what matters to you. You could start by picking three key values, goals, interests, and achievements. If you can, try to further focus on the critical value, goal, interest, and significant track record from your life. This can be challenging to drill down at this level because as human beings we are complicated and have varied backgrounds, interests, values, and so forth. However, this exercise, as frustrating as it may be in the beginning, forces you to objectively look at what you are dealing with (the good, the bad, and the ugly). Then you have to apply honesty balanced with judgment in piecing together the most compelling aspects of who you are. It doesn't get any more self-aware than that.

# A MINI PERSONAL BRAND AUDIT (PBA)

In completing the PBA, be as candid and introspective as you can. It is also extremely important to cite examples when answering each question. The more vivid and specific your examples are, the more effective they will be in enabling you to pull out stories from your background that reflect your brand.

**Passion**

I am most passionate about:

My work inspires me in the following way:

If I could live my passion, I would:

**Values**

What do I value the most about myself?

What do people value the most about me? (Ask colleagues, friends, family.)

What three things do I cherish the most in life?

My values are a fit with my career in the following way:

My values are misaligned with my career in the following way:

**Skills**

My three strongest strengths are:

My three greatest areas of development are (describe what you are doing to improve them):

The most significant impact I have had on a person is:

The most significant impact I have had on a team is:

The most significant impact I have had on an organization is:

**Goals**

My short-term goal is:

My reason for seeking an MBA now is:

My long-term goal is:

Without the MBA, it will be nearly impossible to achieve my long-term goal because:

## Brand Themes

In the course of completing your PBA, you will notice some recurrent brand themes. These themes have to be evaluated to determine whether they reinforce your brand and whether they qualify as major themes (a must-have for your story) or minor themes (elements you could add to your story if there is room).

Brand themes are not just your job descriptions or obvious variables of your story. They are consistent and recurrent elements that reflect who you are at the most meaningful level. Brand themes are not typically what you write in your resume. They are subtler than your job title and job description. Brand themes reflect how you do what you do, the characteristics and values that drive your actions and choices, the distinctive and memorable traits that people around you see in you.

One can argue that brand themes can be fuzzy and "touchy-feely." A tech guy I know happens to be exceptionally charismatic and very outgoing. He absolutely does not embody the stereotype of a reserved, nerdy tech guy. When applying to business school, had he focused simply on his job role or title, he would have been ineffective in conveying his charismatic brand. By tapping into instances that demonstrate how he operates in a team environment and by sharing personal stories, he was able to convey an accurate brand picture of himself: one that is dynamic and engaging instead of limited by his work role.

Your job titles or roles do not constitute your brand themes. It isn't the title or label but the intrinsic and motivating elements behind what you do and your own identity (values, passions) that make up your brand theme. So here are a few examples of what a brand theme is not:

- Smart investment banker
- Ivy-educated engineer
- Top-ranked consultant
- Hardworking private equity analyst

You will notice that these examples are generic and not differentiating. In other words, if you want to build your application around being a smart banker, you pigeonhole yourself with the other thousand smart bankers in the applicant pool. The same goes for each of the other examples. To stand apart, you need brand themes that are differentiating. So although you are a smart banker, one of your key brand themes could be a bridge connector. A bridge connector is someone who thrives on bringing disparate people and teams together to solve problems. They enjoy people, are well connected, and make good use of their social network to create positive impact wherever they are. Bridge connectors do not hoard information or sit on the sidelines when a problem needs to be resolved. They love to jump in and partner with people to bring about results. More than that, they are gifted at working with different types of people and can bring out the best in them. Being a bridge connector is what differentiates you from the pack. Nowhere in your application do you explicitly state "I'm a bridge-connecting banker!" Rather, the stories you choose to recount when addressing the essay questions can convey and reinforce this bridge-connector brand, which then leads the Admissions Board to draw the conclusion based on the evidence.

The challenge in sharing your brand with the MBA Board is that you need concrete examples from your personal and professional life to substantiate any themes you select. One of the laws of personal branding is focus. So with selecting your brand themes, it is important to pick three to four that are most reflective of who you are and what matters to you. You may be wondering, why three or four? Because the application has a limited space, it is important to focus on the most salient themes in your story. Furthermore, you don't want to come off as scattered by throwing in too many attributes and themes. By selecting a few focused themes, you can then use the application essays to reinforce a consistent message that supports your personal brand.

Your recommenders also would need to be aware of the key brand themes you are presenting so that the examples they use to illustrate your story remain consistent with your branding strategy.

At the end of the day, it is less about having the "right" themes and more about tapping into meaningful attributes and elements from your life experiences. Here are just a few examples of brand themes of successful applicants to business school:

## SAMPLE BRAND THEMES

| | |
|---|---|
| "Empowerer" of women | Engendering trust |
| Articulate communicator | Risk taker |
| Global citizen | Multicultural |
| Charismatic leader | Contagious optimist |
| The connector | Unrelenting |
| "Bootstrapper" | Bridge builder |
| Diplomatic rebel | Investor in junior talent |
| Innovator | Entrepreneur |
| Turnaround expert | Idea guy |
| Motivational manager | Astute negotiator |
| Dancer of life | Trailblazer |

These themes are by no means exhaustive of potential themes. Brand themes are endless and are reflective of the candidates' experiences. The examples offered here are only snapshots of potential brand themes from successful applicants. These applicants were able to successfully brand their way into top business schools not because they had perfect stories but because they committed to the introspection necessary to identify their personal brand. Articulating what mattered to them and why they had made the different choices that they made (connecting the dots of their lives) allowed the MBA Board to differentiate them from their competition.

---

# PERSONAL BRAND THEMES

List the four brand themes/attributes that best describe you.
Make sure you cite examples to back them up.

1.

2.

3.

4.

---

Now that you have identified your brand themes, go over them to see if they accurately represent you. What words come to mind as you have read through your responses? Do you notice any surprises? With branding, it is equally important that those around us reach the same conclusions about our brand. Ask two people who know you well (they can be colleagues, family members, or friends) whether the themes you selected are reflective of who you are or if other themes are more relevant to your brand. If there are inconsistencies, then be willing to go deeper to determine whether you need to take steps to better communicate your personal brand.

A major mistake applicants make is that they don't invest in enough introspection to identify their brand themes before embarking on their essays. As a result, many of the business school essays are disjointed, boring, and superficial. Let's explore how a candidate can use a brand theme, global citizen, to sell her personal brand. The candidate doesn't even have to mention the brand theme in the actual essay. Rather, she can select stories that depict her as a global citizen. Let's say she has five essays for her application; she can use two to three different stories to convey her comfort level in international settings. The first could be of a key project she worked on managing an international team spanning two continents; this project shows how her sensitivity to the nuanced cultural differences enabled her to lead effectively. She may then wish to share a personal story about the study abroad program she did in a remote region of the world and her personal "aha" cultural moment. Finally, she may wish to write about her involvement with a nonprofit group that helps immigrants from different regions of the world adjust to their new lives in America. These examples plus the fact that she has lived in many countries around the world, speaks multiple languages, and has recommendations that reinforce her global citizen brand can etch a strong message about who she is in the MBA Board's mind. When you have a clear sense of your brand, you become more memorable and it is easier for whoever reviews your application to summarize your story in a succinct, easily identifiable way.

Once you have identified the themes to your story, it is important to distill them into a summary, the personal brand statement, which speaks to the heart of who you are. Clearly as human beings we are a lot more complicated than a one-sentence statement. I'll be the first to acknowledge this. However, given that you have thirty seconds to make a lasting impression and the fact that the application comes down to a few minutes of review before a decision is rendered, I encourage applicants to go through the exercise of summarizing their salient attributes into one sentence: their personal brand statement.

## Personal Brand Statement

If you had about twenty-five words to describe yourself, what words would you use? Many people refer to this as your one-minute introduction or elevator pitch. We refer to it as your personal brand statement (PBS). The PBS is important because it summarizes who you are in a memorable way. To improve your chance of writing a focused application that reinforces the core of your brand, it is important to have a clear PBS.

The PBS is made up of three parts:

1. Who you are
2. What you have done
3. Where you plan to end up

Here are some PBS examples of MBA candidates who have gained admission to top programs:

- Gutsy Asian female with a passion for empowering women who plans to transform family business by infusing fair-trade practices
- Athletic, team-driven leader with passion for investing who plans to leverage international investing experience to build a world-class investment management firm
- Midwestern energetic female with accelerated cross-functional leadership roles at media company who plans to run an entertainment company focused on educational programs for children
- African American bootstrapper with significant leadership track record who plans to create and run a VC fund to help revitalize inner-city communities

Why is the PBS important? The MBA Board reads thousands of pages of applications and has the challenge of distilling a candidate's information into a descriptive summary, the equivalent of a PBS. After wading through countless application pages, the Board needs to be able to point to a clear takeaway of what they think is distinctive and memorable about you. When candidates start out with a personal brand statement, it serves as a road map for their application. They are able to ask themselves whether each story (essay) reinforces their personal brand statement. Given the limited space allotment of admission essays, a personal brand statement allows you to maintain a laser-like focus when selecting topics to write about as you position your story. Also, by having a clear sense of your PBS before you complete the application, you will be able to refer back to it each step of the application process to determine whether your essays, recommendations, and even the answers you provide in an interview reinforce your personal brand.

So now that you know how important it is to complete a PBA to understand your brand, you know what brand themes look like, and you have reviewed PBS examples, let's practice. Try summarizing your story in one sentence (your PBS), keeping in mind that although there may be different things that you would like to cover, the law of focus is critical.

---

## YOUR PERSONAL BRAND STATEMENT

_____

_____

_____

_____

---

After you have developed your PBS, continue to refine it and work on keeping it succinct (about twenty-five words).

Once you have completed this entire branding process, you are now ready to tackle the application. In a couple of chapters, I address the selection criteria used by Admissions Boards at leading business schools to evaluate candidates. But before I leave this branding chapter, I want to share a few thoughts on Career Changers.

## CAREER CHANGERS

No applicant is more in need of personal branding than career changers. Applicants in this category have to convince the MBA Board that they need an MBA and that the new career goal makes sense given their current experience.

Although MBA Boards welcome career changers to apply, the expectation is that there should be a strong connection between who you are, what you have done, and what you wish to do in the future. A derivative trader, for instance, with little to no community service experience helping nonprofit groups who simply says that she wants the MBA so that she can run a nonprofit organization is going to have an extremely difficult time convincing the MBA Board that her goals are authentic. The immediate questions in the mind of the MBA Board are, how realistic is the goal and does the applicant have elements in her background that reinforce her identified passion of nonprofit management?

Many career services offices have come under fire in the past few years regarding the placement statistics of graduating students. It is not enough to show interest in a new career; applicants today must keep in mind that they will need to find a job in the new career at the end of their program. The bigger the gap between your experience and future role, the tougher it is to convince recruiters to hire you in the new career. Career changers are likely to be rejected if their goals are inconsistent and don't seem credible. I address the consistency and credibility issue in greater detail in the chapter on essay fundamentals.

The first step career changers should take is to find ways to begin incorporating their passion into their lives. If you find that there is a gap between what you want to do and what you do currently, you may be able to create credibility for your goals by using your extracurricular activities and community service involvement to establish a track record of commitment to the new career. Doing this will create more synergy between your passion and your actions.

Successfully positioning yourself as a career changer requires planning, time, and a good dose of patience. Simply stating that you are an engineer who wishes to make a switch to finance will not cut it. It is a huge career leap. Why does a career in finance matter to you? How will you use the new career to effect change? Career changers need to be very specific when making a case for a new career. They have to demonstrate specific knowledge about the new career so that it is clear that it isn't simply a passing fancy. In addition, having congruence between your personal life and your professional life is equally important. The following cases illustrate the importance of creating consistency in one's brand.

## Case Study: Pre-MBA Career Changers

### Ann: Auditor to Real Estate Entrepreneur

Ann had been working as an accountant and auditor for a somewhat obscure company and felt quite dispassionate about her career. She enjoyed numbers and had studied accounting at the university and shortly after became a certified public accountant (CPA). After a few years as an accountant and auditor, she noticed that despite having mastered her responsibilities and having received multiple promotions, she was beginning to plateau in her professional development. More than that, she realized that as she ascended her career ladder, she was becoming more specialized, leaving her less excited about accounting. Ann began to question what was missing. Why was she not excited about the prospect of another potential promotion? Why was she more interested in closing the next real estate deal for her sideline "hobby"? For the past two years,

Ann had been dabbling in buying real estate, but she always considered it a hobby, not her bread and butter.

After completing a brand audit, Ann realized that her true passion was indeed real estate and that an entrepreneurial track was what was missing in her current role, where there was limited room for innovation. Further reinforcement came through her brand audit as she began to recall early memories tagging along with her real estate entrepreneur uncle as he made his Saturday rounds to review his development sites.

Delving deeper into what attracted her to real estate, Ann discovered that she enjoyed the research involved in locating the right deal, structuring the financing, negotiating with lawyers and sellers, and managing the overall process. Ann carefully saved enough money and eventually quit her job to focus on real estate full time.

Because her passion and brand are intrinsically tied to real estate, Ann also became involved in community service organizations to help low-income residents access affordable housing.

Ann has successfully rebranded herself as a real estate entrepreneur in a consistent and credible way. Her passion and goals come from the heart and are clear to anyone who meets her. Her community involvement isn't simply to check off the box on the application but is a result of what matters to her. If she decides to apply to business school in the future, she will have the advantage of applying with a clear and distinctive brand, which will likely lead to a successful application.

### Jenny and Scot: Bankers to Nonprofit Managers

Not all career changers will have the luxury of quitting their jobs and starting a business they are passionate about. So what else could a career changer do to strengthen his or her application?

Take Jenny, an investment banker who had decided she wanted a career in nonprofit management. Her challenge is that she does not have community service experience and her extracurricular activities boil down to some social events that she planned through her sorority in college. Given her lack of track record in volunteering for nonprofit organizations or any related activities, Jenny's goal of starting or managing a nonprofit organization most likely will not pass the credibility test in the application. If Jenny applies without developing a track record at a nonprofit group, her brand will be strongly tied to finance and it is unlikely she will be offered admission at a top-tier MBA program.

Contrast Jenny with Scot. Scot, too, is a banker who wants to run or start a nonprofit organization in the future. He has spent most of his professional career working as an investment banker. However, his extracurricular involvement, both while he was in college and currently in his community, is strongly tied to nonprofit leadership. Scot's track record of having started several socially conscious organizations in college and beyond enables him to pass the credibility test. Clearly, an MBA Board is more likely to admit Scot over Jenny because his socially responsible interest is strongly tied to his brand and he has solid evidence of having started organizations in this area. In fact, Scot gained admission to Harvard and Stanford Graduate Business School!

The lesson here is: if you want to change your career and rebrand yourself, it is best to show a track record through work or outside activities. Are there skills that you currently use in your career that are transferable to your new career? Highlight them in your application. Are there opportunities to work part time or as a volunteer in the new career? A consultant who discovered that her passion is in the restaurant business spent most of her weekends working in a restaurant. She didn't simply fall back on the fact that she worked long hours. She invested the time to gain some exposure to the new career. Some may think this is too extreme, but it made the difference in her acceptance to her top MBA program.

But what about after you gain admission to business school? Career changers still have a tough road ahead of them in transitioning to the new career. The two-year MBA program is ideal for a career changer because there is more time built into the curriculum to allow for hands-on experience in the new career.

## Case Study: Post-MBA Career Changers

*Felix: Engineer to Investment Banker*

Felix was an engineer for five years and was interested in switching to investment banking. After his first year in business school at a top program, he interned for a financial advisory firm during the summer. This experience enabled him to land a position in a small private equity group in his home country. His ties to his country coupled with a name brand institution gave him an advantage in securing this position. His goal is to build up his private equity experience to develop a track record before making a move into a larger, more established private equity shop.

*Valerie: Nonprofit Manager to Marketing Associate*

Valerie is another career changer who used the MBA to land a job at a leading firm that is her passion. She had worked in the nonprofit sector prior to attending business school. She knew from the minute she arrived in business school that she wanted to change careers and set out to build skills and gain experiences that would make her competitive in the career search. Her goal was to switch into marketing. Instead of targeting the summer for internships, she realized that she needed marketing experience to land a coveted internship. She joined the marketing club and began networking with classmates with marketing backgrounds and met with marketing professionals visiting the school. During the winter break, instead of going on a leisure trip with friends, she secured an internship with a consumer goods company. At the company, she made sure to network with key individuals in the marketing and business development group. Her focused efforts paid off as she received a summer internship at the firm. When she graduated from business school, she had multiple offers from the top consumer goods companies.

# CHAPTER FOUR

## Admissions Full Cycle

A CRITICAL MISTAKE THAT MANY applicants make in the application process is not fully understanding the importance of the entire admissions cycle. There are three stages to the admissions cycle, namely, preapplication, application, and postapplication. Each of these periods is important to creating a successful application, and ignoring one of these stages can negatively affect your admission outcome.

Business school application requires a fair amount of time and resources to yield a positive outcome. It is important to give yourself enough time when planning to apply to business school. Beginning to plan for the MBA two years before applying to business school allows candidates to address any holes in their story. Applying shortly before the deadline (while it may work for some candidates) is not optimal because it does not allow enough time for candidates to build up a track record or to address any potential weaknesses in their story. Quite frankly, it is never too early to start preparing for the application. While you are still in college is the ideal time to begin planning for business school. Deciding to take quantitative business classes, acing the GMAT, and ensuring you have a fantastic leadership track record in college are all practical steps you can take to solidify your background before you begin the application to business school.

I'm often asked what happens to the physical application once it is submitted, and I'll answer that question in this chapter. I will also address the steps and process an application goes through after you hit the submit button, the actual evaluation process, and the follow-up process associated with the application after it has been reviewed and a decision is made.

## THE PREAPPLICATION PROCESS

The preapplication stage is when you can do your due diligence to determine which MBA program is the best fit for you. During this stage, candidates can research MBA rankings, review program websites and marketing materials, attend open house events, visit campuses, and refine their brands. What a candidate does during the preapplication period can significantly change his or her odds for admission to an elite business school.

Another important component of the preapplication period is GMAT preparation. The GMAT material covers mathematics, grammar, and other subjects that you probably studied many years ago. When was the last time you were tested on a sentence completion exercise? By taking a GMAT prep course during this period, you can increase your test performance when you take the exam. If you are not satisfied with your score, you will still have ample time to retake the exam.

In addition, starting early gives you the opportunity to take multiple courses to strengthen your quantitative background (especially if your GPA is low or you do not have a business background). I had a male client who was an engineer and who had attended five universities before finally graduating and earned a 2.9 GPA. He was able to strengthen his academic background by taking two business classes and earning an A in both of them. Taking the initiative to attend finance and accounting courses and demonstrating that he had the intellectual aptitude and discipline to handle rigorous coursework was exactly what he needed to do to mitigate the low GPA. He ended up gaining admission to a top MBA program and received several thousand dollars in scholarships.

Lack of leadership is a common reason that applicants are rejected. The preapplication period presents a great opportunity for you to assess where you can improve your leadership track record. Devoting a year or two to address those gaps can make you more competitive in the future when you apply to business school. Early preparation for the application will also allow you to make a candid assessment of your personal brand to determine whether there are admission gaps that exist and devise a plan to tackle them. For instance, realizing that your community leadership is weak will allow you enough time to take on community leadership roles and develop a track record, which will set your application in a positive light. If you have demonstrated little leadership at work, you can use the preapplication period to beef up your professional leadership (whether it is starting a new initiative at work or taking on leadership responsibility to manage junior team members). The brand assessment also can be helpful to those who are career changers. With a two-year head start, you can try to make a move into the industry in which you are interested or at least become involved on a volunteer basis in the area in which you wish to transition in the future. For candidates who lack international exposure, this is the perfect time to request an international assignment or to change jobs to gain more global experience.

Let's take a closer look at the specific steps and variables that can guide candidates as they prepare themselves before embarking on the application.

## Rankings

The four most popular ranking entities for business schools are *U.S. News & World Report*, *Business Week*, the *Wall Street Journal*, and *Financial Times*. My general opinion of rankings is that they are a good starting point to gain perspective on the brands of the programs and how they are viewed by students, alumni, and recruiters. However, I caution applicants about using rankings as the only determinant for their decision to apply to a particular program. The methodologies for ranking business schools vary from one ranking entity to another, and a large amount of the information is subjective. Therefore, it is quite common to have a wide discrepancy between the ranks that are conferred to each MBA program (for instance, a program can be ranked first and tenth by different agencies in the same year). It is also important to remember that just because a program is ranked in the top ten MBA program list does not mean you will fit in there. You should conduct a thorough investigation to ensure that the program will offer you the right environment to grow and meet your professional and personal objectives.

## Open House Events

Each summer and fall, MBA programs embark on an extensive recruitment schedule that includes on-campus information sessions and open house events across the globe. These events are designed to introduce prospective candidates to the MBA program through presentations from MBA Board members, faculty, current students, and alumni. Invitations are extended to prospective candidates living in the area where the admissions events take place. Prior to each event, the MBA Board sends out an invitation to individuals in their inquiry database. I recommend that you provide your contact information to the admissions office as soon as possible so that you can be invited to open house events held in your city. These are beneficial in that they give you access to board members who you may not get an opportunity to engage with outside of this context. Also, for individuals who do not have access to alumni from their MBA program of interest, open house events are great opportunities to meet with alumni and to gain perspective about the direct impact and value of the specific MBA program.

## Marketing Materials

MBA programs are quite savvy with their marketing, often creating glossy brochures and elaborate websites to attract prospective applicants. Relying on the marketing materials of business schools without visiting the schools may only give you a superficial view of the program. For instance, some programs may say they have a global focus, but further investigation can reveal that opportunities to pursue a global education or to study abroad may be severely limited. This is why you can't simply take materials at face value without speaking with alumni and current students and visiting the schools to get a firsthand experience of the program. I can't tell you how many candidates swear that a particular program is ideal for them simply based on the marketing materials they read. I know of a candidate who got admitted to a school in the Midwest that she had set her mind on attending. After realizing it wasn't a good fit, she found herself stuck because it was the only admission offer she had in hand. Because she couldn't remain at her current job, she had to scramble to find an alternative. The result was that she eventually found a job in a far-flung region of the world as she planned her reapplication strategy. The wasted time, money, and angst that she experienced could have all been avoided had she taken the time to visit the programs she was applying to. You can bet on the fact that the second time around she will be sure to visit every single school she plans to apply to.

## Campus Visits

Although the websites of business schools can be useful tools when getting started in application research, it eventually becomes more important to speak with individuals who are products of the programs to get their firsthand perspective. A campus visit allows you to attend classes, experience the faculty and their teaching styles, and interact with current students to learn about the academic and social culture of the program. I have always said that the application to business school is an exercise in marketing; and as you spend more time with the students, faculty, and administrators of a business school, the more familiar you will be with the program's brand. In turn, the more face time you have with your "customer," the MBA Board, the more likely you are to convey your brand. There is a caveat to this: stalking the Admissions Board by camping out at the admissions office will only send the wrong message and therefore have the opposite effect you wish to have. Limit your visits to a couple of trips to campus and ensure that you get full exposure to classes, student life, and the Admissions Board (when available) during your visit.

## THE APPLICATION PROCESS

Application to business school is challenging and can be extremely stressful for most candidates. The combination of knowing that you have a 10 to 20 percent acceptance chance and the engaging, time-consuming nature of the application process presents a fair share of anxiety for applicants. You should avoid skipping any steps in the application process. For instance, during the application cycle, passing up an opportunity to interview at programs for which interviews are an option may communicate to the MBA Board that you are not fully committed to their program. Once you have identified the MBA programs in which you are interested, the next step is tackling the application.

Applications vary from one MBA program to another, and it is important to review each program's application requirements and deadlines to ensure that you fulfill each appropriately. Most leading MBA programs have set deadlines that focus on discrete rounds. To further complicate things, you will find that some programs, such as Tuck, have an early application (priority) deadline that is not binding if you are admitted; on the other hand, Columbia's early decision deadline is binding and is for candidates for whom Columbia is a first choice. To avoid any confusion, get the information from the business school admissions office directly to ensure that you have the exact deadlines and admission policies.

MBA programs have strict policies surrounding the deadlines, so plan to start the application process early. Incomplete applications are typically pushed to the next round and exceptions are rarely granted even when an incomplete application is the result of an errant recommender.

Applying first or second round is preferable. There isn't a fundamental difference between round one and round two, so applicants should apply when they are ready, not because they are trying to "game" the system. Avoid submitting your application in the later rounds. Many programs explicitly state that applicants should avoid applying in the later rounds because most admissions spots are taken by then. It may also become tougher for international students to secure their visa if they apply late. There are a few candidates for whom applying later may not have as detrimental an effect: a classic example is the nontraditional candidate with an excellent GMAT score and academic record and solid track record of leadership. A candidate like this can "round out" the class and, with no academic issues, could be admitted in a late round. Also, someone who is applying from a country that is underrepresented in the applicant pool could get away with a later-round application if they are solid in all three admission criteria. (I'll go into great detail in the next chapter on the admission criteria used to evaluate candidates.) The operative word here is "could." You always run the risk of being rejected if there are few spots available. There are even some MBA programs that have informed candidates that their application was strong but that the lateness of their application affected their admission being denied. Preparing yourself early in the pre-application stage and judiciously executing the application will help you avoid any mishaps.

Because I'm discussing the application stage, I'll go over some specific topics that often arise concerning the actual application in the following sections.

## The MBA Application Components

The MBA application is composed of several items, including the resume, recommendations, essays, transcripts, GMAT, and a completed application. Each aspect of the application is important and carries significant weight in the decision to admit a candidate. The goal for applicants is to present a strong application across all the evaluation materials. The stronger each element of the application is the higher the chance of being admitted. I will discuss each of the application components in later chapters. I would like to give you some insights into what happens to your physical application once it is submitted and the process it goes through before an admission decision is rendered.

## What happens once I submit my application?

In the past couple of years the majority of admissions offices have moved to a paperless application. Moving to an online application model has streamlined the application process and created more efficiency for MBA programs. Operations teams in the admissions offices are now able to spend less time entering application data, thus enabling MBA Boards to quickly begin the application evaluation. Even the submission of recommendations has become more efficient. Instead of relying on the postal service to deliver a recommender letter on time, you can take the guesswork and stress out of the recommendation process by having letters submitted online. Once you identify who will write your recommendations, you can enter their names and email addresses, giving your recommenders access to the online application. The trick, however, is to make sure that the recommender does not submit the recommendation before you have had a chance to discuss your overall strategy and key brand message. This has happened to a few unsuspecting candidates, so make sure to communicate to your recommenders that you plan to discuss your branding before they submit their recommendations.

Once you have submitted your application and all supplemental materials, your status will change to reflect that your application is complete or under review. The operations staff then prints out a copy of your application and creates a folder for you. Applications are not reviewed until they are complete and all required materials have been received.

## Can I influence when my application is reviewed?

The order in which applications are reviewed is random and does not indicate who will receive a favorable outcome. It comes down to when your physical application is created and when the MBA Board member picks up the application bin that happens to contain your application. Let me paint a vivid picture for you to illustrate my point. The operations room is the hub of any admissions office. It is here that the applications are printed, folders created, and bins (containers that board members use to lug applications back and forth between their homes and schools) assembled. Let's say your complete application is printed in the beginning of the week and placed in a bin, and it happens to be a week where a higher number of applications are printed and assembled. Even though your application was printed at the beginning of the week, by Friday, when the MBA Board members stop in to pick up their bins, yours may be in the back, making it logistically difficult to get to. The MBA Board will grab the bins that are up front and make their way to the back. Candidates whose folders were created later in the week will be in bins that are more accessible. The good news is that every application will receive the necessary and thorough evaluation regardless of when it is reviewed. It will receive the same level of scrutiny and multiple evaluations by different board members. So you see, there isn't much a candidate can do with regard to influencing when their application is evaluated. Thus, investing energy into figuring out how to influence the timing on your application review is a useless exercise. A better use of your time is to create an appealing and interesting application that will capture the mindshare of the Admissions Board. Applications to schools with a rolling admissions policy are reviewed in the order in which they are received.

## Can I send additional materials to the admissions office?

Schools vary in their policy with regard to accepting additional materials after the application deadline. It is imperative that you know what the program's policy is so that you are not surprised. A safe assumption is that the MBA program will not accept new materials after the deadline. A few exceptions may exist for wait-listed candidates at some schools, but again, you should check with the MBA program to find out exactly what their policy is and adhere to it.

## What happens if my application is not complete at the deadline?

An email is the most common way that candidates are notified of their incomplete status. If your application status doesn't change from pending to complete, it is worth contacting the admissions office. A top reason for an application remaining incomplete is a delay in the recommendations. It is your responsibility to touch base with all your recommenders to ensure that they submitted their letters on time. If you are like me, a little on the cautious side, you may want to contact your recommenders at least a couple of weeks before the submission deadline to make sure they have everything they need and that they submit their letters in time. Contacting admissions offices multiple times to inquire if they received your recommendation letters or any other materials is not the best way to make a positive impact on them. Be sensitive to the Admissions Board's overstretched schedule and don't inundate them with calls or emails. You are better off controlling the process by staying in touch with your recommenders and making sure that they fulfill their commitment of submitting your materials on time. Giving them more than three months to write a recommendation for you will help you limit any recommendation problems that may crop up.

## How are applications reviewed?

MBA programs vary in the specific evaluation processes that they use in assessing candidates. I am often asked questions regarding how many people evaluate candidates at Harvard, how long applications are evaluated, and the gender of MBA Board members. Those are the wrong questions to focus on because answers to these questions do little to prepare you for presenting a powerful application nor do they influence the admission outcome.

Here is what may be useful to know. Applications are randomly selected for review and are not ranked based on GMAT, GPA, or any other variable. In other words, applications are not sorted based on GMAT scores, with candidates having top scores being reviewed and those having lower scores cast aside. Applications are selected and reviewed randomly. For schools that have students involved in admission, the students are typically involved in reviewing the applications during the first reads. Applications are then passed on to a board member who does a second read. For schools where students do not evaluate applications, the first read is done by an Admissions Board member and then passed on to another Admissions Board member. By the second evaluation, a decision is made to reject, wait-list, further review, or admit the student. Candidates in the admit pile typically are extended an interview invitation. A few candidates may be "rescued" from the reject pile for various reasons (for example, their unique perspective based on their backgrounds and experiences). Those that are in the wait-list pile will be held until applications are reviewed from the next round to see how strong they compare to the next batch of candidates. Some number of candidates will come off the wait list (this number varies from year to year based on how competitive the overall pool is). Applications in the "worth another review" pile will be reviewed by another board member or discussed at committee before their fate is determined. There are MBA programs in which decisions are made in the context of a committee. In this situation, batches of applications are debated and decisions made after board members have had a chance to discuss, or should I say, dissect the candidate's application merits. This is why it is important to have a distinctive brand that the MBA Board can identify after reading your application. This makes it easier for the person who is arguing for your candidacy to make a compelling case on your behalf.

## THE POSTAPPLICATION PROCESS

After you have submitted your application, there are a few things you can do to prepare yourself for business school. For starters, you can register for one or two business classes if you feel you need a refresher, especially if you have not taken such coursework in the past. This could also be helpful if you have been out of school for a long time. At the very least, such coursework is excellent preparation to ensure that you are not too rusty when you begin the business degree. On the other hand, you would be ready should the Admissions Board admit you with the condition that you take business courses.

One of the issues facing applicants once they are admitted is when to quit their jobs. This decision warrants careful consideration. Here's an example that illustrates why planning your exit strategy is important. An overly confident applicant believed that the admission "was in the bag" so she subsequently quit her job before getting an admission offer. Unfortunately for her, she was denied admission by all the schools she applied to.

A related issue to timing your departure deals with how to manage your boss. It is important to remain sensitive when quitting your job. A candidate I know contacted me frantic and upset after her current boss threatened to call the Admissions Board at a top business school where she had applied to rescind his recommendation supporting her candidacy. His reason? He felt that the candidate had not shown good faith by choosing to quit several months ahead of when he expected her to leave. Clearly, she had not managed her boss's expectations effectively, and this put her in a precarious situation.

Exiting before you receive an admission offer is a risk not worth taking. It is equally important to manage the expectations of those with whom you work. As long as you remain at the firm, it is important to convey unrelenting commitment to your job. Should you decide to leave, you should have an exit strategy that you ease your boss into. Because it is important not to burn your bridges (you never know when you will need that former boss again), consider offering to train your replacement. Of course, every situation is unique so you will have to decide what course of action is right for you.

### What happens after a decision is made on an application?

Once a decision is rendered on an application, it is then entered into the application database. The outcome is then communicated to the applicant at the notification deadline. A huge pet peeve for the Admissions Board is when candidates call to find out their decision before the notification date. Not too long ago, overeagerness to find out their admissions decisions led several candidates to illegally access a database in an attempt to discover their admission outcomes prematurely. They paid a steep price because some schools rejected them despite having admitted them. I understand the pressures candidates are under to find out their admission outcome especially after waiting several months. I feel your pain! The best thing to do after you submit your application is to stay busy to keep your mind off of the admission forums and resist checking your email obsessively hour after hour for the interview invitation. But, of course, this is easier said than done.

The day before the notification deadline is a crazy day for all applicants, with many camping next to their computers awaiting news of their admissions decision. These days many admissions directors call admitted candidates to congratulate them prior to or shortly after the notification email has been sent. Often there is a trend in the region that dictates who receives calls first. International applicants who reside abroad may get calls first given the time difference.

Even after you have been admitted, keep in mind that your application can be rescinded should you demonstrate poor judgment. Remember that you are viewed as someone who will reflect positively on the brand of the MBA program. Your admission offer can be withdrawn should anything negative or scandalous be associated with you. So exercise wisdom both with what you say in online chats and blogs, as well as in your life in general.

## What is the application verification process?

After a candidate has received his or her admission offer, the Admissions Board verifies the information presented in the application. Verification of applications isn't new. Admissions Boards have typically verified admitted students' official transcripts and GMAT scores. More recently, however, the MBA Boards have expanded their verification to the career track record of candidates and scrutinize information involving employment dates, history, bonuses, and salaries. Wharton has been doing verifications far longer than most schools but the trend today is that all top MBA programs verify applicants' information at some level. The approach used by each program varies, however. So while some use an actual verification firm, others may opt to do so themselves by making the calls to your former employers. Schools that do not have the bandwidth to verify every single candidate may focus on candidate information that seems far-fetched.

Candidates should take the verification process seriously and ensure that all information provided in their application is accurate; those who don't ultimately learn the hard way. I know of instances where admission offers were revoked due to inconsistency in the candidate's information. This was the case with a candidate who falsified his grade in one class from a B to an A. The outcome was that his admission was rescinded. He would have been admitted anyway with the B grade but his dishonesty cost him a spot at a top business school. Candidates are not immune after they have been admitted either. I'm aware of a situation where a candidate who was already enrolled was kicked out of the program after the school received a late verification report indicating that the candidate had provided false information.

Applicants should pay close attention to information covered in their application to ensure its accuracy. Even casual mistakes can be problematic, so be extremely careful when inputting your information, and if you are not sure, spend the extra time to get the accurate information. My advice to all applicants is to resist the temptation to embellish or exaggerate your story. Falsifying your achievements, career impact, or any other information for that matter can lead to your admission being overturned. Don't take that chance.

The following words from Harvard's website summarize the MBA Board's view of verification:

"The School will verify application information and reserves the right to withdraw any offer of admission already made if there is any discrepancy between the self-reported information and information provided through verification" (HBS Admissions website).

## FINAL THOUGHTS

The application to business school is a marathon and not a sprint. It takes years of "training" and careful execution to yield the desired results. Taking this approach and devoting appropriate time and resources to each stage of the process will give you a better shot at getting into a top institution. Given the significant benefits of an MBA from a top school, it is a missed opportunity to leave any part of this process to chance. Another factor worth a close examination is the admissions criteria that every candidate is evaluated on. I discuss this at great length in the next chapter.

# CHAPTER FIVE

## Understanding the Admissions Criteria

B EFORE I GO ON to discuss the specific application components, I want to review the overall admissions criteria
that are used to evaluate candidates. There have been a lot
of questions surrounding exactly how candidates are evaluated and which aspects of the admissions criteria count the
most when assessing a candidate. This chapter focuses on
the three admissions criteria used by the MBA Board in
evaluating all candidates. I also go into details of the specific
components comprised within each criterion to ensure that
you understand how the Admissions Board views them and
how you can maximize your chances of being admitted.
After you understand the admissions criteria, you should be
able to objectively evaluate your candidacy. This chapter
also provides suggestions of steps you can take to address
any gaps in your application.

Top business schools evaluate candidates across three core
areas, namely:

- Academic ability/intellectual aptitude
- Leadership impact/managerial potential
- Uniqueness (diverse experiences/perspectives and differ-
  entiated personal characteristics)

Some of the greatest myths surrounding the application process are related to candidates' misconceptions of the admissions criteria. I am often asked by applicants which criterion is the most important in the application process. The short answer is all of them. It is important to understand how these three admissions categories are viewed by the MBA Board. Ideally, candidates should try to be strong in all three areas. Given an extremely competitive admissions landscape, the stronger you are across all three criteria, the better your chance of being admitted. So, although we all know someone who was admitted without excelling in the three criteria, I encourage every applicant to present his or her strongest suit and submit an application that presents a compelling case across the entire admission criteria.

Each top MBA program refers to the admissions criteria in a different way, but, ultimately, they evaluate candidates based on these three categories. These statements taken from MBA admissions websites illustrate this point.

---

**STANFORD**

*The three primary criteria for admission to the Stanford MBA Program are demonstrated leadership potential, intellectual vitality, and contributions to the diversity of the Stanford community.*

**HARVARD**

*Our selection process emphasizes leadership potential, strong academic ability, and personal qualities and characteristics.*

**COLUMBIA**

*The committee values academic performance and seeks candidates who demonstrate superior intellectual ability...have developed a strong foundation and/or essential skills for their future professional goals...have proven themselves as both leaders and team players, who are well rounded and interesting, and who have demonstrated the will and ability to actively contribute to the well-being of their community.*

## CHICAGO

*The Admissions Committee looks for people who have demonstrated the ability to succeed through work experience, academic endeavors, and extracurricular or community service involvement.*

## INSEAD

*We expect intellectual curiosity coupled with a desire to learn and stretch yourself in a rigorous academic programme, as well as personal qualities to contribute to the many activities of the Institute.*

## TUCK

*What makes a candidate successful? There is no formula for admission to Tuck. Each decision hinges on the interplay of five principal factors: Demonstrated Academic Excellence, Demonstrated Leadership, Demonstrated Accomplishment, Interpersonal Skills, and Diversity of Background and Experience.*

## STERN

*We seek students who are confident in their ability to master the required material and have the courage to ask challenging questions...who have a proven track record and clear professional goals, both short-term and long-term...who will contribute to the Stern community. We seek students with proven leadership ability, maturity, character, and strong communication skills, who will be active participants at Stern and have a great passion for, pride in, and commitment to Stern.*

Let's take a look at each of the three core areas.

# ACADEMIC ABILITY/INTELLECTUAL APTITUDE

The curriculum at MBA programs is challenging. It is therefore important that admitted candidates have the appropriate academic preparation to handle a rigorous environment. Candidates do not need a business degree from an undergraduate university to apply to business school. In fact, the majority of MBA programs report that business majors make up only about 20 to 25 percent of their class. What's more important is that candidates show that they are intellectually sharp and have the discipline to engage and contribute in a rigorous educational setting.

Whether candidates can handle the rigor of the MBA program is assessed in two ways: their Graduate Management Admission Test (GMAT) scores and their college transcripts. Both of these variables are reviewed in the context of the candidate's life: What opportunities have they had? Are they the first in their family to go to college? How do the GMAT and GPA overlap?

Ideally, you want both the GMAT score and GPA to be very strong. For some applicants, although the GMAT may be lower than the median at the school, the GPA may be significantly higher. The reverse can also be the case. If you find yourself in this situation, there are practical steps you can take to convince the MBA Board that you are intelligent and able to handle a challenging program. In such circumstances, the recommendations become even more critical in the selection process because they can add additional reinforcement of your intellectual ability, curiosity, and analytical and quantitative strengths. Coursework can also alleviate academic concerns, as does retaking the GMAT and earning a higher score. Let's take a closer look at the GMAT and your transcript.

## The GMAT

The GMAT is the entrance exam that is required by all top, full-time two-year business schools in America. A recent trend has emerged with two top business schools (Stanford GSB and MIT's Sloan Business School) giving applicants the choice to submit either the Graduate Records Examination (GRE) or the GMAT. (It will be interesting to see whether other programs follow suit and allow candidates to submit the GRE scores as a substitute for the GMAT.) The professional organization that oversees the GMAT is the Graduate Management Admission Council (GMAC). Once a paper-and-pencil exam, the GMAT has become primarily a computer-administered exam. It is also adaptive in nature: the computer generates questions based on your skill level and your performance on previous questions.

After a candidate takes the GMAT, the score is active for up to five years, so it is important to take the exam as early as possible. The test itself is administered six days a week, with the exception of holidays. Applicants can take the exam up to five times in an academic year (waiting thirty-one days between exams). Business schools do not penalize candidates for taking the exam more than once. In fact, they accept the highest score (check with your school to make sure that this is still applicable).

Candidates who are unhappy with their GMAT results the first time should definitely retake the exam. The fact that MBA programs accept your best GMAT score isn't license to take the GMAT half a dozen times. Two or three times is acceptable. The fifth and sixth time may be overkill. The important thing here is to invest in adequate preparation ahead of time to avoid having to take the exam too many times. On the other hand, if you take it once and you are dissatisfied with your score, and if you think trying a second or third time can significantly improve your score, then that is fine. However, if your score doesn't improve after retaking it two to three times, I personally feel it is more effective for you to focus on other parts of the application where you may have greater control in shaping the "story."

Timing when to take the GMAT is vital since you have to wait thirty-one days to retake the exam. Avoid taking the exam too close to the admission deadline. I know candidates who have scored unexpectedly poorly on the first GMAT, and because of the thirty-one-day waiting period, they missed applying within the first round. Also, remember that the test itself is not cheap. Each exam cost $250, so it is to your advantage to fully prepare for the exam before taking it. You can learn more about the GMAT by visiting www.gmac.com or www.mba.com, where you can register for the exam.

I'm often asked about the ideal GMAT score an applicant needs in order to be admissible. Unfortunately, there are many misconceptions surrounding this subject. The truth is that there is no magic number to guarantee admission.

MBA programs often state that they do not have minimum GMAT scores or cutoff requirements for admission. Although that is true, a GMAT of 300 will not earn anyone a spot at Stanford Graduate School of Business (GSB) or any top ten MBA program; on the other hand, a GMAT score of 800 won't guarantee a candidate admission to a top MBA program either.

The best way to view the GMAT is to recognize that it is a necessary but not sufficient variable in the application. Getting a strong score can keep you in the running for a coveted admission spot, but a mediocre score can end your admission aspirations. Check out the websites of the MBA programs you are interested in to find out where your GMAT score falls compared with the median GMAT score of the entering class. If your score is significantly below that of the median, 640 compared with 706, for example, you should postpone applying and devote more time and resources to improving your score.

The GMAT scores standardize the academic components by providing a benchmark to assess different candidates coming from varied professional and personal backgrounds and experiences. This is especially so when candidates come from schools that the Admissions Boards are not as familiar with. Even for well-known schools, majors and grading systems vary. As such, a 3.7 GPA at one school may be closer to a 3.4 at another school and vice versa. The GMAT score, on the other hand, is an admission variable that provides the MBA Board with perspective of how the candidate scored compared with others who took the test. The other reason MBA Boards care about the GMAT score is that some of the ranking agencies rely on this information when ranking MBA programs. The GMAT has considerable weight in the application process, so give it the attention it deserves.

### GMAT Components and What They Mean to the Admissions Board

The GMAT score is made up of three components: the Analytical Writing Assessment (AWA) Section, the Verbal Section, and the Quantitative Section. The AWA is made up of two essays (one on argument analysis and the other on issue analysis). You will be given thirty minutes for each essay. The overall GMAT score ranges from 200 to 800. The score represents performance in two areas: verbal and quantitative. The Verbal Section is made up of forty-one multiple choice questions that include sentence correction, critical reasoning, and reading comprehension. You will have seventy-five minutes to complete the Verbal Section. Like the Verbal Section, seventy-five minutes is allotted to the Quantitative Section. This section is made up of thirty-seven multiple choice questions covering data sufficiency and problem solving (covering such topics as algebra, geometry, and arithmetic).

In addition to the raw number ascribed to each section, there is a percentile figure associated with it. Admissions Boards pay very close attention to both of these percentile figures. So not only is it essential to have a strong overall score and percentile, it is also important to perform strongly across both sections.

An applicant to business school, Chad, illustrates what a great GMAT result looks like. He has a score of 760. Following is the breakdown of his scores:

| | |
|---|---|
| Overall Score: | 760 |
| Overall Percentile: | 99% |
| Verbal Score: | 42 |
| Verbal Percentile: | 95% |
| Quantitative Score: | 51 |
| Quantitative Percentile: | 99% |
| AWA: | 5.5 |

The first thing the MBA Board will review when evaluating the GMAT performance is how the person fared overall. So, the first note would be that Chad scored 760 and that his score is higher than that of 99 percent of test takers. But they will not stop there. They will then check to make sure that there are no issues between the Verbal and Quantitative Sections. Scoring highly in both sections is important. Chad's Verbal and Quantitative breakdowns of 95 percent and 99 percent show that his GMAT is fine—both scores are above the 90th percentile. Some people are exceptional test takers. With more than a billion people in China, and with a strong emphasis on education, Chinese applicants may find steeper competition when it comes to the GMAT. For instance, although the overall median GMAT of an MBA program may be 700, the median for Chinese candidates may be even higher. This means that an applicant from China with a GMAT score of 700 may be considered much weaker on this evaluation variable. Be sensitive to how your profile fares in the overall GMAT pool as well as the specific demographic group that you fall into.

Besides the overall GMAT score, a candidate's performance in the Verbal and Quantitative Sections is important to the evaluation of his or her application. At a minimum, candidates should aim to score above the 80 percent mark in both sections. But what if there is a discrepancy between the two? Being weak in either the Verbal or the Quantitative Section can raise red flags for the MBA Board. For instance, an international applicant who has a 99 percent in the Quantitative Section and only a 60 percent in the Verbal Section will surely face questions concerning his or her verbal abilities. Candidates in such circumstances should plan to retake the exam and improve their performance in the Verbal Section. Conversely, a nontraditional applicant whose work experience is devoid of quantitative exposure and whose quantitative score falls in the 66th percentile will have a tough time convincing the Admissions Board that he or she has a strong enough quantitative background to thrive in a business school. Such a candidate can address this issue by retaking the exam and by taking quantitative classes and having a strong performance in them.

The AWA score ranges from 0 to 6 (6 being the highest score). AWA scores of 4.5 and above are considered fine. A high AWA (5.5) will rarely earn the applicant any major points. However, a low score (3.5 or lower) will raise questions regarding a candidate's writing ability. Although important, the AWA has traditionally been the least scrutinized component of the GMAT at most top business schools. This is changing somewhat as schools concerned about inconsistencies between applicants' writing ability and their actual essays may opt to compare writing style of essays from the AWA with the actual admissions essays. Anyone who chooses to use an advisory firm should maintain the integrity of their writing: never resort to hiring writing professionals to write your admission essays. A candidate with an AWA score of 3 whose essays read like that of a Pulitzer Prize–winning journalist will have a major problem explaining the inconsistency.

## BASIC GMAT TIPS

Start early. Plan to take the test at least a year before the deadline. Take a couple of practice tests to see how you perform.

Invest in a GMAT prep course if the score is below the median score of your target MBA programs.

Consider taking the GMAT while you are in college. It is easier to take an exam while you are still in studying mode. The GMAT score is active for five years.

Retake the exam if you are not satisfied with your score. The majority of MBA programs accept your highest score. (Check the specific programs to make sure their policy doesn't change.) GMAC reports that more than 20 percent of GMAT test takers retake the exam in a given year.

The GMAT range of admitted students at the MBA program should serve as a guide. Scoring below this range does not automatically disqualify your application. The strength of the rest of your application will be taken into account.

You can take the GMAT once every thirty-one days, so plan accordingly to ensure that you don't miss your application deadline.

Many test prep programs are available to help applicants boost their scores. The most popular ones are Princeton Review, Kaplan, Veritas, Bell Curve, and ManhattanGMAT. I strongly recommend that candidates do their due diligence to assess which one will best provide them with the support and preparation they need in order to nail a strong score. I encourage you to also check out my interview with Andrew Yang, Managing Director of ManhattanGMAT, at the end of this book.

# ENGLISH LANGUAGE ASSESSMENT
# (TOEFL AND IELTS)

International candidates who studied at institutions where English isn't the medium of communication are required to take an English Assessment exam. There are two main language exams that international students take for admission to business school: the Test of English as a Foreign Language (TOEFL) and/or the International English Language Testing System (IELTS). TOEFL is the more common and accepted test, although some MBA programs accept the IELTS in lieu of the TOEFL. Both exams assess international candidates' ability to speak and comprehend Standard English at a college level. Because the precise requirements for exempting from this exam vary from school to school, international candidates should visit each program's website to confirm which test is required. For instance, at Wharton, international candidates need to take the TOEFL, whereas Chicago GSB and UCLA's Anderson School accept either the TOEFL or the IELTS.

The TOEFL, the older test, has its roots as far back as the mid-1960s and is more widely accepted in the United States. The test is offered both through a paper-based and computer-based format. The TOEFL scores range from 0 to 300, with selective MBA programs requiring scores north of 250.

The test is composed of four sections, namely, Listening Comprehension, Structure and Written Expression, Reading Comprehension, and Essay Writing. The result is valid for two years. MBA programs do not accept expired scores, so make sure your scores are valid when you apply to business school. You can also arrange to have your scores sent directly to the school by providing the program's test code. For more information on the TOEFL, visit www.toefl.org.

The IELTS is a relatively new exam started in 1980. Applicants can register for a computer-based exam on its website (www.ielts.org) or sign up to take the exam at a test center, although only a limited number of locations are available. Test scores range from 1 to 9, with scores north of 6.5 required at top business schools that accept the IELTS.

## The Transcript

The college transcript plays an important role in the MBA admissions evaluation. The Admissions Board places great weight on candidates' academic track record because it reveals their performance over a period of time. The cumulative GPA isn't the only thing that matters when assessing a candidate's transcript; the trends of the grades are examined for consistency. So for instance, someone with an overall GPA of 3.5 who has straight-A grades in the first three years and C and D grades their last year can raise major flags for the MBA Board. Equally problematic are situations where the candidate's academic performance is like a roller coaster where they perform well in one year and poorly the second year. Transcripts with consistently strong grades over the course of the entire academic experience are ideal. If you are reading this book and are still in college, then you should do everything you can to make sure that your performance is in an upward trajectory. One thing is for sure, finishing weak is one of the hardest issues to overcome with the Admissions Board. Therefore, MBA candidates should avoid having their weakest grades their last year of college. It is easier to explain away a weak start than a weak finish.

The rigor of the academic experience is also taken into account when evaluating candidates' transcripts. No Admissions Board wants to admit a candidate who would flunk out of business school. Therefore, the college transcript is carefully scrutinized to ensure that the candidate has taken a challenging academic program and performed well. The GPA of each candidate provides the MBA Board with a general sense of how the applicant has handled academic challenges; this is then used to extrapolate how the applicant will perform in business school. A strong GPA enables the MBA Board to answer the question, "Can this candidate cut it academically?"

But the Board goes beyond GPA. They review the major academic strength of the school as well. For instance, the MBA Board recognizes that some majors, such as physics or computer engineering, may typically offer fewer 4.0 GPAs than less rigorous majors. Also, the MBA Board is aware of the significant differences that exist between schools when it comes to grading. Some schools are known for grade inflation; others are known for their tough grading policy. As a result, the Admissions Board is sensitive when evaluating a 3.0 GPA from a school with little grade inflation versus a 3.7 GPA from a school where a significant population earns high grades.

You demonstrate commitment to your area of study when you have taken challenging courses and even pursued independent study or honors research. However, it is equally important not to be too narrow. By taking courses outside of your major, you can show that you are not just a physics or computer geek. This will help differentiate you from other candidates with similar majors. The Admissions Board can also see through candidates who have taken easy classes just to pad their GPAs.

Applicants should educate the Admissions Boards when they have pursued an unusual academic program, especially if it is highly selective and rigorous. One way you can do this is to include a short sentence in your resume to highlight that point. An example is being the first in your department to complete a dual degree in an unusually short time frame. If you are one of the two people from your school to be inducted into an Honors Society, you should also state that in your resume. Equally interesting is taking the initiative to track down a professor from another institution and convince her to oversee your senior thesis if it is in an area that isn't covered by faculty at your school. Being willing to step beyond your academic comfort zone can be a differentiator that can give you an edge in the admissions process. To demonstrate how important Admissions Boards view the academic college experience, take a look at Harvard's essay question, which was introduced in the past couple of years: "What would you like the MBA Admissions Board to know about your undergraduate academic experience?" In asking this question, the interest lies in *academic experience*, not the social clubs and activities the student has been involved in. MBA Boards at the end of the day want to go beyond the letters and numbers of your transcript and aim to understand the motivations that drive you to pursue knowledge, your thought process behind your academic decisions, and the insights that you have gleaned that have molded you into the person you are today.

## Internationals

Many top business schools invest a lot of time in visiting different countries during their marketing cycle. They use these trips to learn about the schools and companies that employ the applicants from that region, and as a result, they are well-versed on the academic differences that exist among many of the international universities. Internationals coming from schools that do not give GPAs or class ranks do not need to worry; the MBA Board will not penalize your application for this. If in doubt, check with the MBA program to find out how it wants you to handle this situation (whether to leave it blank or provide an estimation). The Admissions Board is familiar with the grading systems at non-U.S. schools. They understand that a first class is rare and depicts exceptional academic achievement while a third-class performance obviously raises significant concerns about a candidate's academic ability. They also appreciate the academic rigor of a degree in engineering from a school like Imperial College in the United Kingdom or Indian Institute of Technology.

*Explaining Transcript Inconsistencies*

Health issues (on a personal level or involving a family member) are often the reason for a candidate's academic decline. A candidate I know had a tough two semesters when her mom was struggling with a life-threatening illness. This resulted in a big dip in her transcript her sophomore year. Luckily, she was able to turn this trend around, and for the remaining two years of college, her grades were consistently above a 3.5 GPA. Other candidates have spotty transcripts because they worked full time to support their education. Then there are situations where a candidate has low grades as a result of not effectively balancing academic studies and leadership involvement. Regardless of what the scenario is, candidates need to address any gaps or hiccups in their transcript. Using the optional essays to do so is the ideal strategy. The way you describe the situation can be telling. Demonstrate maturity by owning up to what happened and avoid making excuses. But don't go to the other extreme by groveling and overemphasizing the issue, which could cause the Admissions Board to fixate on it.

## BASIC TRANSCRIPT TIPS

If your GPA is low, you should take two or more quantitative courses and earn an A in each of them. Financial accounting, economics, calculus, and statistics are good options. MBA programs vary in terms of the courses they recommend, so inquire directly to the programs to identify their preference. This is most pertinent if your undergraduate degree is in a nonquantitative area.

Use the optional section of the application to address why your grades were less than stellar in college. Make sure your response reflects maturity and self-awareness. Whatever you do, avoid blaming others and take responsibility for your weak academic grades. Lower grades at the start of college are easier to explain than consistently weak performance for four years.

Your recommendation is another great place to convince the MBA Board that you have the intellectual horsepower and ability to handle a challenging academic program. To offset a weak transcript, recommenders can stress your exceptional analytical, quantitative, and technical skills as well as your ability to grasp new information and come up the learning curve quickly. The more specific and detailed these examples are, the more successful you will be in reassuring the MBA Board that your weak college academic performance will not dictate how you will perform in their program. Equally important is allaying any concerns that the MBA Board has about your maturity, and the recommendation letters can be effective in doing this.

Retake the GMAT if you have low grades. This way, your GMAT can mitigate the MBA Board's concerns about your weak academic record. It is fair to say that a combined weak academic college performance and GMAT score presents a challenge that is very difficult to overcome in the evaluation process. What this means is that a candidate with a 540 GMAT and 2.9 GPA will likely not be admitted to Columbia or any top business school for that matter. On the other hand, getting that GMAT score above 700 can often result in an admission offer at a top business school, despite a 2.9 GPA.

Excellent performance in a graduate degree can sometimes help offset the MBA Board's negative perception of low undergraduate academic performance. I don't advocate taking a master's program solely to boost your academics. If there is a graduate program that appeals to you and will provide you with tools that fit with your long-term goals, then by all means pursue it. However, be careful not to take a graduate program that then calls into question whether you still need an MBA. You certainly do not want to be pigeonholed as a degree collector. I've been asked often by candidates if they could apply to a top MBA program although they have an MBA already from a less-selective institution. The answer is no. Hoping to apply at a later date after earning an MBA at another institution is not acceptable. Similarly, candidates are not able to transfer from one top MBA program to another. Unlike undergraduate admissions, where transfer opportunities exist, MBA programs do not typically accommodate transfer requests. Admissions Boards are sensitive to this. A candidate who is admitted to Kellogg and then decides she doesn't like it will have to stick it out as opposed to transferring to Columbia.

Addressing the academic component of the admission evaluation is a necessary part of the application. But once you have scaled this academic hurdle you still need to address the remaining two admission criteria: your leadership track record and the uniqueness criteria.

## LEADERSHIP IMPACT AND MANAGERIAL POTENTIAL

You cannot read through the website of a top business school without coming across the word "leadership." Admissions Boards are all looking for leaders with a track record of effecting change and improving any environment where they are.

Leadership isn't limited to formal titles such as vice president or manager. Leadership is measured based on the level of impact a candidate has. This is why admitted early career candidates, those with less than two years of work experience, can still show remarkable leadership despite very junior titles at their job. The MBA Board wants to learn about situations where you initiated something that didn't exist, convinced your superiors about an opportunity, created a tool or product that improves the way business is done at your firm, or managed a process, project, and person who had a fair share of challenges and delivered a successful outcome at the end.

Leadership can also be seen in your knowledge arena. For instance, becoming a resident expert at something (above and beyond your job responsibilities) that creates value for your group or firm shows leadership. Although many candidates may not have had formal management experience, their exposure to leading small teams can offer interesting insights about their leadership potential. It is always important to show your self-awareness of your strengths as a leader and the areas you could further develop as you grow in your management responsibilities. But equally important for a candidate is to show self-awareness of why a particular leadership impact or experience is personally meaningful. The "why" and "how" are as important, if not more so, than the "what."

The MBA Board evaluates leadership on three dimensions that I call "The 3 Cs of Leadership," namely:

1. College leadership
2. Community leadership
3. Career leadership

## College Leadership

Although it may be a few years since you graduated from college, your college leadership is an important variable when assessing your candidacy. In the ideal admission world, candidates should be strong across all three leadership areas. From my experience, however, most admitted candidates are strong in at least two out of three of these leadership dimensions. What

I've observed is that college leadership and career leadership are often very strong, leaving a gap in the community leadership. The main reason for this is limited time. Many candidates are working eighty plus hours each week, making committing to community service activities on a regular basis impossible. This is where the college leadership comes into play. Many candidates have an excellent track record of leadership while they were in college. These candidates will have to rely on their college leadership and career leadership track record to impress the Admissions Board.

But what if your college leadership is weak? Some candidates with weak college leadership track records may have a compelling reason, such as having to self-fund their education. For some, it could be a result of partying too much in college. Regardless of why, candidates with a deficit in their college leadership must focus on strengthening their community and career leadership before applying to business school.

Do keep in mind that college leadership isn't simply about formal titles in student organizations. Although those are fine and represent the bulk of college leadership examples candidates have, there are many acceptable leadership examples at the college level that are a result of someone taking initiative. An example is the student who has to work to fund her education and sees an underutilized system or a potential market that her employer isn't capitalizing on—by stepping up to present this idea to her bosses and helping to implement it, she will demonstrate a strong leadership track record.

For many candidates reading this book, college was a distant experience, so you can't do anything to change the college leadership (but you can focus on community and career leadership). However, for those of you who are still in college, it is never too late to start creating leadership impact. Are you an athlete? Could you serve in a leadership role on the team? How have you helped your team become stronger and closer? You don't have to be the captain of the team to do this. Is there a problem that exists that you can resolve even without a formal title? Is there an interest you have that matters to you for which there is no formal organization at your school? If so, don't hesitate to start this organization. If you enjoy teaching/tutoring, is there a way to move beyond your typical tutoring role to one where you can manage the other tutors? Perhaps the opportunity to teach a class could present itself? My point here is that you need to raise your game. Don't be shy to step up and put your leadership stake in the ground at your school. And don't fixate simply on title but on impact—that's the true test of leadership!

---

### COLLEGE LEADERSHIP EXAMPLES OF SUCCESSFUL MBA CANDIDATES

Strategic director at a college credit union, where he instituted new initiatives that led to expanded services for students

On-campus position that gave the student experience managing student employees

Founder of an art organization that gave students opportunity to showcase and express their creative talent

Teacher for a freshman seminar that pushed and stretched her students to develop new ideas and explore alternative conclusions

Portfolio manager of student fund resulting in 20 percent return

Captain of varsity sports team

Instituting regular dinners for international students at parents' home to help create a sense of community for classmates

---

## Community Leadership

To strengthen your community leadership, you can join a nonprofit organization and assume a leadership role in it. Most nonprofit organizations are in great need of human resources and money. You can have a major impact as a volunteer. Be careful that your involvement isn't seen as trite. Simply participating in an event once every few months does not qualify as strong evidence of leadership. Opt for tangible contributions. A concrete and significant leadership example could be applying your marketing experience to write the marketing plan and launching the marketing strategy for a nonprofit organization. Another example could be using your business development professional experience to help a community-based organization establish strong relationships with partner firms as a way to build revenue.

Do not underestimate the power of getting involved at your alma mater. By initiating recruitment activities for your college, you can demonstrate your leadership skills by establishing relationships, leading a team, and executing a plan. This is exactly what Stacy, a candidate, did. She noticed that many students from her alma mater did not pursue a career on Wall Street. Graduating from a nonselective university, top banks did not recruit at her school. Stacy created a career support program that educates and mentors students and alumni from her university on career opportunities on Wall Street. This experience stretched Stacy's leadership abilities, as she had to attract and manage disparate alumni from varied industries. She learned how to sell her idea with conviction as she dealt with her school's administrators and career services personnel. She also honed her negotiation and communication abilities through this project. To crown her involvement, Stacy received an alumni award for extraordinary service.

Applicants can also opt to serve on the board of a nonprofit organization to help provide strategic leadership advice. A great organization that places talented young professionals on the boards of nonprofit organizations is BoardNetUSA (www.boardnetusa.org). I don't recommend joining a nonprofit board simply to check the box. The Admissions Board can see through this. You want to be authentic. So if you should decide to pursue this option, make sure to select an organization that ties to something you are passionate about. And while you are on the board, it is key that you initiate activities that yield real solutions to improve the organization.

If you don't find an organization that appeals to you, then consider creating one. Starting an organization, even a nonprofit, can enable you to build an excellent leadership track record. Juan returned to his home country, and after noticing that there was no formal internship program to employ smart college students during the summer, he set about creating one. Not only did this experience provide interesting content for his essays, but more importantly, it gave him an opportunity to give back in a meaningful way. Juan had moved to America when he was young and had benefited from many formal internship programs. He wanted to give other students from his country a similar opportunity. The passion with which he spoke of his project was infectious, and it was easy to see how this was a labor of love for him. This leadership experience influenced his positive admission outcome.

I often hear candidates lament over their limited time for community service. As a new mom, running a full-service consulting practice, and writing this book, I recognize the time constraints that most professionals face. However, it isn't about quantity, but quality. Pick something that really speaks to your heart and find a way to make a meaningful contribution. An applicant I know wanted to deepen his community involvement and chose to partner with a group of internationals who had a mission to commit $100 a month for one year, with a goal of raising funds that would be disbursed to two selected organizations in his home country. It worked. He fulfilled his commitment, got his friends to join, and had the satisfaction of seeing two nonprofit organizations expand and offer more services to the poor.

Regardless of which path you chose to take, it is more important that you have one community involvement where you have had significant impact and depth than to have a lot of activities with no impact. It is not enough to be a member of an organization. MBA programs are looking for leaders and want to see evidence that you have had an impact on people's lives and on an organization. Even if you are applying this year, it is never too late to get involved in community leadership. What is important is making sure that whatever you choose reflects your passion and brand.

## COMMUNITY LEADERSHIP EXAMPLES OF SUCCESSFUL MBA CANDIDATES

Board leadership of a not-for-profit hospital

Business development and marketing volunteer for Street-Squash (an inner-city sports nonprofit organization that builds up the self-esteem of teenagers through squash)

Founder of tutoring program in an inner city

Board leadership of the Asian Task Force

Leader of Women's Initiative for National Domestic Violence Organization

Sunday school teacher and accountant for church

Executive leadership team of an international business forum

Publicity Chair of a national association

Founder of first-ever scholarship program and alumni fund at alma mater

President of the Nigerian Business Forum

Founder of philanthropic private equity enterprise

Raised significant money to help family member battling life-threatening disease

## Career Leadership

The career leadership carries the most weight when evaluating a candidate's leadership experience. That is why most top MBA programs request that students provide recommendations from supervisors who can attest to their professional experience and trajectory. (Early career [EC] candidates are an exception to this. In EC situations, the college and community leadership are elevated in the evaluation process.)

When considering career leadership, you should always focus on the actual impact you have had, not simply on your title. Go beyond your job description to demonstrate your contribution and make sure to address why you chose to take the leadership steps in the first place. If the leadership role involves working with people, that's great. Opportunities where you managed a team allow you to clearly show your leadership abilities. It isn't just about how many people you have on the team; the important thing is that you demonstrate your insights into how people operate, how to motivate them, and what your leadership strengths and developmental needs are.

The MBA Board wants to know that you have challenged yourself and that you take initiative. They are interested in understanding your motivations and the type of leader you are. Team dynamics are pivotal to leadership. How do you handle conflict? How do you deal with disappointment and failures? Many of the top business schools will demand that you address these questions. At the heart of these types of questions is a desire on the part of the MBA Board to make sure that you are mature enough to learn from tough situations, have a healthy emotional intelligence, and can work well with people regardless of the circumstance.

I often hear MBA candidates complain that their jobs make it tough to show leadership. Investment banking analysts who work in a hyper-hierarchical environment are a good example. Let's look at a few ways an investment banking analyst can demonstrate career leadership.

- An investment banker who sees an opportunity to create a new training program can stand out in the applicant pool based on her commitment to others and her ability to transfer her knowledge to improve the experience of her peers. If the program is already established, she can seek ways to improve it and could be selected to lead training as well.
- Another example is the investment banker who sees opportunities where others see obstacle. For example, by using his Spanish language skills and knowledge of Latino culture, he can add value when working on projects in Latin America, an area that the company may not have much exposure to.
- Then there is the investment banker who raises her hand to work on that tough project that seems mired in challenges or to work with the difficult managing director that everyone avoids and is able to successfully "manage up." A commitment to excellence and a strong track record of delivering impeccable results can capture the attention of the Admissions Board, as seen in the investment banker whose work experience is significantly accelerated because he is hand picked, as a result of having developed a reputation of excellence, to work on high-profile deals with significant responsibility.
- Equally interesting and differentiating is the investment banker who steps up and operates as an associate and manages her peers and new analysts to greater success.

I think you get the point. In each of these instances, the focus is on how the person used her particular situation to achieve, as opposed to the circumstance itself. The preceding leadership examples are not just for investment bankers but are applicable to candidates from any industry. It is important to figure out the unique experiences you bring to the table and then capitalize on them to differentiate yourself from the pack. The following are a few examples of the types of leadership track records one can have to stand apart in the application process.

---

## CAREER LEADERSHIP EXAMPLES OF SUCCESSFUL MBA CANDIDATES

Initiating and leading the business development that landed the firm a client that increased revenue by 20 percent

Conducting the entire valuation of the highest profile transaction at firm worth EUR 1.1 billion due to strong analytical track record

Operating in the role of an associate while still an analyst

Building a training program, hiring a team of international analysts, and creating a formal analyst culture at firm

Co-establishing the leveraged finance practice in another country

Managing the consulting team that introduced and implemented an automated management tool for clients worldwide

Investing in a struggling employee and helping that person develop into a confident and successful leader

Creating a utility tool to improve the tracking system of a shipping company

Managing employees on an assembly line and improving efficiency by 25 percent

Reducing human product errors from 10 to 4 percent at pharmaceutical firm by introducing a new tracking system and training employees to use it

---

So with the academic and leadership criteria out of the way, candidates are left to tackle the last of the admissions variables: their uniqueness. Unlike the other two admissions criteria, the uniqueness admissions criterion allows the greatest flexibility for candidates to market themselves in a powerful way.

# UNIQUENESS (DIVERSE EXPERIENCES/ PERSPECTIVES AND DIFFERENTIATED PERSONAL CHARACTERISTICS)

The third admissions category that MBA Boards use in evaluating candidates is the uniqueness of your brand. Business schools are looking for individuals who are a fit with their brand. And nowhere is this more evident than through your personal characteristics and unique perspectives.

This aspect of the evaluation is by far where applicants have the most flexibility and influence. To a large extent, applicants' academic history has already been formed. Their leadership track record and management experience have been established. The insights that applicants offer into who they are and why they have made the choices they have made to date can land them a coveted admission spot in a top business school.

A good way to illustrate this point is by looking at investment bankers, a group of candidates who are overly represented in the application pool. The following fictional example speaks to the power of the unique perspective applicants bring to their application.

Five hundred investment bankers apply to an MBA program. Ten percent are accepted. That means that 450 investment bankers will be rejected. What is unique and interesting about the fifty who are admitted? It is the personal characteristics and unique perspective that they offer that often sets them apart from their competition. All candidates, regardless of their industry background, should ask themselves how they are different compared with other candidates from similar backgrounds.

The personal characteristics and unique perspective is different for each candidate. For some applicants, they are interesting in the fact that they are the first in their family to get a college education. Their initiative, vision, and "bootstrapper" background differentiates them from their competitors who have had a lot of opportunities given to them. For other applicants, it is the innovative nature in which they approach their work that is distinctive. Even candidates with the more unusual examples of having been raised on a farm in Iowa or growing up in Alaska or Chechnya can offer interesting and different viewpoints to the class based on their diverse personal life experiences.

This is an application to business school, so you should highlight the different perspective and experience that you bring in the context of how it can add value to the class discussions and student community. Uniqueness for its own sake isn't what MBA programs are after. Rather, what is attention-worthy is how growing up in Mongolia and working in the United States in the pharmaceutical industry has influenced your desire to return to Mongolia to open the country's first health- and nutrition-focused business (like GNC). The unique vantage point you have of the economic landscape of Mongolia and the subtle cultural obstacles that you will need to overcome are the types of stories that will allow you to present convincing and differentiated essays.

But the reality is that most candidates do not come from exotic backgrounds and do not have profound experiences such as experiencing combat in Afghanistan, Iraq, or Bosnia. If you happen to fall in one of these unusual backgrounds, great. Leverage it to show how you will offer a different viewpoint to the MBA program. However, if you find that your background is more along the beaten path, there are tangible things you can do to stand out in the pool as well.

For instance, have you traveled abroad or lived in different countries? You can capitalize on your international experiences and lessons learned and insights drawn from working in diverse environments. Are you an avid sports person and enjoy challenging yourself? You can describe your experience training for the marathon or the process of climbing Mt. Kilimanjaro and the team dynamics from that experience. How did this situation change or shape you? Drawing lessons from these types of experiences and connecting them to what you will bring to the particular business school can be appealing to the Admissions Board.

If you come from a privileged background, it is important to know how to present your experience. Be careful not to sound spoilt or entitled. Also, when recounting experiences, you are better off choosing things that do not play into a stereotype. For instance, if asked about a mistake you made, you are better off selecting an example that shows personal awareness (realizing you are fallible), instead of one that simply shows bad judgment (crashing your parents' Bentley after a night out).

Here are some additional examples from candidates who have succeeded in branding their way to their dream business schools:

- Raising five siblings without parents allowed a candidate to demonstrate his initiative, management skills, and maturity.
- Health problems led a candidate to develop his knowledge of Parma industry/health policy issues. As a result, he became passionate about the business side of drug development and transferred this interest into thought leadership at his firm.
- Being raised by entrepreneurial parents gave a candidate exposure to running businesses and an appreciation for the discipline, creativity, and innovation required to start a business in the future.
- Witnessing her mother's domestic abuse fueled one candidate's commitment to empowering women.
- A hunger for a global education led a candidate to leave her home country, attend college in the United States, and convince her firm to send her to Europe to gain international work experience.

Successful candidates do not fall within prescribed categories or profiles. Rather, they have understood the admissions criteria and have successfully presented their own unique experiences to show how they will create value to the MBA program. The good news is that most of your competition is not perfect. They have gaps or weaknesses that they have to address as well. It could be weaker GMAT scores or GPAs, lack of exemplary leadership, or a vague sense of their brand (what is distinct or unique about them). Investing time in assessing and addressing any gaps that exist in your application will strengthen your MBA candidacy. And in no place is the brand more telling than in the essays. The next chapter explores the MBA application essays in detail and offers insights on how to tackle them effectively.

# CHAPTER SIX

## Essay Fundamentals

HAVING COVERED THE THREE main admissions criteria used to evaluate MBA candidates, I would like to turn the focus to the different components that make up the application. The first is the MBA essays. MBA Boards have historically stressed the power of the admissions essays in the application process. Unlike any other aspect of the application, the essays are the one area where candidates have the most control in representing themselves. After all, undergraduate grades are already predetermined, and there is a limit to how far a GMAT score can change (it would be unlikely for someone who scores consistently at 500 to jump to 750).

With the exception of meeting the applicant for an interview, the essays are the best way to reveal each candidate's brand. Essays are blank canvases that provide candidates with an incredible opportunity to create a Picasso. In my admissions experience at Harvard and Carnegie Mellon, I have observed numerous instances where one candidate's application stands apart from others with identical backgrounds based simply on the treatment of the essay topics and the type of information the essays reveal about the candidate's brand. These successful candidates understand that presenting their experiences in the form of stories allows them to paint a vibrant picture of themselves, as opposed to simply stating facts in a dry way.

Applicants to business school must be comfortable going into depth when describing who they are and what matters to them. It is impossible to submit a powerful application without revealing personal aspects of who you are. That said, applicants need to be wise about the personal stories they share with the Admissions Board. Not all personal experiences are appropriate to discuss in your application. A good litmus test to determine whether a subject is worth including in your story is to ask yourself what it reveals about you as a future business leader. Raising your five siblings shows maturity and "management" ability. But you would be hard pressed to make a compelling case that overcoming a rough breakup with your first love reveals something meaningful about your leadership. The essays for business school are a test of applicants' judgment. Make sure that whatever personal insights and examples you provide do not raise red flags about you. A sure way to guarantee that your application gets dinged is by exhibiting poor judgment.

Unlike other graduate programs where the standardized scores drive the admission outcome, to a large extent, business schools' essays can significantly influence the admission decision. So applicants who are serious about being admitted to a competitive business school should ensure that their essays are well written and embody a strong personal brand.

## MBA ESSAY OVERVIEW

Time is a major factor in presenting a winning application, so start early. The average number of essays at top business schools is four. Therefore, you should allocate enough time to tackle each essay thoroughly. To be safe, give yourself at least four months to complete two to three applications. If you are going to apply to more schools, then you should consider applying in two different rounds (three applications during the first round and two applications or more during the second round) to better manage the process. With admission to top schools becoming more competitive, more candidates are applying to a greater number of programs to increase their chances of gaining admission to at least one school. A greater number of applications means that you will need to budget even more time to ensure that you can give each application the attention necessary to yield the results you seek.

Getting started on the essays can be daunting for many applicants. So take a deep breath and exhale. The MBA Board does not expect you to write like a Pulitzer Prize–winning journalist. You are not tested on how creative or excellent a writer you are. The main emphasis is on how substantive your leadership impact and managerial potential are, whether you have taken advantage of opportunities available to you, and your awareness of the drivers behind your personal and professional decisions and success.

That said, you should not present a shoddy essay full of grammatical and spelling mistakes. Make sure that you revise your essays as many times as needed to produce well-written finished products. It is generally a good idea to have someone you know who is a great writer, for instance, an English major, read through your essays to catch any writing errors.

Before tackling the MBA essays, you should go through a brand audit to identify the most compelling parts of your story. You should also go through a brainstorming exercise to organize your experiences. Successful essays require a fair share of introspection. We encourage applicants to adopt a brainstorming model we refer to as SOARS (Situation, Obstacle, Action, Results, and So What). Investing time in framing your questions in this format will allow you to tease apart your story in a coherent and tangible way, making it

possible for you to focus on the more compelling examples in
your story. Once you have completed the SOARS model, you
will be ready to begin writing the essays. Always do an outline
before tackling an essay. An outline is important because it
allows you to tease apart the important parts of the event.
When writing an outline, you should always aim to flesh out
these key points:

1. What is the situation you wish to discuss?
2. What was challenging, difficult, or unusual about it
   that is worth mentioning?
3. What steps did you take to address or resolve the issue?
   How did you do it? What role did you play?
4. What was the outcome of your involvement? Why did
   you make the decisions you made or take the actions
   you took? It is important to stress specifics of the
   result. If it is quantifiable, then don't fail to show the
   before-and-after outcome you were able to create as a
   result of your involvement.
5. So what! Be clear on why anyone reading the story
   should care about it. What was meaningful about this
   experience? What did you learn about yourself? Why
   does it matter to you? This is where you reveal your
   insights and self-awareness to the MBA Board.

Candidates to business school are not limited to following
this outline. If another process works for you to effectively
outline your essays, then that's great and you should use it.
What's important is that you take the time to assess whether
the story you have selected is compelling enough to feature in
your application. Using the SOARS model to brainstorm essay
topics will quickly reveal to you whether the story is strong
enough or whether it lacks substance. The other point I wish to
make about using the SOARS outline for your essays is that you

are not limited to using it chronologically. It's a tool that helps you with brainstorming but should not become confining; that is, you should not feel bound to structure all your essays chronologically. You can vary the sequence to support whatever creative approach you wish to pursue.

Let's take a few minutes to complete the SOARS Model below. Feel free to come back to it to refine the story as different ideas come to you.

## EXPARTUS SOARS MODEL

| Situation | Obstacle | Action | Results | So What! |
|-----------|----------|--------|---------|----------|
|           |          |        |         |          |
|           |          |        |         |          |
|           |          |        |         |          |
|           |          |        |         |          |

# CHARACTERISTICS OF WINNING ESSAYS

With establishing a process to outline the essays out of the way, let's review what makes for winning essays. While there isn't a formula to gain admission to business school, there are certainly variables or ingredients that distinguish applications that are admitted from those that are rejected. I will examine those variables closely in the next section.

## The PGII Factor

A common question from MBA candidates is, "What sets apart winning essays from bland and ineffective ones?" Having evaluated thousands of MBA essays at Harvard, at Carnegie Mellon, and through my consulting practice, EXPARTUS, I have identified the fundamental ingredients that successful essays embody. These winning essays have what I call the PGII Factor. They include:

1. Passion
2. Guts
3. Impact
4. Insight

Essay questions that embody these four ingredients create a solid and powerful backdrop from which the MBA Board can assess you. Let's take a closer look at each ingredient.

### 1. Passion

As you are preparing for your essays, ask yourself whether you have clearly identified your passion. Take a few minutes to complete the passion survey from the earlier chapter. Keep in mind that if your essays do not convey your passion, there is a good chance that they will be bland and boring, thus increasing the likelihood that they will put the MBA Board to sleep. Do you simply do your job, or do you bring great enthusiasm and energy to everything you do both at work and beyond? Your attitude reflects your passion. Think about what difference you have had in your company, in the organizations you have been involved in, in your community. Your essay has to convey your passion for what you do (whether in your work, your personal life, or community); your long-term goals have to connect with what you say matters to you. Connecting these pieces to why you are pursuing an MBA is a very important part of the application process.

## 2. Guts

You can't talk about winning essays without seeing clear evidence of guts and courage to take personal and professional risks. Having guts is not about unplanned, haphazard stunts. MBA Boards are an extremely savvy bunch and can see through gimmicks masked to appear like courage and risk taking.

Take two people (Bob and Don) who apply to business school. Both of them have a successful career in the finance industry, and their academic backgrounds are equally strong. Bob has been with the same finance firm for five years. His essay has few examples showcasing his stepping up and having a significant impact beyond what a typical associate does at the firm. Can you imagine how many "Bobs" are in the applicant pool? The Bobs of the applicant pool have made it easy for the MBA Board to deny them admission.

Contrast this with Don, who has chosen to leave his firm to start a real estate company, which is his passion. Even if Don's business folds, the MBA Board isn't as focused on the failure of the business as they are in what motivated Don to leave a safe job to start a business and the lessons he learned through the process. The MBA Board is also interested in learning the impact Don's business had on others. Most important, the Admissions Board wants to learn how his entrepreneurial venture has developed his leadership and managerial potential. His maturity and growth will very well set him apart from other talented candidates vying for a spot in the competitive admission pool.

I am not advocating that the only way to show guts is through an entrepreneurial endeavor. If you are an entrepreneur, by all means, go for it. However, for the majority of the applicants, you can demonstrate your risk taking within your firm by stepping up and going above and beyond your prescribed role. For instance, as a financial analyst, you may realize that your firm falls short in its training and professional development of new analysts, so you volunteer to start an analyst training and mentoring program (if none exists) or to overhaul the existing one. If you are in Equity Research, for instance, and you have a lean group, you could raise your hand to cover more industries above and beyond what is expected of you. Perhaps you are in the strategy group at your firm and you disagree with the firm's plan to shut down a business unit and see it as a missed opportunity. So you take the initiative to conduct a thorough analysis, and identify how a counter approach can add value to your firm. You have the guts to present an alternative plan, present data to back up your thoughts, and deliver a convincing argument to your senior management. Behind the scenes, you build bridges and get key people to champion the idea. Your idea not to shut down the group is accepted. The outcome? The group ends up being a major money maker for your firm.

So what if you are an engineer? You could demonstrate your guts by volunteering to lead a system improvement project that involves other departments. Or you could initiate a new safety mechanism that improves the way an assembly line operates.

Other ways candidates can show guts is by being willing to explore a different business environment. The American consultant who opts for an international project in Singapore will get a broadened perspective that can make him more competitive when it comes time to apply to business school. I know a candidate working in the United States who pushed to be transferred to a European country to work because she knew it would push her outside her comfort level. I'm not advocating that everyone jump ship for an international assignment; this is an option for applicants for whom such a move is in line with their brand and goals.

Even a simple step of leaving a lucrative consulting career, for example, to become a soccer coach at your alma mater can reflect a gutsy move on your part. But you have to show how this move fits into your longer-term goal. And of course, it also has to fit with your passion for athletics. If your long-term goal is to work for companies like Nike or the U.S. Soccer Federation on the business side, you can make a compelling case for the tie-in with sports and your career move to coaching. You should be careful, however, if you are simply making a move to impress the MBA Board. In the event that the admission doesn't pan out, you have to be comfortable living with your decision. So whatever decision you take, make sure you choose roles that you are passionate about and that fit with your long-term goals.

Demonstrating guts is about:

- Raising your hand to take on additional responsibility
- Seizing an opportunity to affect change
- Having the confidence to speak up and sell your ideas
- Taking a path that is untried and different

## 3. Impact

A major mistake MBA candidates make with their essays is failing to quantify their impact. Impact simply comes down to your track record. What was your specific role in bringing about change or improving a process or product? Note that impact isn't limited to organizations; it also expands to people—taking the intern trying to navigate a large bureaucratic organization under your wing, helping the co-worker who is having a tough time grasping how to read and interpret balance sheets, mentoring the consultant whom everyone views as the weakest link on the engagement team and who is about to quit as a result of his or her frustrations. These are all individuals that many of us have encountered at some point in our career. The question is what role we chose to play: did we engage someone and make a difference to improve his situation when we saw him struggling, or did we simply focus on our own individual success? These types of experiences make for very interesting essays.

The opposite mistake that candidates make relating to impact is exaggerating their role. MBA Boards can deduce when the truth is being stretched, and this is a major turn-off, which will adversely affect your admission outcome. So tell the story with specific details of your involvement but shy away from stretching your account in attempts to make your essay sound impressive.

## 4. Insight

The law of writing winning essays in the application process is to *show don't tell*. It's not enough to tell the MBA Board how great your accomplishments are, but you must show them how you have accomplished something and what you learned from the experience. Awareness is king in the admissions process. What you have done is important, but equally important is why you have done the things you have done and how you do what you do that is unique to you.

Be committed to showing the MBA Board why the things you have done matter to you. Simply stating that you have leadership and management abilities is not enough. What kind of leader are you? What is your managerial style, and how do you rely on it to bring out the best in the people you lead? Are you a leader who leads in front? Perhaps you are charismatic in your leadership style. Are you more of a "quiet" leader who leads from behind? You need to have a clear sense of your style and have stories to back it up to reinforce your point. It is your self-awareness that sets you apart from all the other applicants who, at a first glance, have the same background.

## The Power of the Six Cs

In addition to the PGII Factor, successful essays tend to have the following six attributes:

- Captivating
- Credible
- Compelling
- Consistent
- Clear
- Concise

When writing your essay, you should always ensure that your essays embody these six characteristics.

*Captivating*

The essays must capture the attention of the Admissions Board. It is said that it takes thirty seconds to make an impression (good or bad), and once someone makes up their mind about you, it takes much more time and effort to reverse that impression. The MBA application should be approached from this mind-set as well. The application as a whole and the essays in particular are your opportunity to say, "Hi, my name is Vanessa, and you need to pay close attention to my story." A captivating essay will make the MBA Board sit up and remember your story many applications later.

Remember that the MBA Board has several thousand essays to read and limited time to make their recommendations. So your essay should be anything but bland. The last thing you want is to put the board members to sleep when they read your essays. Let your personality come through. Don't be afraid to take some risks (tempered with judgment) by allowing the different aspects of your personality (brand) to come through. You want the MBA Board to identify with you when they read your application. So, simply said, the essays need to be engaging, interesting, and personable.

While captivating essays are important, you have to also be honest. There is no room to stretch the truth in an attempt to be interesting. Fabricated stories are grounds for automatic rejection. Given the climate of corporate malfeasance and cases of falsified applications, MBA Boards are extremely sensitive to honesty and authenticity.

## Credible

Candidates should always ask themselves whether their story is believable. Given your background, is it reasonable to expect that you will achieve what you outline as your career goals? Avoid grandiose and unrealistic goals. Essays need to maintain a balance: while your vision has to be big enough to warrant an MBA to achieve it, it still has to be achievable. For instance, saying that you will be the Donald Trump of Africa but having little evidence of real estate passion will leave the MBA Board skeptical of your ambitions.

Some career changers fail the credibility test by picking future careers that are a big leap from their current role. If you are an information technology (IT) manager, you will have a tough time convincing an Admissions Board that you will become a brand manager at Proctor & Gamble. This doesn't mean that you can't make major career changes after you graduate from business school. In fact, most graduates of MBA programs are career changers. The challenge is that at the application stage, you have to show that your goals are realistic. If you select a new career you wish to pursue, make sure you can show that there are some ties from your background, interests, and experiences that make it believable.

## Compelling

Your essay needs to convey a compelling rationale for why you want an MBA. You need to be convincing. What is your long-term vision/goal, and is the MBA necessary to achieve it? Be sure that you have thoroughly examined why you want the MBA and how the degree will help you succeed in your career. If your career ambition is simply a small incremental step, it is unlikely that the MBA Board will give you a spot to go into a middle management role when there are candidates who are looking to use the MBA to have transformative impact and change.

## Consistent

Essays that are consistent reinforce the brand of the candidate. In the chapter on selling your personal brand I discussed the importance of doing a brand audit and identifying the brand themes, which are the basis for the essays. By identifying key brand themes to your story, you can write essays that build on each other in a way that reinforces your overall brand message. This is an area where applicants err: they write essays without a unifying story (theme) behind them. The unfortunate outcome is that their application is unmemorable, making it challenging for the MBA Board to advocate for their candidacy.

## Clear

With limited time, Admissions Boards need to be able to ascertain the main thrust of each story. Essays that lack clarity are problematic because the board members will be unable to extricate the brand message of the candidate. To ensure that your essay is clear, make sure you address the who, what, when, how, why, and so what (impact). By getting to the point and using this format, you can eliminate unnecessary aspects of the story, enabling you to present a clear picture of who you are in your essays. After reading your essays, who you are should jump off the pages. Also, you should ensure that you have answered the question being asked in the most straightforward and direct way possible. A case in point is the question about describing your defining leadership experience and addressing your strengths and weaknesses. Many candidates address the first part of the question and ignore the second part about their strengths and weaknesses (especially the latter). Make sure you have answered all the questions fully and write with as many specific examples as possible to ensure clarity of your story.

### Concise

The issue of conciseness is related to clarity. Get to the point quickly so the reader can get a clear message of your story. I'm often asked whether the MBA Board cares about word count and how far off one can deviate from the limits. My advice is to always adhere to the essay word or page limits. At a basic level, it is a sign of your ability to follow instruction. At a deeper level, it reflects your sense of equity. (Why should you have an edge over candidates who followed the instruction and stayed within the prescribed limit?) In my experience, I have found that in most cases, less is more. Rambling essays or essays that are lengthy rarely engender positive feelings from the overworked Admissions Board. This is why it is important to start essays using an outline as opposed to "a brain dump," where you start off writing anything and everything that comes to mind. And of course, I can't stress enough the importance of revisions. I knew an applicant who submitted twenty-plus pages for his first essay to Stanford Graduate School of Business (GSB). Suffice it to say, he didn't gain admission. Extra essays and supplemental documents such as newspaper articles, CDs, and portfolios are inappropriate unless the school specifically requests them.

## ESSAY TYPES AND STRATEGIES TO TACKLE THEM

In this next section, I address the various essays covered in the MBA application and provide suggestions on how to deal with them. I have also included actual examples of essays used by applicants. I recognize that some essay topics may overlap across multiple categories but for the purpose of this book, I

have broken the essays into four groups.
The four essay categories are:

1. Career essays
2. Impact essays
3. Who you are essays
4. Miscellaneous essays

## The Career Essay

Although all the admissions essays are important, it is rare to bomb the career essay and still get admitted. Failure to nail your career essay is likely to yield an unfavorable admission outcome. The career essay category asks candidates to discuss their professional decisions and experiences to date, to explain why they want an MBA and why this is the right time for them to pursue it, and to indicate why they are interested in the particular MBA program in the first place. Some MBA programs word their career essay broadly (What is your career vision and why is this choice meaningful to you?—Harvard Business School [HBS]) while others are very specific (What are your short-term and long-term career goals? How will Columbia Business School help you achieve these goals?— Columbia). It is important to note that cut-and-paste jobs are not the most efficient way to succeed in the admissions process. If a question is asking specifically for your short-term and long-term goals, do not simply recycle the career vision essay; it will be obvious to the MBA Board that you copied an essay from another school. I'm not advocating writing five separate career essays for your five applications. But it is important to pay attention to how the question is worded and even when you use original content from a previous application, take the time to give it a fresh touch so that it answers the specific question being asked.

Your particular industry or sector doesn't matter. What is vital is showing that you have thought through your career goals and the steps you anticipate will be necessary to achieve them. Candidates need to be very specific when addressing their career essays. There is little room for vague and broad career goals. Generic career goals only signal to the Admissions Boards that you are either unsure about what you want to do or that you do not know enough about the professed career path. In either case, you make it easy for the MBA Board to discount your application. So be as specific as you can when addressing your career goals. A statement such as, "I will become a general manager after business school" is too vague. But saying, "I wish to join a rotational leadership program in an apparel company like Gap after business school, and long term, I plan to become the president of a retail company in South America" is a very specific and clear career goal. There is a caveat to this, however. Schools that ask for your career vision as opposed to your short-term and long-term career goals tend to be more open to broad statements like "I plan to return to Latin America to help change the pharmaceutical industry." Harvard Business School is one such example that doesn't penalize candidates for not specifically outlining the steps they will take to achieve their professional objectives.

Furthermore, all candidates need to make a strong case for why a particular MBA program is the best fit for them given the set of experiences they have had to date. This is where many candidates fail. The temptation to copy and paste paragraphs from previous essays is often too strong to resist. Avoid falling into this trap. Take the time to understand the nuanced differentiation or brand of each MBA program before tailoring your rationale for an MBA accordingly. Campus visits, sitting in on classes, and speaking with alumni and current students will help you zero in on exactly why a particular MBA program is a fit for you. I know a candidate who had applied to multiple schools and visited the programs only after gaining admission. To her horror, she realized she didn't fit in at the programs where she was admitted. She was forced to decline her admission offer and radically transform her professional experience with hopes of reapplying the following year.

The issue of timing is also a factor here, so be ready to address why now is the right time for you to pursue the MBA. Even if the question of "why now" doesn't come up, it is wise to explain your thought process regarding why you feel you are ready for the MBA and why this is the ideal time for you to enroll as opposed to a few years from now.

Another important element to keep in mind when thinking of the career essay is demonstrating awareness of the industry you plan to pursue. This issue is most pertinent for career changers. The more knowledgeable you are about the industry and how the MBA will equip you with the skills to succeed, the more likely your story is to be believed. It is also useful to show how the skills you have built from prior professional experience will be relevant in your career after business school.

Finally, no career essay will be complete without showing that you have been successful to date in your present career. The idea is that if you have been extraordinarily successful where you work currently, there is a good chance you will be successful in a new career. One of the biggest problems candidates face in the application process is making the case that they will be successful in a vibrant career after business school when they have worked at a few mundane jobs and have lackluster impact and track record. Should you find yourself in a situation like this, it is critical to hold off on applying to business school and focus on "rebranding" yourself to build a more compelling professional track record. Doing so will reduce the likelihood that your application will be rejected!

It is unlikely to have a winning application if you don't nail the career essays. So although all the essays are important, I encourage you to devote extra time to make sure your career essay is spot on.

Here are the questions on the MBA Boards' minds when reading your career essay:

1.  Who is this candidate?
2.  What has she achieved?
3.  Is it compelling?
4.  Is she on an upward trajectory where she is taking on more responsibility and creating more impact, or has her career stalled?
5.  What are her career decisions, what steps has she taken, and is there a logical connection to her goals?
6.  Is she a good fit for our program?
7.  What will she contribute to our program?
8.  Is she mature, and will she be able to operate in a team environment?
9.  Does her career goal make sense, and will she be marketable after business school?
10. Are her aspirations transformative, and will an MBA help her achieve her goals?
11. Does getting the MBA now make sense: did she leave applying to business school too late, or is she applying too early and needs more work experience?

Answers to these questions will help the MBA Board determine whether to admit or reject the candidate.

Let's review a sample career essay and examine what makes it effective.

### Sample Career Essay:

*Think about the decisions you have made in your life. Describe the following:*

(a) *What choices have you made that led you to your current position?*

(b) *Why pursue an MBA at this point in your life?*

(c) *What is your career goal upon graduation from NYU Stern? What is your long-term career goal?*

*"Sassy, sexy, and stylish" is how Baby Phat describes their brand. I would also add "profitable" as the brand produced sales of $18M and profits of $4M in its first year. It is this recent success of "Baby Phat" and my contribution to it which in part have led me to change my career direction from finance to marketing.*

*I began my retail finance career at New York and Company, a leading women's apparel company. As Store Financial Analyst within its real estate group, I learned to assess and forecast the performance of potential new stores and recommend which ones to open. I later pursued greater responsibility, in managing profitability company-wide, as a Senior Financial Analyst at Coty. Initially responsible for seven brands, I now oversee the budgeting process for our entire portfolio of 25 brands.*

*It was through my work with Coty's marketing teams that I realized that my true passion lay in marketing. For example, during one project I provided financial and profit scenarios to our marketing director to aid in a decision whether to pursue a re-launch of the "Coolwater" fragrance or to design a new brand. I created a model that illustrated the cost and profit implications of redesigning the product package and collaborated with the marketing staff to determine the required levels of advertising support. As a result, instead of the costly creation of a new brand, we decided to reignite interest in this mature brand and "Coolwater's" sales ranking rose from 30th to 15th. Though my work assisted in the decision, it was the strength and creativity of the marketing which ultimately led to this success. This project showed me the power of marketing to revive a product at the end of its life cycle and inspire a new generation of customers: I was captivated!*

*After the engaging "Coolwater" project, I asked to work with the marketing team on providing budget guidelines for the launch of the "Baby Phat" fragrance. After studying past launch spending for comparable products, I discovered our marketing team initially tends to overspend to achieve brand awareness through national advertising. Later, when customers need more purchasing incentives by, for example, offering "free gifts," the team is likely to underestimate its cost of goods sold expenses. When presented with my analysis, the marketing team corrected their budget allocation and, as a result, "Baby Phat" gained momentum at the launch with minimal waste of funds and an efficient use of its promotional arsenal.*

*With the realization that my true passion lies not in finance but in marketing, I now feel a sense of urgency in my desire to make the transition to begin my career in this field. As a career changer, I will need to immerse myself in the subject and I believe that the Stern MBA provides ample opportunity to do so, not only through classroom instruction, but also, as importantly, through a real-world setting.*

*Post MBA, I would like to work in brand management for a consumer packaged goods company. As brand manager, I aim to grow a brand and develop a comprehensive marketing plan which appreciates both financial and creative concerns. This experience would provide me with some of the requisite skills to achieve my long-term goal of managing a diverse portfolio of products. I am confident I would enjoy synthesizing disparate information, as in the "Coolwater" analysis, to mold a brand through strategies including line extensions, package innovations, and product positioning. I believe my experience in the fragrance industry, in addition to an MBA education, will serve to benefit my new career path.*

*Assessment*

This applicant is a career changer who plans to go from finance to marketing. The first thing to his advantage is that he has worked in interesting industries (apparel and fragrance). His work in finance has exposed him to other functional areas such as marketing. And because he plans to switch careers into marketing, it provides authenticity to his career goals. He does a good job of showing examples of the work he has done, balancing his specific roles and contributions. He shows his career progression by describing how he started out running analyses and performance forecasts to managing his new company's profitability. When it comes to addressing his career goal, he doesn't equivocate. He states specifically that he wants to become a brand manager of a consumer packaged goods company. Because he shows awareness of what marketing entails by describing projects he worked on with the marketing team at his company, the reader is able to believe his career aspirations. This is a career changer who has passed the credibility test.

## TIPS ON HANDLING CAREER ESSAYS

Answer the question directly. State exactly what your goals/vision are up front. Then help the reader to understand why you have these aspirations.

Avoid regurgitating your resume. Instead of mainly highlighting what you have done, take the time to explain why you made the decisions you made, the key achievements, and how the experiences have brought you closer to your career ambitions.

Be very specific when stating your career goals. Spell out the industry, the role, and even the region you wish to work. If there is a company you have identified that fits your goals, highlight it.

Provide evidence to support your career goals. Make sure your work experience and life in general backs up your career goals.

Of all the MBA essays this is the one that least lends itself to creativity.

Demonstrate your knowledge of the industry, including its growth, opportunities, and challenges, and how you plan to make a contribution.

Make it clear why you need the MBA: show how the goal you have is significant, requiring an MBA to get there.

Address why each particular MBA program is the right fit for you. Be very specific and avoid generalities.

Balance talking about what you will get from the program with what you will contribute to it.

## Some Recent Career Essay Questions

*Fuqua:* Why are you interested in the Duke MBA and how will it help you achieve your goals? Please also discuss your career path, including your short and long term professional goals.

*Yale:* Please describe your short and long term goals and how your previous experience and an MBA will help you achieve these goals.

*Darden:* What matters to you most, both personally and professionally, and how does an MBA relate to these priorities?

*Haas:* What are your short-term and long-term career goals? How do your professional experiences relate to these goals? Why do you want an MBA from Berkeley at this point in your career?

*Wharton:* Describe your career progress to date and your future short-term and long-term career goals. How do you expect a Wharton MBA to help you achieve these goals, and why is now the best time for you to join our program?

*Stanford:* What are your aspirations? How will your education at Stanford help you achieve them?

## The Impact Essay

You will be hard-pressed to complete an MBA application without addressing your professional impact. There are specific essays that ask you to describe your impact. Examples of such essays include the following: What are your greatest accomplishments, and what did you learn from these experiences? Describe an impact you had on a person, team, or organization. When did you tackle a situation that was problematic, and how did you turn things around? When have you used innovation to solve a problem?

Earlier in this book I discussed the ingredients of successful essays: passion, guts, impact, and insight. Besides the specific impact essays that you will face in the application process, you should always aim to describe the impact you have had in different situations in all your essays (whenever applicable).

---

### *Sample Impact Essay*

*Describe your impact on a person, team, or organization.*

*After moving to Houston, I was shocked to find no platform for mentoring and developing junior employees, particularly college hires. The pervasive hierarchical system placed little value on investing in junior talent, leading to dismal retention history.*

*Upon inquiry to create a program for developing junior talent, I was repeatedly told - "It cannot be done! Many before you have tried for years." I decided to try anyway.*

*Months of deadlocked negotiations followed. I started seeing why others had quit: the bureaucracy was unyielding! Keeping my team motivated was also proving to be challenging. Finally, we convinced NXO's CEO to meet with HR and my team. As we sat at his desk, I drew from every debating experience to persuade them and quell any fears of losing their investment given our low retention rate. Eventually, we won them over. We also negotiated funding, making the employee development program the only fully funded employee club at NXO.*

*Within weeks, NXO had 400+ members. We oversaw the first cross-site mentoring program for all members, initiated partnerships with community service organizations, and held networking events. The retention rate is also up 20%.*

*I consider building the employee development program significant because I successfully led a team and navigated the seemingly insurmountable bureaucracy to invest in junior talent at NXO Corporation.*

---

## Assessment

This essay is refreshing in that it isn't your typical work-related accomplishment. This applicant's brand themes are innovator, tenacious, and empowerer. The story he shares shows how he creates a program that didn't exist because he saw a need that wasn't being met (lack of systematic mentorship of new talent). Despite little support, his persistence pays off and he is able to build an employee organization that has created a cohesive community among new employees. He does a good job also of showing the impact he had instead of telling you what he had done. It is always a good idea to tell a story that shows what you achieved rather than simply stating that you are great at negotiation or innovation. Such statements come off as trite to the MBA Board. Always show the reader what you did and the motivations to do it rather than stating the obvious.

---

### Another Sample Impact Essay

*In discussing Columbia Business School, Dean R. Glenn Hubbard remarked, "We have established the mind-set that entrepreneurship is about everything you do." Please discuss a time in your own life when you have identified and captured an opportunity.*

*In June 2007, I turned a big problem into a big opportunity. One of my biggest clients was going through a futures delivery cycle and was exposed to very high overnight market risk. Having lost several hundred thousand dollars overnight, he was threatening to take his business away from my firm. His point was perfectly understandable: If the prime broker is notified of his positions at 11p.m., why should he have to wait until 7a.m. the next morning to find out? His argument made perfect sense and I assured my client that I would find a solution.*

*I took it upon myself to conduct very thorough research; however the results were discouraging. This procedure took about eight hours to complete and the same timeline was present at every single competitor. I had to come up with an innovative plan to change such a widely used procedure for the first time and I had to convince management that it was absolutely necessary. After countless informational conference calls, I came up with a proposal on how to avoid this risk. I suggested that we modify the existing software and staff an employee in our Chicago office overnight to coordinate trades with our Tokyo office.*

*Now that I had the plan, I needed to get it implemented and this was the challenging part. As a new associate in the firm, I did not have the authority to hire a new employee, or hand out new responsibilities to our team in Tokyo. I strategically chose to approach my manager's manager since he had the authority to implement my idea. Given his experience at our firm he knew the right people and introduced me to the global head of futures. Mike D, who had over 30 years of experience with the futures business, directed a lot of questions to me testing my knowledge of the product but I had already done my due diligence. I knew all the answers regarding the time spent on each step along the way, the systems used, and the cost/benefit implications of the plan. By the end of this long discussion, Mike was intrigued and wanted to check the feasibility of my plan by talking to his team leaders. I not only persuaded my supervisors, but also impressed them with my complete vision from idea to execution.*

*I made a substantial impact because I leveraged my connections across the firm, which I have successfully built over the years and for the first time on Wall Street addressed the delivery risk with a global approach. I was proud to inform my client that I delivered the results that I had promised and effected change. The new procedure not only helps my client save approximately $1.2MM per year but also gives my firm a competitive edge.*

---

## Assessment

The value of an essay like this is that the leadership impact focuses on seeking out opportunities to create value for the client. This candidate could have given up when she realized there were obstacles in the way and that what her client needed hadn't been done before. Instead, she rolls up her sleeves, creatively identifies a solution, and then lobbies the decision makers to buy her idea. She demonstrates strong emotional intelligence, tenacity, and ability to creatively solve problems. The fact that her solution led to a new procedure at her firm that helps her clients save money to the tune of over a million dollars is an added boon.

---

### TIPS ON HANDLING THE IMPACT ESSAY

Be sure to show the challenge that was involved in achieving the impact. The obstacle could be getting something off the ground; selling/communicating an idea to a skeptical boss; managing people who are resistant to a vision; coming up with a novel business solution to a client's problem; or simply convincing your team to take a different approach to a problem. When tackling an impact essay, be sure to be as specific as possible in describing your impact and your actual involvement.

Do a lot of soul-searching to make sure you select the best representative example. What you may consider great impact may come across as not that impressive. The circumstances surrounding the situation are important. For example, if you are an investment banker with an annual salary and bonus of over $100K, you may want to rethink whether contributing $5000 to your brother's education is the best example of your leadership impact. The achievement has to transcend your own personal gain. So the impact you had should have a positive effect on your colleagues, customers, or the organization.

*Some Recent Impact Essay Questions*

*Michigan:* Describe your most significant professional accomplishment. Elaborate on the leadership skills you displayed, and the impact you had on your organization.

*Wharton:* Where in your background would we find evidence of your leadership capacity and/or potential?

*Stanford:* Tell us about a time when you went beyond what was defined, established, or expected.

*Haas:* Give us an example of a situation in which you displayed leadership.

*HBS:* What are your three most substantial accomplishments and why do you view them as such?

## The "Who You Are" Essay

"Who you are" essays are designed to help the MBA Board understand you in a three-dimensional sense. It allows them to get a sense of your values and passions—what makes you tick. They want to gauge your ability to handle adversity, overcome challenge, and bounce back in the face of failure. Ultimately, the question on the MBA Board's mind is whether you are self-aware (whether it's dealing with your developmental areas and strengths or it's connecting the dots together from your experiences). When tackling these types of essays, be willing to reveal your character and the type of student and alumnus you will become.

These types of essays require candidates to reveal a deeper level of insight and information that isn't covered in their resume. An example is how growing up as the oldest child exposed you to responsibility at an early age, shaping your leadership style and your propensity for stepping up to lead from the front. Another candidate who grew up in a home of entrepreneurs can share insights about why she gravitates to innovation and comes up with creative solutions in her career. Both examples are valid backgrounds that reveal the context that has shaped the candidates' lives. It is less about what your experiences are and more about your awareness of how they have shaped who you are in a personal and professional sense.

Being willing to open up and share stories that present your personal side is the surest way to show the MBA Board who you are. But remember: judgment is key. There is a balance between telling the Admissions Board about hardships that have shaped your character and offloading detailed personal information that may not have much bearing on the application. I once read an application where the candidate described getting over her boyfriend breaking up with her as one of her greatest accomplishments. This may be a struggle that the candidate experienced, but it is certainly not appropriate to write about this topic for a business school application. At best, it calls into question your judgment.

You should also watch out for details that are red flags to the MBA Board. For instance, saying that you are highly impatient or prefer working on projects solo do little to endear you to the Admissions Board because teamwork is at the heart of business school education. Also, essays that push blame to others instead of taking responsibility for a breakdown of a process or project reflect poorly on the candidate.

"Who you are" essays can be further divided into two groups: self-assessment essays and values and influence essays.

### *"Who You Are" Essay One: The Self-Assessment Essay*

What sets you apart from other people? What are your strengths and weaknesses? What type of leader are you? What attribute has influenced your success? These types of essay questions are designed to see how self-aware you are. The purpose isn't to identify perfect candidates. However, these essays are tricky in that they require you to provide an honest assessment of yourself. For instance, the MBA Board wants to know how self-aware you are of your weakness or developmental area. The MBA Board relies on these types of essays to gauge whether you have a balanced perspective of yourself. A major red flag for the MBA Board is when there is a discrepancy between how you describe yourself and how your recommenders describe you. For instance, if you say you are conscientious and thrive in fast-paced, pressure situations and your recommenders say you are highly disorganized and need to develop your ability to handle pressure, you have a problem. Be honest with your assessment and make sure your recommenders are on the same page.

Equally important is selecting real weaknesses that you are working to improve. Don't insult the MBA Board's intelligence by choosing topics that come off as superficial, for example, saying you need to become less of a perfectionist. Here's an authentic example: "I have a propensity to overanalyze things. This comes from my natural tendency to be less of a risk taker. Doing intense assessment enables me to mitigate the risk and gives me a comfort level to pursue a new direction. The fallout of this weakness is that there are a lot of business situations where there isn't enough time to do intense research and I have to become more comfortable with making decisions without gathering all the data I'd like...." You get my point. This is a real weakness; the person understands that it can inhibit his progress as a business leader. What would strengthen this example is going a step further to describe how the weakness is being addressed. Let's look at an actual self-assessment essay.

---

### Sample Self-Assessment Essay

HARVARD ESSAY: *Provide a candid assessment of your strengths and weaknesses.*

*Maturity, adaptability, and leadership are my core strengths. When I was ten, my parents left Africa to work in Saudi Arabia. Living with little supervision in a boarding school in Africa for 5 years helped me mature quickly. At eighteen, I became responsible for my younger siblings who continually looked to me for guidance and direction as we all tried to adapt to life in the U.S. Currently, I supervise people that are twice my age, some of whom have over 20 years of experience in pharmaceutical production. My maturity has enabled me to successfully lead and manage these experienced line employees while earning their respect.*

*Living in 4 different continents has afforded me many opportunities to adapt to different cultures, people, and ways of thinking. Over the past 3 years, I have had 7 different job functions in 2 different companies. I have worked under different management styles, and in different regions of the country. In each position, I have quickly adapted successfully to new hierarchies, situations, and environments.*

*Throughout my life, I have shown an affinity for leadership. In high school and college, I took on several leadership roles. In my professional career, I have addressed challenging situations at work, leading several teams to success. At Pharma Co A, for example, I led a campaign to end the waste of expiring drugs. I also created and led a successful human error management campaign. Recently, I initiated a similar plan at my new company, Pharma Co B.*

*My two main weaknesses are incomplete business knowledge and my learning to balance relationships with line employees and making tough business decisions. To become a successful pharmaceutical business leader, I must get a better grip on marketing, finance, and strategy. But as a line manager, I must learn to keep adequate emotional distance between me and the employees under my watch. While at Pharma Co A, I once hesitated before reporting an operator who on more than one occasion fell asleep on the job (his mistake, had I not discovered it, would have cost the company $750,000). In hindsight, this was a very expensive mistake which if not addressed could have caused the factory to shut down. But because I had befriended a number of the line operators, it was, at first, a tough call to report him. As I take on more management responsibility, I must learn to better balance my investment in the employees and keeping a business productive and successful.*

---

## Assessment

This essay is written by an engineer and is less creative in its style. It is a matter of fact essay, representative of the candidate's personality. He provides specific examples when laying out his strengths and weaknesses. He does a good job setting the tone for his experience raising his siblings. One doesn't get a sense that he is looking for sympathy or brownie points. Rather, he uses the experience to show his maturity and strong leadership and management abilities, which are anchored in a series of personal experiences from his family situation. His weaknesses come across as authentic. As an engineer, he conveys the practical business skills that he lacks, which is more a function of his role as opposed to his personal weakness. Had he stopped there, he would have missed an opportunity to show the MBA Board a glimpse into who he is and his awareness of his developmental needs. By describing how he struggled with balancing managing people and holding them accountable and then citing a specific example to drive home his point, he presents an interesting essay that shows depth of character. He could have also shared another developmental weakness instead of selecting one about having incomplete business knowledge.

---

## TIPS ON HANDLING THE SELF-ASSESSMENT ESSAY

Be candid about your strengths and make sure you have substantial evidence to back them up.

On the weakness side, use real weaknesses, not something trite such as, "I work too hard" or "I need to delegate better."

Make sure that the essays you write reinforce the main brand message you want to convey about yourself. For instance, if your brand is a perpetual optimist, your weakness could be that you need to temper your optimism because you may fail to devote enough time anticipating downsides and potential problems when working on projects. And of course the value of a weakness is to tell a story where it occurred and then acknowledge your awareness of the weakness and show how you turned things around.

Be comfortable in your own skin. This is an important variable in successful candidates. You want to show that you have a good understanding of why you have made the decisions you have made and have the capability to learn from mistakes as well.

---

*Some Recent Self-Assessment Essay Questions:*
*Darden:* Please choose one phrase that describes you from the set below and support your statement using concrete examples. Professionally I am: (a) involved globally, b) committed to diversity, c) socially responsible.

*Kellogg:* Each of our applicants is unique. Describe how your background, values, academics, activities and/or leadership skill will enhance the experience of other Kellogg students.

*Wharton:* Tell us about a situation in which you were an outsider. What did you learn from the experience?

*Wharton:* Describe a failure or setback that you have experienced. What role did you play, and what did you learn about yourself?

*HBS:* Discuss a defining experience in your leadership development. How did this experience highlight your strengths and weaknesses?

*"Who You Are" Essay Two: The Values and Influence Essay*
Similar to the self-assessment essay, the values and influence essay probes what matters to you as it relates to your beliefs, philosophies, and influences. These essays cover such topics as the following: Who are your role models? What experiences have influenced your development as a leader? Which business leaders do you admire and why? Describe a situation that has had a transformational impact on who you are. What matters most to you and why? When were you an outsider? Describe a situation when you experienced culture shock.

These types of essay questions are trying to understand the experiences that have shaped who you are, your value system, and the people who have shaped your life and worldview. The values and influence essays also aim to ascertain what type of a business leader you aspire to become. Don't just focus on what or who. Take the time to express why you feel the way you do. The MBA Board wants to know that you have very clearly defined values and awareness around the forces that have shaped you personally and professionally. This gives them a clearer picture of who you are as a person beyond your accolades and job titles.

---

### Sample Values and Influence Essay

*Each of our applicants is unique. Describe how your background, values, academics, activities, and/or leadership skills will enhance the experiences of other students.*

There are four distinct attributes of my personality that have guided my life: guts, creativity, leadership, and passion. I plan to bring these attributes to X program to enrich my classmates' lives and anticipate a two-year period full of growth and development.

Growing up in suburban Detroit, I came to understand there were 4 major religions in our community: Christianity, Judaism, Islam, and University of Michigan Football. As my friends donned the colors of maize and blue, and made plans of who was going to live with whom, my college dreams expanded far beyond the boundaries of my backyard. I wanted a different experience. X University presented the opportunity to stretch myself, gain new experiences, and make new friends. In college, I selected Engineering Psychology, a major few had heard of because it combined the liberal arts discipline of psychology with the mathematical and analytical foundation of engineering allowing me to blend my analytical right brain nature with my creative, expressive left brain spirit. A university experience far from home, an unusual major in the engineering school, a semester abroad in Spain living with an extended Spanish family, and many adventurous trips and outdoor expeditions reinforced my belief in the importance of taking the right risks and pushing myself outside of my comfort zone. I plan to share this free-spirit and lessons gleaned from many of these experiences with my classmates at X program.

As a child, I had an active imagination and loved performing in shows and dance recitals. I sought interesting and creative ways to entertain myself. I pursued jazz and ballet for 11 years and found creative outlets in college through X University's Hip Hop Dance Troupe performances. My work at X firm is exciting because of the *creative brands I get to work with. I rely on my creativity to create new and innovative product lines. X MBA program is a dynamic environment that attracts driven, committed, and creative individuals from a wide array of professional and personal experiences. I love that about X program and it is precisely why I'm convinced that it is the perfect program for me. I look forward to starting a dance club for X program students. I am excited to share my creative background and experiences with other X program students and teach them how business challenges are best tackled through creative solutions and innovative thinking.*

*I have always thrived in leadership situations, whether in formal settings at work or in less formal settings in the outdoors. As an outdoor enthusiast, I am faced with numerous situations that stretch my leadership and teach me new skills. I have enjoyed sharing many of these lessons with others. Algonquin Provincial Park in Ontario, Canada, provided a wonderful opportunity to lead youths on canoe trips. I spent many of my summers motivating and leading 10-16 year olds through difficult, and sometimes dangerous situations. The wilderness of the park was the perfect backdrop to encourage kids to empower themselves through these outdoor excursions while developing their reliance on their team. The external factors of weather and wildlife constantly impose new and various challenges. I embraced the challenge, led responsibly, and found gratification in my ability to competently execute the objective. These lessons have taught me the importance of team work, being able to laugh at adversity, have fun, and take a negative and make it a positive. These elements are very analogous to the circumstances one encounters on a regular basis in business. I look forward to joining the Outdoor and Service club where I would lead and coordinate the trips servicing the first year student community through team building outdoor adventures. In my professional life, I have learned not to be bound by my early career status and that being a leader is not about title. I've learned that leadership is about being gutsy, taking risks, influencing teams, and creating opportunities. During my work on developing X firm's candy line, I have had experiences to lead teams of graphic designers and candy developers, while creating new opportunities for healthier product innovations. I will bring my strong sense of leadership to the X program community.*

*During my college experience, I was fortunate to develop my main passion towards children by volunteering at a day care for under privilege children that was run by the X university community. Playing activities and reading stories with the children helped me keep my own life in perspective. It was there that I realized that my future career would somehow impact children's lives. Working at X firm, I've had a very tangible impact on the lives of kids and the lessons I've learned will enrich my MBA classroom conversations. I wish to continue my involvement with children through various volunteer organizations at X MBA program.*

*It is these four distinct attributes that have made me the person I am today and will help me enrich the learning experiences of my fellow X MBA program students.*

---

### Assessment

This candidate is very outgoing, people-driven, and comfortable in her own skin. Showing your point instead of simply stating it is also important in an essay like this. She does a good job of that when she says:

> *Growing up in suburban Detroit, I came to understand there were 4 major religions in our community: Christianity, Judaism, Islam, and University of Michigan Football. As my friends donned the colors of maize and blue, and made plans of who was going to live with whom, my college dreams expanded far beyond the boundaries of my backyard.*

She could have simply stated, "Pushing myself outside traditional boundaries is a value that matters to me." Instead she shows it by using the preceding illustration. The use of the four religions in Detroit shows her sense of humor, which is done in good taste. Candidates always need to be careful when using humor so that it doesn't backfire. She does a good job of showing how the choices she has made were driven by her natural curiosity and desire to stretch herself instead of playing it safe (whether moving to the East Coast instead of going to U of M like all her friends, or selecting her major, which combines psychology and engineering). Even her industry, entertainment/media, is unique. One gets a sense that she brings passion to anything she does, whether it's working with young people through the outdoor adventure programs or a day care for underprivileged kids.

Finally, by describing her commitment to dance (eleven years of dancing ballet and jazz and performing with the Hip Hop Dance Troupe), she shows her creativity and discipline, traits that would be attractive to the MBA Board. The essay is a bit on the long side, but overall, she does a good job of bringing in different things that she does that matter to her without simply listing them. She manages to inject her spunky personality in her essay, ensuring that she doesn't come off as a bland candidate.

## TIPS ON HANDLING THE VALUES AND INFLUENCE ESSAY

The trick to writing a values essay is to make sure it doesn't come across as clichéd. Remember, all 5000 applicants to that MBA program will also answer the same question. Can you imagine how the board members' eyes would roll when they read the 255th essay in a row about how I value making a difference in society or my family is the most important thing in my life? With these essays, it is important to try to take a fresh angle to the story. Stay away from the beaten path unless you feel it absolutely is essential to who you are.

When writing the role model essay, also avoid choosing clichéd responses such as "My grandparents [or parents] have shaped my values to become who I am today" (a lot of people will choose the same example). If you must choose this, then offer a unique and interesting angle. For example, instead of the typical story of parents who worked hard and made it, a different take is a story of multiple failures and a persistent spirit that has shaped your worldview. Don't manufacture a story if it isn't part of your experience, but I caution you to avoid choosing the first "usual suspect" story that comes to mind. Devote enough time to select a topic that truly represents a differentiated and unique insight into who you are as a person.

When it comes to essays that ask for a business leader you admire, don't be afraid to select a lesser-known, but accomplished, business leader. Yes, you may admire Jack Welsh, Bill Gates, or Meg Whitman. However, are there other business leaders who you identify more closely with who are not as prominent? A young woman whose brand was retail entrepreneurship chose to focus on a widow who was thrust into running her husband's retail business after his untimely death. The business started with a few million dollars in revenue, and she grew the revenue to more than a billion dollars. By eschewing the more prominent business leaders, this applicant focused on a less famous but extremely successful business leader who connected to her retail brand. Her story was refreshing and gave her an opportunity to share new information with the MBA Board that set her apart from applicants who were mired in clichéd stories. The size of the role model's achievement isn't as important as articulating what you admire about the person. So don't feel that you have to only choose individuals who have achieved enormous financial success.

Tackling the "who you are" essay requires incredible focus. It is tempting to try to dump everything into the story. Given limited word counts, you can ace this essay when you have done a thorough brand audit and can hone in on three to four brand themes that reflect what matters to you. You will often hear Admissions Board members say at information sessions that your essays should reflect who you are. Nowhere is this most pertinent than in essays that ask you to describe who you are and what matters to you. This Stanford essay is one of the most challenging application essays out there. It requires the deepest level of introspection, and candidates cannot hide behind any props. It is as bare and open as it gets. Most applicants struggle with this essay because they haven't invested enough time into the self-assessment necessary to unveil the core elements of who they are, and nor have they identified the appropriate specific stories to paint a vivid picture of who they are—their brand. Be willing to take a risk and share stories that honestly represent your brand.

*Some Recent Values and Influence Essay Questions:*
*Stanford:* What matters to you most and why?

*Columbia:* Please tell us about what you feel most passionate in life.

*Haas:* If you could have dinner with one individual in the past, present, or future, who would it be and why?

*Chicago:* If you could step into someone else's shoes for a day, who would it be and why?

## The Miscellaneous Essay
The miscellaneous essay category is the fourth type of essay that candidates encounter in the application process. These

essays are broad in terms of specific topics they cover. The MBA Board may want you to weigh in on a political situation to assess how you develop an argument and provide evidence to back it up. On the other hand, these essays could also be personalized, providing you with a chance to speak to anything else in your story that is compelling that you were unable to address in other application essays. You can also use these types of essays to explain any gaps in your work experience, academic weaknesses, or potential questions that the Admissions Board may have about your candidacy. Topics covered by miscellaneous essays can touch on a global issue, what you do with your spare time, or anything else you wish to cover in your application. Here's an example of a miscellaneous essay that asks candidates to address how they spent their time in college.

---

### *Sample Miscellaneous Essay*
*HARVARD ESSAY: Tell us about your undergraduate academic experience.*

*I was one of three African-American females in my class at a small England boarding school and elected to attend the University of Pennsylvania because its large, urban, diverse atmosphere represented the opposite of my high school environment. At Penn's Annenberg School for Communication, I customized my communication major to focus on Latin-American and Afro-American cultures, the former of which I studied during a semester-abroad program in Oaxaca, Mexico. For both cultures, I focused on history with special emphasis on various forms of expression, including folk music and literature. One representative class from my course of study was "Without Struggle," a seminar that required completion of faculty-guided research. My project focused on the benefits and disadvantages of Dubois House—Penn's Afro-American-themed college house—for which I designed a survey, analyzed the raw data, and drew conclusions. This experience gave me the strong foundation to excel in "Basic Communication Research—A Quantitative Data Analysis Course." These two classes combined to give me the confidence to serve as a teaching assistant for "Without Struggle" my senior year. As a TA, my leadership style evolved from simply providing my opinion to learning to encourage students to draw their own conclusions.*

*During college, I did not properly manage academics, extracurricular activities, and employment, spending disproportionate amounts of time on the latter two at the expense of the others. Unfortunately, my grades in some quantitative courses reflect only my misbalanced study schedule, not my true academic fervor. Recalling how I harnessed my study abroad experience to achieve Spanish fluency, I chose a post-undergraduate employment that would yield "fluency" in another foreign subject: finance. After graduation I joined Goldman Sachs as a Sales Trader and learned about stock market supply and demand in real-time; further, I developed sharp quantitative skills by monitoring the financial markets. Now, as an Equity Research team analyst, I build valuation models by evaluating financial statements and I am the lead associate for eBay and Amazon, stocks that respectively trade over 20 million and 6 million shares daily. I supplemented this comprehension by excelling in a course, "Financial Statement Analysis," this past summer. During this time I also maintained my volunteer and leadership responsibilities, effectively demonstrating my maturity and improved ability to multi-task, juggling real-world duties with scholastic commitment. I will utilize both of these personal qualities to balance leadership positions and academic achievement at HBS, without ever sacrificing one for the other.*

---

## Assessment

This essay is written by a candidate who was concerned about her academic track record. She had to strike a fair balance between describing her academic experience and providing evidence that she has the analytical and intellectual rigor to handle a challenging MBA curriculum. She begins the essay by demonstrating her resilient spirit as one of three students of color in an unfamiliar environment. She then introduces examples of her quantitative and analytical skills by describing her data analysis course in college, the financial statement analysis course after college, and her career in a blue chip firm, Goldman, where her day-to-day role involves its fair share of quantitative and analytical computations. I like the fact that she owns up to her "failure" in college for not balancing her time well. However, what is important to highlight here is that she strikes a great note between owning her mistake and not groveling. By introducing her work experience in sales and trading and equity research at a blue chip firm, she is effective in providing additional evidence that shows that she is in her element working in an analytical environment. Finally, she proactively takes a finance course and does well to reassure the MBA Board that she has what it takes to handle quantitative coursework.

Let's look at another example of a miscellaneous essay, this time one that deals with a candidate who is reapplying to business school.

---

### *Another Sample Miscellaneous Essay*
*I wish the Admissions Committee had asked me: Why I chose to reapply to Kellogg.*

*While I was disappointed that I did not receive an admission, my drive and commitment did not deter me from applying to the class of 2006. The reapplication process allowed me a period of reflection enabling me to take a step back to reassess my life. Furthermore, it provided me with an opportunity to focus on my set goal. At work I have taken on additional responsibilities by managing more people, along with centers, which now focus on retail chain strategy. Within the community, I have become more actively involved in a women's empowerment group. I have also increased my GMAT score by 80 points and in the spring of next year, I plan to build an alternate transcript by taking accounting, calculus and statistics courses.*

*One key reason I am reapplying to Kellogg is the outstanding program in entrepreneurship. In 1965, my grandmother became the first sole distributor of the Guinness brand of liquors in Africa and my father is a leading African entrepreneur. There is no telling to how great a business woman my grandmother could have become had she had the proper formal business school education. As an adult, I observe my father's business prowess and though admirable, would be far superior had he had formal business school education. I am reapplying to Kellogg not to become a moderately successful entrepreneur or to become a good business person. I am reapplying to Kellogg for the opportunity to learn how to become a thought leader, an innovator and a superbly successful business person. I am reapplying to Kellogg to major in entrepreneurship and International business and to have the opportunity to take advantage of the Kaizer Institute of Entrepreneurial Studies.*

*My first interaction with the Kellogg culture was at the prospective students information session in November 2002. I also interacted with Kellogg students during the planned trip for Dean Jain in Africa. During my on campus visit in October 2003, I had the opportunity to attend Professor Anderson's New Product and Services class and Professor Christine Nordhielm's Big Picture lecture. Both classes showcased Kellogg's first-class educational standards as both professors were insightful, challenged the status-quo and pushed us the students to think strategically and out of the box. Also during my trip, I had multiple interactions with students, and members of the administration. The culture of excellence and collegiality I observed during these interactions were exceptional and I feel that Kellogg was truly an environment that embraces teamwork, unique attributes and openness to new ideas. Upon my return home from Evanston, I took a look at my experiences and it is unequivocally clear to me that the Kellogg School of Management is a perfect fit for my personal and professional growth. And this is why I am reapplying to the Kellogg School of Management, Class of 2006.*

---

## Assessment

This essay does a good job setting up the expectations of the Admissions Board. The applicant immediately outlines what is different with her application the second time around by showing that her GMAT has gone up and that her work experience has expanded, thus increasing the likelihood that the board member reading her application would take her reapplication bid seriously. She then follows up by talking about coursework she plans to take. Although this is fine, ideally, it would have even been more compelling had she taken the classes already and had excellent grades to report.

Every candidate to business school has to make the case about what he or she finds attractive about the particular MBA program. As a result, Admissions Boards read these essays over and over again, a *Groundhog's Day* experience. The challenge, however, is keeping the essay fresh and connecting it to your unique background. This essay does precisely this. She connects her personal life (her grandmother's and father's entrepreneur backgrounds) to how she hopes to develop into a better entrepreneur at Kellogg. She also shows that she understands what the program offers by describing specifics of her campus visit, particularly attending classes. The only additional feedback I would give her is to highlight insights she developed from the classes that she can compare to her professional experience working in Africa.

## TIPS ON HANDLING THE MISCELLANEOUS ESSAY

The reapplication essay is an important essay because it gives you a chance to make a case of what is different, and with more than 80 percent of applicants being rejected, it is only reasonable to expect that some would reapply at a future date.

Don't underestimate the importance of the miscellaneous essay, even if it is allocated only 250 words.

When crafting a question, make sure it is appropriate and doesn't raise any red flags about your candidacy.

Use the optional essay or craft your own essay question to address a gap in your story. For example, if you are a reapplicant, you may wish to use this essay to address why you are reapplying and what is different about your application the second time around. If you are applying very early in your career, you may want to use this essay to show why now is the ideal time for you to pursue your MBA.

*Some Recent Miscellaneous Essay Questions*

*HBS:* What else would you like the MBA Admissions Board to understand about you?

*Yale:* Please develop a question/topic of your choice and answer it in essay form.

*Haas:* What steps have you taken to learn about the Berkeley MBA program, and what factors influenced your decision to apply?

## COMMON ESSAY MISTAKES

I have compiled missteps that applicants often make when writing their MBA essays. As you tackle your essays, always ask yourself whether you are falling into one of these traps. Avoiding these essay errors can improve your admission chance.

1. Engaging in Essay Brain Dump: Writing your essays without first doing an outline will ensure that you create disjointed and ineffective essays. Use the SOARS model to frame up the outline before tackling any essay.

2. Being Bland and Generic: Failure to nail down your marketing will increase your chances of producing boring and undifferentiated essays. Do a brand audit to understand your overall positioning. I can often tell when an essay is written without a clear brand message: they are boring and don't communicate a message about the applicant.

3. Being Selfish: Focusing too much on "I" can make you come across as arrogant; balance your individual accomplishment with your team involvement.

4. Going Back Too Far: Selecting accomplishments from a long time ago, for instance, during high school, especially after you have been working for seven years, may not come across as compelling; if you must go back that far, it is important to make sure the example is significant and has special meaning in shaping who you have become as a leader.

5. Using Clichés, Sermonizing, and Stating the Obvious: The MBA Board knows what conventional wisdom says. They care about what you personally think or believe.

6. Overusing Quotes: There is a place for quotes in the essays, but think long and hard before using up precious words to quote some Greek philosopher or business leader. The MBA Board is interested in your original thoughts, not those of a dead poet.

7. Not Answering the Question: If the question asks for leadership impact, be sure to tell a story that clearly depicts you as a leader. If the question asks for weaknesses, give examples of real weaknesses. Don't skirt around the issue. You will only annoy the Admissions Board if you do.

8. Being Unmemorable: Choose vivid stories that resonate with the Admissions Board. Unusual stories or a different take on a common topic can be interesting and capture the mindshare of the Admissions Board.

9. Not Pacing Yourself Strategically: Don't try to do multiple essays for different schools at once. Tackle the essays one school at a time and complete them before working on another school's essays. Similarly, you should not underestimate how much time and work are needed to assemble a strong application. Give yourself at least four months to complete the essays and add another month or two when factoring in other parts of the application (including managing recommenders, campus visits, interviews and so on).

10. Using Humor Inappropriately: Don't be funny for the sake of being funny. Always exercise good judgment with your essays. Recounting the antics that you and your friends found funny will not win you any friends on the MBA Board. Subtle humor is more effective.

11. Being Too Rigid: This is the opposite of the inappropriate humor mistake. It is important to open up and share personal (appropriate) stories that give the MBA Board insight into who you are and what matters to you. Focusing all your essays on your professional life misses the chance to show the full range of your personality, character, and motivations.

12.  Trying to Be Creative for the Sake of Being Creative: Sometimes, less is best. Artificial essays with whistles and bells can backfire. I'm not against being creative but make sure that your creativity fits with the brand of the school and that it comes off well instead of appearing gimmicky.

13.  Being Repetitive: It is important to bring up different stories to show the breadth and depth of your personality, experience, and perspective. Using the same example over and over again will suggest that you have a limited experience base.

14.  Not Understanding the Program's Brand: Take the time to understand the brand of the school and what that means for your essays. Kellogg, for example, is a program that is significantly tied to teamwork, so essays that ask about leadership impact should show team partnership instead of focusing on your "lone-ranger" leadership exploits.

15.  Having Too Many People "Weigh-In" on Your Essays: Beware the too-many-cooks phenomenon. It's helpful to get feedback from someone who knows you very well, especially if that person is a good writer. But it's another thing to have your twenty friends, former colleagues, and that relative who happened to graduate from the same business school a decade ago review your essays. At the very least, you will get a hodgepodge of feedback that will yield a disjointed set of essays.

16.  Doing a Drive-By Application: Don't be in a rush to complete your application. Rather, focus on producing excellent applications. The best applications are a result of intense introspection, focus, and multiple revisions.

Applying good judgment when it comes to all your essays will help you get closer to your admission goals. Good judgment means not being stubborn and insisting that you will write the essay about the speech you gave to five people that was the "best speech this side of the hemisphere." Just because you think the world of something you did does not mean that it is essay-worthy. If you can't point to the tangible impact your actions achieved, you may have to think twice before selecting that topic for your essay.

## FINAL THOUGHTS ON THE MBA ESSAYS

One thing you probably picked up from reading these sample essays is that there are different writing styles and that the topics can vary quite broadly. Two candidates can write about a personal accomplishment of buying a house for their parent, and one person's essay soars while the other person's essay falls flat. The difference is in the positioning of the story. Approach your application by writing heartfelt and insightful essays that take the Admissions Board into a deeper awareness of your motivations and what you care about. This approach will make your application stand apart. You need to use good judgment when selecting your admission essay topics. The same applies to the treatment of each essay. Your decision to write about how your relationship with your fiancée is your greatest accomplishment needs to be seen through the business school lens. How does that tie into who you are as a leader? Whatever example you choose, make sure it fosters your story that you are a leader and someone who can get things achieved with and through other people.

It is also important to "own" your story. It can't be manufactured. The essays that grab the attention of the Admissions Board can be a very simple achievement, written in a straightforward style with little creativity and poetry. These essays are successful because they give the Admissions Board a glimpse into the heart of a candidate. No matter what your life experiences are, make sure you devote enough time to introspection before tackling the admissions essays. Doing so can be the difference between a congratulatory phone call from the director of admissions and the depressing email informing you that you have been denied admission.

# CHAPTER SEVEN

## The Resume and Professional Record

THE RESUME IS ANOTHER important part of the application. It is often one of the first things that the Admissions Board looks at in your application packet. Think of it as a snapshot of your work, your life journey, and what stands out about you. It reveals to the MBA Board your professional and educational accomplishments, as well as any interesting and unusual things you have done or are currently involved in.

Most top MBA programs require a resume, so plan to update yours early in the process and invest enough time in it to ensure that it adequately reflects your brand. Unfortunately, many applicants do not pay enough attention to their resume, thus missing an opportunity to sell themselves to the MBA Board.

Candidates often question how much work experience is necessary to apply to business school. Deciding how much information to include on the resume can also be tricky. Those with more years of experience wonder if they should submit their seven-page curriculum vitae (CV) that covers every job they have ever held. On the other hand, candidates with limited work experience worry that they don't have enough information to highlight in their resumes. Although the average number of years of work experience is four to five years, there is no set requirement. Seasoned and early career candidates are both admitted to the nation's top business schools. Regardless of where you fall on the age and work experience continuum, the key is to make sure that your career is on an upward trajectory and that you can make a compelling case for why you need an MBA now. Ideally, you should keep your resume to one to two pages, unless the school requests a more comprehensive curricular vita. Be as succinct as possible and focus on the most important impact and contributions you had rather than including ten bullets of each responsibility you had in a particular job. Using active verbs and eliminating any redundancies will help you create a focused resume.

The resume for business school is different from the resume an individual uses to search for a job. Unlike job resumes, application resumes should contain limited jargon and acronyms (the person reviewing your application may not know the intricacies of your industry). Also, you do not need to include a reference, summary, or objective section. They only use up precious space. The MBA application in general calls for brevity and the resume in particular needs to be short and to the point as it typically gets only a few seconds to about five minutes of the MBA Board's attention. I recognize that producing a succinct resume poses its share of challenge to MBA applicants. I'll focus the next section on the critical components of the resume.

## THE FOUR COMPONENTS OF THE RESUME

Determining what to include in your resume can be difficult for many applicants. Many who struggle with this issue end up including everything they can think of, which does nothing to strengthen their application. Some candidates make the opposite mistake: they make the resume too short and leave out interesting and unique things about themselves—things that can differentiate them from their competition and instead focus on solely the academic and career aspects of their resume.

I will discuss the key things to include in the resume. For starters, the resume for business school should have four main components: professional experience, education, activities (leadership), and interests/other.

## The Professional Experience Section

The professional experience section is about achievements you have had in your career and your roles, not simply regurgitating your job description. It is important to communicate your professional career progress by emphasizing the quantifiable aspects of your job.

The types of questions you should be thinking of when creating your resume for your business school application are: Did I get an early promotion? Was I the only analyst from my group invited to work on a high-value, complicated deal? Did I have an unusual opportunity to manage groups of people, even peers? Did I initiate something that has now become the standard at my firm? Have I had opportunities to lead and work across functional roles? Have I led diverse or global teams? Have I been able to create value at my firm? These questions are designed to help you focus on the tangible contributions you have had at your firms.

MBA candidates are challenged with the amount of detail they should cover in the professional experience section. Prioritization is key in this process. Anticipate that you will have about four to five bullets at most for each job, so think long and hard about the most important achievements you wish to highlight and ascertain whether they reinforce your personal brand. A rule of thumb is that the further removed you are from the position, the fewer bullets you allot to it. Another useful tool in saving space is to provide a sampling of deals or projects you have worked on instead of devoting extensive space to every major project you have worked on. So for instance, an investment banker can select three to four major deals she has worked on to show diversity of industries and breadth of experience instead of every single deal she has worked on.

The professional experience section should be in reverse chronology, with the most current job first. If you work for a lesser-known company, consider including a sentence that describes what the firm does, its market size, and what makes it compelling.

You should indicate your job title and show whether your role has grown over time. You should also make it easy for the MBA Board to follow your progress. Make sure the information of your tenure—your years at the job—is clear and easily identifiable. Ensure that the dates are easy to see.

Internships are valuable work experience that should not be ignored; in fact, they can be critical for early career candidates with limited work experience. That said, however, the longer you have worked, the less important it is to provide detailed information on every internship you have held in your life. You will need to make trade-offs on what specific information to focus on and what information to minimize. Experiences that reinforce your personal brand should be highlighted (especially if you have strong examples of leadership and impact), rather than roles that do not reinforce your brand message.

For college students, the work experience section is even more important because you have to make a strong case with limited experience that you have the potential to "hold your own" in a business school. You should highlight your internships and show what you were able to do besides doing what may be considered grunt work. This section of the resume is where you can show your maturity and initiative. If, for instance, you worked during your school year, you should definitely highlight the work you did and the value you created. If you were involved in an entrepreneurial venture, you should make sure that you communicate the size of the business, the achievement, and your role so the Admissions Board can gauge whether you have enough professional insight to be admitted. The good news is that there is no age or work limit, so instead of focusing on the quantity of years of experience, show the impact and quality of contribution you had in the time you have worked.

## The Education Section

The education section typically comes after the professional work experience section. The exception to this applies to applicants who are still in college or who have less than a year of work experience. The first point you need to convey in the education section is where you went to school and your graduation year. It is worth including that you graduated early if that was your situation. It is also important to highlight your major, class rank, GPA, and any dual, double, or specialized degrees that you pursued. You should also mention any graduate degrees you have earned, as well as business coursework you have taken (especially if you did not take business classes in college). The education section is also where you discuss your awards, for instance, being on the Dean's List or any scholarships and honors awards you received. If you received any unique and highly selective awards or honors, you should quantify this to help the Admissions Board understand its selectivity. You should also include your study abroad program in this section.

Some additional points related to your GPA: The GPA you reference on your resume should match up to that on your official transcript. Inconsistencies, especially when the GPA on your resume is higher than your official GPA, raise questions about your integrity.

Research papers published in professional journals should be mentioned in this section as well. For example, someone whose honors thesis is selected for presentation at a national professional association should highlight this achievement.

If you transferred from one school to another, it is important that your resume reflect this change. I'm often asked whether an applicant is obligated to include the schools attended if he or she didn't graduate from there. The simple answer is yes. You don't want to misrepresent yourself. So, if you left school after a semester or two and transferred to another school, you should include this information. Many MBA programs ask for all the schools you have attended, so not providing this information can come back to haunt you.

Other unique situations that are worth mentioning in the education section of your resume can be self-financing your education or being the first in your family to graduate from college.

## The Activities Section

The activities part of your resume is also very important. When you are thinking of your activities, you should think primarily in the context of leadership: does it highlight your leadership attribute, character, or achievement? Remember the 3 Cs discussed earlier. You should keep them in mind when addressing the resume in general and the activities section in particular. Showing a track record of consistent leadership not only in your career but in your community involvement and during your college years places you on a different level compared to your competition.

The activities section allows you to communicate how you are different from each candidate in your category who works in the same industry/firm. Are you involved in extracurricular activities that matter to you? Pick the ones that reinforce your brand message and where you had the greatest impact. You will be limited by space, so be selective on how far back you wish to go. The longer you have worked, the less far back you should go. A professional with ten years of experience should not go as far back as high school to highlight the summer Habit for Humanity project he worked on. It will raise flags about the absence of more recent community involvement. Your college activities are acceptable.

MBA Boards are interested in candidates who have a life outside of work and who are more than academic geniuses. The reality for many applicants is that they will have strong leadership activities while in college but these often taper off once they start working, especially for those in the financial services and consulting industries. Even if you are no longer involved in a particular activity, if you had significant impact during your college years, you should highlight this in the activities section. Quality is also more important than quantity, so focus on the activities that mean the most to you rather than having a laundry list of peripheral involvement.

Applicants should go beyond listing their activities. They need to provide information that communicates the depth and scope of their involvement. Stay away from activities where your only involvement is as a member. Focus on those where you demonstrated leadership and impact. Applicants to business school often have a lot of leadership activities during college. Many of them showcase their leadership through activities such as managing the student investment portfolio, leading new initiatives through student senate, or supervising more than 100 students as resident assistants.

Leadership roles can also come from athletics. For instance, you may have been the captain of your soccer team. Did the team's ranking improve? Did you institute any initiative to improve teamwork and training regimens? Highlight your influence through this formal leadership role. Not all activities include formal leadership titles, however. So even if you were not the captain of your team, playing on a varsity sports team is an accomplishment to be proud of. You can highlight things such as the number of games played, team rank, any awards you received that set you apart (for instance, being ranked fifth in the nation among female doubles tennis players).

Activities can also come from your community involvement. The duration of your involvement is important (highlighting continuity and commitment), but if you do not have a history of long-term participation, you can offset this by focusing on your impact. Some of the exceptional leadership activities that I have come across over the years have been achieved in the span of less than a year. Whether you choose to serve on the leadership board of a nonprofit organization, you start an organization to help immigrants assimilate into a new society, or you volunteer in an organization that does social good, the important point to convey in the activities section is the quantifiable contributions you have made and why it matters to you in the first place.

## The Interests/Other Section

Similar to the activities section, your interests/other section also allows you to stand apart from your competition. There are no ideal profiles in this section. The important point to convey is that you are interesting and have a different point of view or perspective you can offer to the MBA class. One of the main admissions evaluation criteria is uniqueness. This information can cover aspects of your brand that differentiate you from other candidates. For instance, are you internationally minded? If you are, you can show your commitment to international business by highlighting your multilingual abilities (especially if you have achieved fluency in them). Honesty is very important, so avoid exaggerating your skills. If you are conversant but not fluent in a language, then say exactly that.

If you have quirky and interesting things in your brand, by all means capitalize on them in this section. Think about what the interest you profile says about you. Ask yourself whether it sets you apart or reinforces a stereotype that already exists about you. A simple example of this can be seen in the case of an engineer who is passionate about salsa dancing. His commitment comes through his four years as a dance instructor. The stereo-type of the smart but bland technical individual goes out the window when you envision him gyrating to pulsating merengue music. Why is this important? It shows that this applicant not only has a life outside of work but is highly adaptable and can connect with different people.

Traveling is an interest that falls in the usual suspect cate-gory. If you choose to discuss traveling as an interest of yours, make sure you go beyond, "I like to travel and see new cities." This is a major cliché and gets you zero bonus points. A better way to convey this could be leading a trek to a remote area that isn't your usual hot spot. If your travel led to your interest in a particular region and you decided to work there, then it is worth mentioning. Here's an example of this:

> AVID TRAVELER: *Trip to Costa Rica during college break led to discovery of eco-tourism and influenced decision to work in Costa Rica for a year after graduating from college.*

There are other interesting things about your background that you may wish to address in the interests/other section of your resume. A few examples are captured here:

- Growing up in an interesting region, especially one where there are ongoing global political issues (for example, Sudan, Zimbabwe, Rwanda, Bosnia, Afghanistan, Nepal)
- Unusual upbringing can also be interesting to feature in the interests/other section: growing up in a blue collar family in the Midwest; being the first in your family to attend college; raising your younger siblings because of family issues; living in different countries; growing up on a farm or an Indian reservation
- Running multicountry marathons in cities that have a special meaning to you

Skills, awards, and certifications are also important elements to flag in the interests/other section of the resume. Similar to other parts of the resume, you have to determine whether the information you are highlighting will resonate with the brand of the school. Schools that are highly technical will likely appreciate your technical achievements in mastering programming languages or in building a complicated system network more than schools that are not.

If you are a financial analyst, having passed all three levels of the chartered financial analyst (CFA) exams is an important accomplishment to share in your resume. The same thing applies to other certifications, whether the CPA for accountants or the Series 7 and 66 exams to sell securities.

If you have received awards for something you do outside of work this is also the appropriate area to mention it. For example, I knew a banker who happened to be very dynamic and was selected to be a national spokesperson to promote positive and educational achievements for teenagers. These types of eclectic achievements are worth mentioning in your resume. A consultant interested in teenage empowerment can highlight her experience launching the first-ever teenage-focused television programming in her country. If she received an award for her work, then that is even more compelling.

If you are not sure what should make it into the resume and what should be cut out, start by writing down everything and then cut down drastically anything that doesn't reinforce your brand, showcase your leadership, or differentiate you from others. Don't be shy about getting feedback from alumni from the MBA programs you are interested in with whom you work or getting the opinion of a professional admissions consultant.

But beyond the four resume components, candidates to business school are often at a loss regarding how narrow or broad they should keep their resume. This issue goes to the heart of the next section—deciding between breadth and depth when positioning the resume.

## POSITIONING THE RESUME: BREADTH VS. DEPTH

I am often asked whether it is better to have worked for one company or in the same industry in similar roles (depth) versus having multiple positions in different industries and/or roles (breadth). The simple answer is that it depends on each candidate's particular situation. There are admitted candidates who worked at the same firm and in the same functional area for several years. These individuals' backgrounds showcase their depth of experience and commitment to their industry. The challenge for applicants with significant depth is to show that they have not stagnated at the same company or job. It is important to show that your responsibility and contribution has grown even though you have remained at the same firm. An investment banker who worked three years as an analyst and then gets promoted to associate with responsibility for managing analysts is an example of a candidate with depth of experience.

Equally admissible are candidates with breadth of work experience. These candidates have resumes that reflect different job positions. Sometimes the roles can be different in terms of function or in terms of industry. An example of a candidate with breadth of work experience is the accountant who worked for Ernest and Young, then joined the Peace Corps after a couple of years, and then decided to work for a foundation. The challenge that a candidate with breadth of experience faces is making sure that the story is cogent, that is, that the resume connects the different roles in a way that makes sense to the MBA Board. Candidates from professional backgrounds with a lot of breadth have to show that their career path has been well planned and isn't haphazard and random.

Regardless of where you fall on the breadth/depth continuum, make sure that your work experiences focus on your brand, demonstrate that you have developed new skills even within a focused role, and that you have had an impact on the organizations, teams, and individuals you have worked with. But more than that, candidates should show that the choices they have made in their career make sense and show logical progression.

The focus should be on the most compelling things about you. Remember that the resume is an extension of your brand. Make sure it is consistent with the rest of your application. Are your brand attributes and themes represented in your resume? When the Admissions Board reads your resume, it should confirm the conclusion they have already drawn of who you are. The sample resume that follows provides a picture of what a winning resume looks like. (Because this candidate has started a nonprofit organization, he felt a need to include Volunteer Experience as a separate section, which is fine.)

---

## SAMPLE RESUME

John Johnson
555 Sandy Lake Ave, NY, NY 10000
jjohnson@expartus.com; (212) 555-5555

**PROFESSIONAL EXPERIENCE**

COTY PRESTIGE New York, NY                    2003–2007

**Senior Financial Analyst—Financial Planning and Analysis Group**

Managed sixteen brand P & Ls totaling $105MM in sales, generating profits of $10MM annually with $53MM marketing budget. Collaborated with marketing and sales teams to build annual company budget and forecasts. Determined profit impact from changes in revenue and advertising/promotional expense forecasts.

Provided marketing team product launch budget guidelines after analyzing historical expenses of new campaigns.

Enabled senior marketing directors to fund new programs after conducting actual-to-budget variance analyses.

Led meetings with U.S. and global marketing teams to ensure use of promotional inventory to generate sales.

NEW YORK & COMPANY New York, NY          2001–2003
**Financial Analyst—Store Finance & Real Estate Department**
Analyzed return on investment and financial viability of building new stores to assist in company brand expansion. Assessed cost-benefits of downsizing/remodeling stores to maximize individual store productivity.

Assisted in reorganizing divisional field sales by geography to gain cost efficiencies.

Evaluated retail environment and sales trends to forecast store performance and aggressively control expenditures.

Recommended closing of 30 stores that led to $3 million savings.

MERRILL LYNCH New York, NY          1999–2001
**Compliance Associate—Global Securities Research and Economics Group**
Enforced compliance with SEC laws and regulations as liaison between analyst research teams and investment banking counsel. Edited research reports to remove restricted insider information under highly time-sensitive conditions.

**VOLUNTEER EXPERIENCE**
TOP HONORS, INC (a not-for-profit organization that provides free tutoring to low-achieving students)
New York, NY          2002–2006
**Co-Founder and Chief Operating Officer**
Built budget model to determine financial needs and secured funding from Citigroup and Columbia University. Managed

effective use of resources to operate weekly sessions under budget.

Fostered relationships with schools to ensure consistent student enrollment levels. Educated 120+ children since inception.

Developed and executed guerilla marketing campaign to triple tutor volunteer staffing in first 2 years. (Recent student scores resulted in 44 percent improvement.)

**EDUCATION**

NATIONAL TAIWAN NORMAL UNIVERSITY,

Taipei, Taiwan                                            1997–1998

**Certificate of Study, Mandarin Chinese language program**

UNIVERSITY OF PENNSYLVANIA,

Philadelphia PA                                          1993–1997

**Bachelor of Arts dual majors in communications and economics**

Awards: Time-Warner, Inc. Community Leadership Award and Scholarship · Taiwan Ministry Scholarship for one year study abroad

Activities: Marketing coordinator for Penn Health Services · English department writing tutor

**OTHER**

Languages: Proficiency in Mandarin Chinese and Cantonese

Software: Excel (advanced), Visual Basic programming, Hyperion/Essbase, MS Office

# COMMON RESUME MISTAKES

1.  Jargon-filled: A resume for admission to business school is very different from a resume for an application for a job. Unlike work resumes, which are full of industry terms, resumes for an MBA application

need to be short, jargon-free, and clear. Avoid acronyms that have little meaning to people outside your industry.

2.  Empty Adjectives: Superfluous language without tangible numbers to back it up offers little insight into exactly what you have achieved professionally. Also, speaking in generalities does not reveal your actual impact. Winning resumes always quantify the change you brought about or the impact you had.

3.  One-dimensional: MBA Boards are looking for candidates who are multidimensional. Don't hesitate to put that quirky hobby or organization you have been volunteering for in your resume. Being smart or working at a blue chip firm isn't enough to land a coveted admission spot. Use the resume to represent what else you have done with your time outside of work.

4.  Jumping Around: Leaving your job in less than two years can be a red flag to the Admissions Board. Obviously this advice is helpful only if you are planning to make the jump. For those of you who have already left your firm after a brief stint, look for a subtle place in your application to address this issue. But equally important is to connect the dots to show that the next move was a strategic decision that fits within your overall career goals.

5.  Dishonesty: This goes without saying, but I can't stress the importance of not inflating your involvement and impact enough. The MBA Board can see through any attempts to "pad" your story. Also, don't be tempted to leave out positions where you worked for a brief period. Hiding the truth has a way of coming back to bite you when you least expect it!

6.  Too Lengthy, Rambling, and Cluttered: A five-page CV is not acceptable for an MBA application (unless

the school explicitly says it's OK). A busy board member does not want to spend hours pouring through your CV. Keep your resume to one to two pages and focus on the impact and results you delivered. Avoid manipulating the font size to try to jam everything into the resume. Anything smaller than a 10-point font is difficult for the reader to read. Leave lots of white space to make the resume attractive and inviting. At the end of the day, a cluttered resume is less inviting to read.

7.  Mistake-Ridden: A shoddy resume will reflect negatively on your brand. Avoid spelling mistakes and grammatical errors. Make sure your numbers are accurate so that you don't have to explain yourself when the school verifies your application after you have been admitted. Inconsistencies in your story can be reason for an admission offer to be rescinded.

8.  Untailored: Every school is different. For instance, when applying to MIT Sloan, a school with a strong innovation and technical brand, you may be well served to include information about the highly technical courses you took in college or the technical project you managed during your internship. On the other hand, it may be more compelling to use the limited space to address the marketing projects you worked on if you are applying to Kellogg or Michigan, programs with strong marketing brands.

9.  Failure to Educate: If you have an unusual industry, firm, or role, make sure you provide a short description under the professional employment section to educate the reader about your experience and impact. This will help the MBA Board understand that your company isn't a hole-in-the-wall and that your impact was significant. This is particularly

important for internationals whose companies may not be as well known in the United States.

10. Boring: Although the resume is not an essay, it needs to be interesting and well written to capture the attention of the Admissions Board. Make sure you use active descriptors and avoid using passive sentences. Action verbs are the best way to describe your experiences.

11. Poor Judgment: In an attempt to make the resume stand out, never resort to gimmicky or cute tricks: they are likely to fail! Stick to the facts and keep the entire resume professional. Your email address should avoid things that call to question your maturity, such as "spunkychic@gmail.com" or any other inappropriate email addresses. Save those for your friends only. Your resume will stand out based on the merit of your work rigor, initiative, and impact.

Now that you are armed with a solid resume, you are now ready for your audition. The resume summarizes your story and an interview allows you to expound on it. Next to the essays, your interview is your next best chance to "sell" yourself.

# CHAPTER EIGHT

## Interviews: How Interviews Are Viewed by the MBA Board

*Your admission interview is both evaluative and informative: it is not only an opportunity for us to learn more about you, but also for you to learn more about Stanford.*

THE PRECEDING QUOTE FROM the website of Stanford Graduate School of Business (GSB) captures the essence of admissions interviews at top business schools. An interview is a two-way conversation in which you are given a chance to assess the MBA program to see if it fits your brand; in turn, the interviewer uses the meeting to determine whether you are a good fit for the MBA program.

You have to put your best foot forward and sell your uniqueness. Let's look at a quick example. Susan has an average GMAT score, but her leadership across college, community, and career is significant. She also has glowing recommendations that offset her GMAT score. In an interview, she is articulate, dynamic, and likable. She knows exactly why she wants an MBA and is able to convey precisely why the particular program fits her goals. During the forty-five-minute conversation, she is able to communicate what is distinctive about her and win over her interviewer. Suffice it to say, she is admitted to her dream school despite having a GMAT score that is below the median of the entering class.

Candidates like Susan understand that the interview does matter. It doesn't make sense to spend all that time on your application and then drop the ball when it comes to the interview. MBA Boards use the interview to assess a candidate. Even when the interviews are by invitation only, 30 to 60 percent of candidates who are interviewed receive an admission offer (depending on the school). So you should view the interview as a practical step that brings you closer to your admission goal.

An interview allows the MBA Board to verify the authenticity of your "story." It's also a way for the MBA Board to learn anything about you (positive or negative) that didn't come through in your application. The main value of the interview is that it can actually sway an admission decision when the MBA Board is on the fence about a candidate. So don't underestimate the importance of the interview and take the time to prepare appropriately.

Most admission interviews at top business schools are based on your resume. An exception to this is Harvard Business School (HBS), which reviews the entire application of each candidate and generates follow-up interview questions based on the actual application.

Top business schools place a high premium on the interview and it is important for applicants to fully understand each MBA program's interview process and policy.

## INTERVIEW POLICIES

Interviews at MBA programs are either open (any applicant can sign up) or by invitation only. Interviews usually last thirty to forty-five minutes, so there is little opportunity to ramble or waste time chatting. Make sure you keep your responses short and to the point. A recent trend in admission shows many MBA programs moving toward interviewing more of the class (HBS and Stanford GSB are examples of programs that interview their entire admitted class). MBA programs like Columbia GSB interview a large portion of the class, but not all admitted candidates are interviewed. Also popular is a move from open interviews to invitation-only interviews, demonstrated by schools like Chicago GSB. However, there are still a few top MBA programs that maintain an open interview policy (for instance, Tuck and Kellogg). To be safe, visit each school's website to confirm their interview policy because they can change from one year to the next.

Regardless of whether a program has an open or invitation-only interview policy, you should take the time to prepare for an interview. I will discuss the preparation steps candidates need to take later in this chapter.

## Invitation-Only Interview Policy

Programs that have an invitation-only interview policy invite candidates in whom they are interested for an interview. These interviews are typically conducted on campus (by board members or current students), in your city of residence (by alumni and board members), or over the phone. Most interviews focus on your resume, with the exception of an interview with Harvard. The design of the questions allows the interviewers to understand the decisions you have made, your self-awareness, the impact you have had in the workplace, and the way you do what you do that is uniquely you. An invitation to interview is welcome news to any candidate, but it isn't a guaranteed admission. Therefore, you should view the interview invitation as an opportunity to "sell" your story in person to the MBA Board. Preparing thoroughly and nailing the interview can result in the admission outcome you seek.

## Open Interview Policy

For an open interview, you should make arrangements to visit the school as soon as possible to take advantage of this opportunity. It's likely that your interview will be conducted by a current student who serves as an admission ambassador. Because an open interview typically involves a review of your resume, you should be prepared to walk your interviewer through your resume and provide him or her with insights into the career choices you have made and the impact you had in each position. Equally important is using the interview to reveal your personality and the activities and organizations you are involved in outside of work that make you an interesting individual. I caution applicants to never pass on the interview, even if the school states that it is optional. Ignoring the interview will likely suggest that you are not serious about the school, which makes it easy for the Admissions Board to discount your application.

But when you interview, you should take every opportunity to impress on the MBA program that you are a great fit and will make a strong contribution to the class. Think of every interaction with the MBA program as a "mini" interview. Before your interview, you may wish to attend an information session or student happy hour to learn more about the program. Believe it or not, you are still being evaluated even when you are out of the interview setting. Outliers will always stand out. So individuals who happen to be extremely articulate, dynamic, or have unique backgrounds will be remembered from the pack. Also memorable are candidates who are selfish (ask multiple questions during an open house event), ask inappropriate questions, or seem pushy or arrogant. Even when you are interacting with current students, you are still being evaluated. A former colleague from a top MBA program recounted how a prospective student he had interviewed attended a student happy hour and got drunk, danced on the table, and bragged about how he had the interview in the bag. Suffice it to say he didn't get the congratulatory admission call. Finally, the proliferation of technology has made it possible for many candidates to interact with each other in online communities. Rest assured that the Admissions Board is reading the blogs and communication exchanges in these sites. So be very careful what you share. It can come back to haunt you!

## WHO SHOULD INTERVIEW ME, AND WHERE SHOULD I INTERVIEW?

I'm often asked whether there is a difference between on-campus and off-campus interviews. From an evaluation standpoint, there is little difference. Candidates who reside abroad may find it cost-prohibitive to travel to campus for an interview on short notice given expensive travel costs. They may opt to be interviewed by an alumnus (or a board member if this option is available) in their city or over the phone. All of these interview modes are weighed the same. With that said, given the option, I personally would prefer to interview with a board member over an alumnus or student.

In addition, if you know that you express yourself better in person, then you should choose a face-to-face meeting instead of a phone interview. The extra money spent for your travel expenses will be worth it if the outcome is an admission offer to your dream school. A phone interview may be a bit more challenging because the interviewer does not have the benefit of seeing your nonverbal gestures to "fill in" communication. If you opt for the phone interview, make sure you speak clearly, get to the point quickly, and avoid interruptions.

Even if you choose to interview in your city, you still need to investigate the school closely by making a visit. There is no substitute for sitting in class and observing the teaching method, quality of faculty instruction, and interactions between students to better assess whether the program is right for you. A pet peeve of the Admissions Board is interviewing a candidate who resides in the same city as the MBA program and finding out that he has not taken the time to attend a class. Don't give the MBA Board a chance to question your judgment.

Another point worth discussing about interviews is that current students can be protective of their program and, in some instances, may be inclined to act as "gatekeepers." Be aware of this, and don't take offense if you encounter a student interviewer who seems unusually tough. Focus on conveying your brand, achievements, and the specific value you would bring to the program. Stay optimistic and hold your ground when faced with a difficult and belligerent student interviewer.

So, regardless of whether you end up with a "save the world" alumnus, an overzealous student, or a jaded board member, remain calm and make sure you communicate your personal brand effectively.

## WHAT DO INTERVIEWS ASSESS?

Without a doubt, the interview is a critical part of the evaluation process. Understanding what exactly the interview evaluates can help candidates prepare and ace the interview. Following are the key variables being assessed in interviews for business schools.

### Likeability

Yes, interviewers want to know that you are someone they can imagine sitting with in class. If they sense any sign of arrogance, awkwardness, or personality issues, they are likely to pass on your candidacy. It doesn't mean that everyone has to fit into a cookie cutter mode. So be yourself, but know that the interviewer wants to admit individuals who come across as positive, inviting, and personable. A member of Mensa who is uncommunicative may be denied admission if he or she comes off as arrogant or as a bookworm with little personality.

### Intelligence

Intelligence is important. The interviewer will check to see if you grasp things quickly. He or she may spend a good amount of time asking clarifying questions about your academic experience. If your GPA is lower than average, be prepared to speak to the rigor of the coursework and own up to why the grades are not exceptional. You may also be asked about your GMAT score, so be comfortable speaking about it regardless of whether it is in the high percentile or lower than average. How you address this question is key. If your score is low, you don't want to seem defensive by trying to justify it. Instead, focus on the positives to your story, such as the quantitative courses you took, the A grades you earned, a strong GPA, and rigorous analytical work experience. Conversely, if your score is in the top 95th percentile, don't gloat either. Candidates may also face questions about trends in the business world, or may be asked an open-ended question that forces them to analyze a business situation. Here's an illustration: "Describe in a couple of minutes a trend you see in your industry and tell me how you would go about capturing the market opportunity." What the Board is looking for is to understand how you think, whether you are sharp on your feet, and if you have a sophisticated awareness of issues going on in the business world.

## Rigor and Impact of the Job
Your work experience will receive significant scrutiny in most interviews. Interviewers usually focus on specific questions about your career that are designed to reveal what your specific role was and the size of the impact you had in each position. Be ready to discuss your exact role and the results you generated. Make sure to quantify your impact whenever possible. When answering career impact questions, be careful not to sound arrogant.

## Leadership
Leadership is a very important aspect of the interview. The three Cs of leadership (college, community, and career leadership) are evaluated during the interview. Remember that

leadership is not only about title. It's about initiative, innovation, influence, and thought expertise. As noted previously, show the impact you had in each position. Use vivid examples to illustrate your points instead of rattling off lists of leadership roles; focus on the most compelling examples and tell short but direct stories to connect the dots between each experience.

## Communication Ability

Communication ability is very important, especially for MBA programs that are primarily case based. Whether English is your first, second, or third language, the interviewer will scrutinize your communication skills. Practicing prior to the interview will allow you to communicate your thoughts in a conscientious and logical way. If you are verbose, it behooves you to really practice a succinct delivery. If you come across as unfocused or, worse, as an incompetent speaker, you jeopardize your admission chances. Nervous candidates can also get into trouble by talking too much and not answering the interview questions. One candidate who was very bubbly rambled so much during her interview for a top program that her interviewer only managed to ask her a few questions during the entire interview. The candidate came across as flighty and was denied admission to the MBA program.

## Personal and Professional Maturity

The maturity question is a big one. In an interview, be prepared to express the thoughtfulness that has gone into the decisions you have made professionally and personally. Even if you have gaps in your story (for example, a lower-than-average GPA, limited community leadership, even loss of your job), how you respond to the question will communicate your maturity. Candidates who are just starting their careers are also under significant scrutiny when it comes to maturity. They have to convey that they have thought through their career goals and have a sound rationale for why they want their MBA now.

## Self-Awareness

MBA candidates who meet all three admissions criteria can still be denied admission. Such cases are often the result of a lack of fit or an interview that didn't go well. It's one thing to have a stellar packaged story, but how you stand up to the face–to-face evaluation of an interview can determine your admission outcome. A perfect package that doesn't represent who you are will quickly unravel in the interview. Candidates who have all the necessary attributes but lack insight into their goals and the decisions they have made (including the decision to pursue an MBA) will also struggle during the interview. On the other hand, a candidate who may not be exceptional on paper can use the interview to tip his or her admission decision to a positive outcome by demonstrating extraordinary insight and self-awareness. Just as with essays, in which insight is as important as what you have achieved, the self-awareness that you exhibit in an interview is critical in differentiating you from your competition.

## Team Dynamics

As with likeability, you should anticipate that the interviewer will want to assess how you operate in group settings. Be ready to talk about your team projects and how you function in groups. (Are you a leader who steps up immediately, or do you lead from behind?) The important point here is to show that you are not a solo player. Even if your job has limited group interaction, look for ways to introduce how you have sought out that type of interaction (even if it is outside of your job) to reassure the interviewer that you are comfortable when operating in team environments.

## Composure and Presence

The interview reveals information about who you are in person. It can confirm the brand you presented in your application, or it may completely call it into question. This is why it is important to present an authentic brand in your application. Also, be aware of how you come across in face-to-face interactions. The following story reinforces this point. A candidate was reviewed, and the consensus was that she was a WOW ("walks on water") candidate. But after the interview, her interviewer expressed surprise at how extremely laid back and almost disengaged she seemed when compared with the vibrant individual who came across on paper. Interestingly, and fortunately, the recommendations the candidate provided were strong enough to influence her being admitted. Had her recommendations been average, she may not have been admitted. Make sure you are excited, engaging, and interesting during your interview. Try to infuse energy when you interview, even if you have a laid back personality. I'm not advocating being fake. Feigning an outgoing personality when you are an introvert is not wise. But it's important, even while being laid back, to show that you can be engaged in a dynamic classroom environment.

## Fit and Knowledge of the Program

The interviewer will often grill applicants to make sure that they have thought through exactly why they want admission into the MBA program. The more clarity you have about what you need to achieve your long-term goals and the more you are able to connect this with the MBA program, the stronger your case will be for why the program is a fit for you. Candidates who have not visited the campus or sat in on a class leave themselves open to questions about their commitment to the program. Take the time to research the program extensively before interviewing so that you can articulate precisely why the program is ideal for you. Be ready to talk not only about what the program will give you but also about what you will contribute to the program if admitted. Some MBA programs go to the length of asking you about the actions you took to research their program. "What steps have you taken to learn about the Berkeley MBA program, and what factors have influenced your decision to apply" (Source: Haas website).

# HOW TO APPROACH AND PREPARE FOR THE INTERVIEW

Following are some tasks that will help you prepare for the interview ahead of time.

## Jazz Up Your Resume

Remember that the business school resume is less about job description and industry jargon and more about your potential as a leader and business manager. Therefore, you should create a resume (ideally one to two pages) with detailed evidence of how you have managed people and developed new products or transformed a process, and finally, show the impact that you have had professionally and beyond. The chapter on the resume reviews the specific details necessary to create an excellent resume.

## Talk to Products of the Programs

Most companies have employees who are alumni from top MBA programs. Don't be afraid to invite them for lunch or drinks to learn about their MBA experiences and the subsequent impact on their careers. Current students can be a huge asset in helping you prepare for the interview as well. Finally, even fellow prospective students can be helpful by sharing their interview experience. (Online communities like Business-Week.com can give you a sense of the types of interview questions candidates are facing.) I will add one caveat to this: do exercise wisdom when listening to other applicants, because some may be eager to psych-out their competition and everything they share may not be accurate. I once had a flustered client call me at 11:45 p.m. in a panic. A fellow applicant who had interviewed on the same day had gotten in her head by making her doubt her responses and her overall interview performance. It took a few minutes of reminding her of her strengths and what she had to offer before she realized she had been manipulated by the other applicant.

## Know Your Story and Sell Your Personal Brand

Reread your application to ensure that you remember all the facets of your story. Make sure the following four themes come through as you present your story: passion, guts, impact, and insight. Share with the interviewer tangible examples of impact you have had—demonstrate self-awareness not simply by talking about *what* you have done but by focusing on *why* you have made the choices you have made and the lessons you have learned along the way. It is also important to demonstrate that you are confident enough to take a risk (that you have guts) and step up to a challenge instead of simply executing on your job description. Finally, come with great energy and share your passion with the interviewer.

## Experience the MBA Program Firsthand

Throughout this book I have stressed the importance of visiting the MBA program you desire to join. Attending classes gives you a firm handle on the MBA program's unique positioning and value proposition. This credible vantage point will enable you to speak authentically about your specific interests and what you will do while in business school. Ideally, you should have already visited the campus and attended classes prior to applying to the MBA program. The interview visit then ends up being a "confirmation" as opposed to a first-time visit where you are still gathering facts about the program.

## Dress Appropriately and Pay Attention to the Nonverbals

Be conservative when it comes to your interview attire, and go with neutral colors such as black, blue, and gray suits. Female candidates may wear a skirt or pantsuit. Some candidates have asked me about the freedom to express themselves. My response is usually something along the lines of, "This time next year do you want to be entering your dream school or do you want to be going through a reapplication process?" Given the level of competition involved in applying to a top business school, I would not take any unnecessary risks. When it comes to interview attire, I recommend playing it safe. If you are a creative type and that's a key aspect of your brand, then limit your creative expression more to the accessories you wear for the interview (for example, choose a tie or scarf in a tasteful color instead of a flashy red suit). You want your interviewer to focus on your leadership contributions, not on your fashion-forward style.

## Practice, Practice, Practice

I can't stress enough the importance of practicing for the interview. Have someone you know pose interview questions to you and time yourself. Solicit feedback after the mock interview to identify areas where you need to improve, and be willing to address any feedback you receive. Some people assume they are excellent interviewees and therefore fail to prepare for the interview. This can be a grave mistake. Regardless of whether you consider yourself a "natural" or you dread the interview, you should prepare for it. As with anything in life, the more practice you have the better. Candidates often tell me that they perform better after their first interview. You may want to interview first at MBA programs where you have an increased chance of being admitted (your safety program) than at stretch schools where your admission chances are slim. The more experience you have with interviewing, the more likely you are to improve your interviewing skills.

## Go into the Interview Well Rested

Avoid going to work on the day you have an interview. If you absolutely have to go into the office, then do yourself a favor and set up the interview in the morning. Then return to the office in the afternoon. I can't tell you how many times I've heard of applicants who went into work on the same day of their interview and encountered an extremely stressful day. Being frazzled before the interview is avoidable, so give yourself every advantage possible by going into the interview well rested.

# FUNDAMENTAL INTERVIEW QUESTIONS

I have compiled a list of popular interview questions that candidates for business schools will likely encounter. I have broken them into five categories. I recognize that some questions can fall into multiple categories, but for the sake of simplicity, I have them organized in one group. These questions do not purport to be exhaustive in the interview question domain. It is more a collection of fundamental questions that every candidate should be ready to face regardless of his or her unique circumstance and experience. Use these questions as a starting point but I encourage you to also look closely at your own story to assess whether there are gaps or flags that are likely to solicit inquiry in an interview.

## 1. General
- Walk me through your resume.
- What will you do if you don't get into business school?
- What will you contribute to our MBA program?
- What do you think will be your biggest challenge at our program?
- Why did you select the recommenders?
- What programs did you apply to?
- What is your first-choice school?
- Why should we admit you given the steep competition?
- Why are you interested in our program?
- Is there anything else you wish to tell me about yourself?
- What do you want to be known for in life?
- What else do you wish I had asked you about your candidacy?

## 2. Professional
- What are your short- and long-term career goals?
- Why do you want an MBA?

- Describe your career decisions to date and highlight your greatest impact.
- Why did you select the firms where you have worked?
- How has your leadership style evolved over your career?
- How would your supervisor (colleagues) describe you?
- What do you think your boss would say are your biggest weaknesses (strengths)?
- When did you work in a team and what impact or role did you have?
- What was your most exciting project at your firm?
- Describe your international experience.
- Describe a professional failure you have had and what you did to overcome it.
- In your career, when have you made a mistake? What did you learn from it?
- What drives you to seek new challenges and opportunities? In your career, when did you take an unusual path or make a decision that was not popular?
- Tell me about a time when you created a product or process that added value to your firm.
- When have you worked in a difficult team and how did you overcome the challenge?
- What do you believe constitutes a great manager and are you one?
- What do you like or dislike about your job?

## 3. Personal
- Tell me about yourself.
- What motivates you to succeed?
- Who do you admire the most and why?
- How would your former classmates describe you?
- What three adjectives best describe who you are?
- What would you change about yourself and why?
- How do you handle change?

- What is your favorite book, and what do you find interesting about it?
- What has been your biggest self-discovery?
- What is the challenge you've sought that scared you the most?
- What accomplishment are you most proud of and why?
- What are your strengths and weaknesses?
- If you could live anywhere in the world besides where you live currently, where would it be and why?
- If you could be a superhero, which one would you be and what would you do with your special powers?
- What talent do you wish you had and why?
- Describe an ethical dilemma you faced and how you addressed it.

## 4. Extracurricular

- What do you do for fun and how do you spend your free time?
- What leadership impact have you had outside of work?
- What community service organizations are you involved in, and how have you created value there?
- What clubs do you plan to join if you are admitted?
- How do you lead differently in your career versus in your community?

## 5. Education

- Describe your academic experience in college.
- Why did you choose your major/school?
- How did you perform academically?
- Which awards did you receive?
- What decisions do you regret making during college?
- If you could change one thing about your education, what would it be and why?

# COMMON INTERVIEW MISTAKES TO AVOID

1. Don't be disrespectful to the receptionist or students. Every encounter you have with someone affiliated with the MBA program is a potential interview.

2. Don't try to dominate the interview. This is guaranteed to backfire. Let the interviewer cover all his or her questions.

3. Don't talk too much or ramble. Be concise and to the point.

4. Don't be too forward, and don't ask the interviewer personal questions.

5. Don't be too informal. Address the interviewer as Ms. or Mr. unless they specifically invite you to refer to them differently.

6. Don't forget to bring water to drink. Your mouth may get dry as a result of nervousness so be prepared.

7. Don't interrupt the interviewer. Even if you have an unreasonable interviewer, you'll get no bonus points for antagonizing him or her. Calmly wait for an opportunity to assert your points and brand message.

8. Don't use slang or informal communication, even if the interviewer does. (Remember, you are the one being interviewed.)

9. Don't communicate insecurity and lack of confidence by giving a weak handshake and unsteady eye contact.

10. Don't come off as unfriendly. Smile when appropriate. No one likes a sourpuss.

11. Don't be late for the interview. Aim to be there at least fifteen minutes early.

12.   Don't dress inappropriately. Ill-fitting and outlandish attire send the wrong message about you and your brand.

13.   Don't be negative, and never complain or criticize someone you worked with or your company. Ditto for other MBA programs. Do not criticize another competitor program. It sends the wrong message about you.

14.   Don't worry too much about the interview. Focus on being yourself.

---

## INTERVIEW REMINDERS

The admission interview is not optional; you should always interview if the school offers you the chance.

The interview is a marketing exercise, so go prepared to sell yourself/your brand.

Know the MBA program thoroughly and communicate what you will bring to the program.

Dress appropriately—a well-tailored suit is key even if your job has a casual dress policy.

Be prepared for the interview; invest time to nail down your responses to two to three minutes so that you don't run out of time. If the interviewer asks follow-up questions, then that is your cue to drill deeper in your response.

The physical resume speaks to your brand, so make sure it is updated and reflects your main leadership impact; don't forget to use quality paper and eliminate errors.

Wrap up the interview with an intelligent question or two about the MBA program. (Program websites, press releases, and faculty knowledge papers present interesting information about new trends and activities at an MBA program.)

Always follow up with a thank you card or email, which should be sent the day of the interview.

## SOME FINAL TIPS ON THE INTERVIEW

Know your story (brand), and make sure you don't leave the interview without communicating key points of why you are unique and interesting: your value proposition. Ensure that you communicate specifically why you fit into the program and what you will bring to enrich the student community. It's possible to face an ineffective interviewer. Regardless of who interviews you or whether they ask you productive questions, you have to be prepared to lead the conversation back to major points that reinforce why you are a great fit for their program. Being clear on the four or so brand themes you wish to cover and having specific short stories to reinforce them will help you leave the interviewer with a strong sense of who you are.

But the interview isn't enough to help you close the deal. The MBA Board will be looking for a third-party validation of your story (your essays, resume, and interview) before they admit you. Let's spend some time in the next chapter reviewing everything you need to know about the recommendation to make it a winner!

# CHAPTER NINE

## Transforming Your Recommenders into Brand Champions

I HAVE READ NUMEROUS RECOMMENDATIONS in the ten years I have been in admissions and academia. The one fundamental difference between excellent recommendations and mediocre ones is that the former are written by individuals who are champions of the candidate, have worked closely with them, and have a clear understanding of the unique value they offer personally and professionally.

Building a powerful brand in the marketplace, whether at work or in your personal life, requires that you have brand champions who are invested in you. These brand champions are committed to helping you refine your brand and are phenomenal marketing agents of your brand.

So who are brand champions? They are individuals who are interested in your professional and personal success. They understand what you stand for, your passion and values, and your skills, accomplishments, and goals for your future. Most important, these individuals are committed to seeing you succeed, are willing to speak up on your behalf to promote your career, and are quick to bring you on board for projects with high visibility and importance.

Not all recommenders are brand champions. In other words, just because someone writes a recommendation letter on your behalf does not mean that they understand who you are, what matters most to you, and how you envision the MBA to help you achieve your life goals. I have read many recommendations that have had damning consequences on a candidate's admission outcome. Choose wisely and make sure whoever you select is truly an avid supporter.

I'm often asked whether the recommendation is important in the evaluation process. The simple answer is absolutely! The recommendation gives the MBA Board a chance to hear from someone who knows you very well to see if he concurs with the story you have shared about yourself in the application. A recommendation letter that is negative or off-track from the story you told in your application at best communicates to the MBA Board that you lack wisdom and at worst provides a third-party justification to reject you.

## THE POWER OF BRAND CHAMPIONS

Most MBA programs require two recommendation letters as part of the application process. Harvard and Stanford Graduate School of Business (GSB) are an exception to this, with both programs requiring three recommendations. Ideally, the recommendations need to come from supervisors who can attest to your business experience, managerial potential, and leadership. The exception is Stanford, which requires that one of the three recommendations come from a peer.

Because the essays are composed of self-reported accounts, your recommendations are a sure way for the MBA Board to verify the authenticity of your story. All things being equal, the recommendation that stands out can be the deal clincher. For instance, the MBA Board may be on the fence about admitting a candidate, but a powerful recommendation that articulates how the candidate is unique, compelling, and a fit to the school's brand can tip the decision to her favor. The recommendation adds a rich texture to your story by providing insights (backed by specific examples) of *how* you have done what you have done instead of simply stopping at the achievements alone. Effective recommendations also educate the Admissions Board of the context in which the candidate works. By learning what's unique about the company, your role or your impact, the Admissions Board is in a better position to evaluate your story.

This is why it is critical to cultivate relationships early with individuals who can become your brand champion. Many applicants to business school ignore this important step until a few months before they start applying to business school. I had a client once whose entire business school application almost crumbled because of her failure to develop relationships with her former bosses. It required some scrambling to track down and reconnect with former supervisors. You can imagine the panic that this applicant felt at the realization that she didn't have adequate professionals to write recommendations for her. Luckily, we were able to do significant damage control and she applied in a later round. Although anyone can find someone to write a recommendation letter for them, cultivating relationships with superiors and colleagues (both in the professional and the community context) can be challenging and requires careful strategy. At the end of the day, recommendations that stand out typically come from individuals who are champions of a candidate's brand.

I have also reviewed many rejected candidates' applications, and more often than not, the recommendations are average at best and weak in most instances. Because the competition for business school admission is so tough, it is important for candidates to manage their recommenders and to select the right people to champion their applications.

# FIVE CRITICAL STEPS IN DEVELOPING BRAND CHAMPIONS

## 1. Know Your Brand

Be clear about your personal brand. You should be able to articulate your brand in one sentence, your personal brand statement (PBS). What you value, your skills and track record, and your passions and goals are all encompassed in this statement. Remember, if this isn't clear in your own mind, then most likely the people you work with have the wrong brand attached to you. Here are two examples of a PBS for a career changer:

> *"A hard-working Boeing engineer"*
>
> *"An innovative engineer with a passion for creating business efficiency who plans to turn business problems into solutions through consulting"*

The first PBS is limiting and pegs you as an engineer rather than someone who plans to transition into consulting. The second PBS is more robust and positions you as a career changer. You will want to make sure that your recommenders understand that you are evolving into a different career, consulting, and that you enjoy solving business problems, not just executing tactical engineering systems.

## 2. Choose the Right Brand Champion

For starters, ideal brand champions need to be in positions of power. That doesn't mean that your peers and subordinates shouldn't be aware of your brand. They should! Everyone you come in contact with, both professionally and otherwise, should be able to perceive a consistent message from you about your brand. But for the purpose of the MBA application, your focus should be on superiors, particularly supervisors who can provide tangible and detailed information about you that reinforces your brand.

However, you shouldn't simply go for title alone. Avoid using the CEO or managing director of your firm who can barely remember your name because their recommendations will offer limited details about your managerial potential and unique, differentiating personal attributes. Rather, it is important to have a relationship with the person that goes beyond interacting with them a couple of times a year. When it comes to selecting a recommender, ask yourself the following questions:

- How does this person feel about me?
- Have I worked closely with her on a project?
- Has she complimented me based on the results I produced?
- What types of evaluation has she given me in the past?
- Did she go out of her way to assist or support me in some capacity? (The more people have gone out of their way to show a commitment to you, the more likely they are to become a fans.)

A clear indication of whether someone is supportive can be seen in the case of a managing director who specifically requests that you work on her deals and invites you to client meetings. The more exposure she has to your work other than the grunt work that everyone else at your level is involved in, the more compelling a case she can make about your brand and unique value. Assuming that there has been enough regular contact with her and that she has indicated that she does care about your professional success, it is then important to make sure that you keep her abreast of your achievements and goals. Such individuals make ideal brand champions.

## 3. Regularly Communicate Your Brand

Seize every opportunity to make your brand champions aware of what you are involved in. Update them on your key achievements and plans and solicit feedback from them. A young man I know is brilliant at marketing his brand to his brand champions. He told me that he sends an email quarterly report to his "Board of Directors," the name he uses to describe everyone in his network he considers brand champions. The purpose of these quarterly reports is to inform them of his professional and personal life developments. Although the bulk of his work experience was in investment banking, that does not stop him from successfully positioning his brand as an inner-city investor. His community involvement and career change has been primarily in venture capital, with a focus on distressed communities. This is what he stresses in his communication. Every three months I receive an email from him giving me an update about his activities, and they always reinforce his brand as a "spiritually grounded, inner-city community investor."

Obviously, email communication isn't enough. Face-to-face communication is even more powerful. So set up meetings with individuals you have identified as brand champions and begin to discuss your brand and vision with them before asking them for a recommendation to business school. Waiting two months before admission deadlines is leaving it too late.

## 4. Demonstrate the Value of Your Brand

The fastest way to develop brand champions is to establish a track record of excellence. At your job, you should aim to perform at the highest level possible, regardless of how minute or grand the project is. Your performance of excellence will precede you and begin to get you brand equity. Here is how it works: You are an analyst in the general pool, but you develop significant knowledge in a particular area that most of your peers do not have. You get selected to work on a deal that allows you to draw from that knowledge base, and your performance on the project is without reproach (you work late, you produce results with little to no mistakes). Soon, senior leadership begins to request for you when they are working on important deals. By working on these types of deals, you get more visibility and experience. Your reputation grows and the cycle continues. I've used investment banking to illustrate this point, but the same principle applies to any industry and position. The takeaway is that regardless of your job, title, or industry, you should make sure you produce excellent results. Your impact should contribute to the bottom line of the company or your group. You have to walk a fine line between coming across as arrogant and self-promoting and being confident in your accomplishments and not being afraid to raise your hand to take on more challenges.

## 5. Take Action

What do you do if you realize that you do not have brand champions? All hope is not lost. First, take stock of all the potential brand champions that you already have in your network: your former bosses, clients, even other managers you have worked with on projects in the past. Once you have developed your list, the next step is to prioritize it. Select five people you wish to develop a stronger relationship with, then design a plan of how to approach them. This is the tricky part. It will require time and a good dose of patience. You need to be subtle about it. Do not approach them immediately to ask for recommendations. You need to capitalize on what you have in common. If you are still working with the person, begin to seek opportunities to work on projects together where he or she will be able to observe your work up close. By working with your potential brand champion on a project and producing excellent results, you will increase your chances of this person becoming your avid supporter. You should seize every opportunity to share your brand when interacting with your brand champion. For example, if you are a career changer and you are engaged in a volunteer capacity for the new career, you should discuss your involvement outside of work to help your brand champion better understand your brand.

If you are no longer at the same firm, then touch base to simply find out how your former bosses are doing and to bring them up to speed on your progress. Under no circumstance should you request a recommendation the first time you contact someone you have been out of touch with. It is impolite, and it also is likely to yield a weak recommendation. Ideally, give yourself a year to reconnect with individuals who will write your recommendations. The more time you have to develop these relationships prior to the application, the better.

---

## QUESTIONS TO ASK BEFORE
## SELECTING RECOMMENDERS

Do they understand your brand, and are they avid fans?

Do they have an MBA? If not, do they understand the value of an MBA?

Have they written recommendation letters before? Are they good writers? Have the people they recommended gained admission to top business schools?

Are they open to your providing them with information about your brand, accomplishments, and rationale for an MBA?

Do they have time to write an excellent recommendation letter?

Are they supportive of your school choice? (I once spoke to a recommender who was writing a letter for a candidate to X business school, and he told me he thought the candidate was a fit for Y business school and that he didn't see him at X business school. Yet here he was, writing a recommendation for him for X business school. Clearly his recommendation would not be the most compelling.)

Do they have enough in-depth interaction with you to provide evidence of your leadership?

Are they senior enough in title to have a broad perspective of what your role is and how it fits into the company?

Are they optimists? You don't want anyone approaching your recommendation from a "half empty" perspective.

Are they punctual? Avoid procrastinators who have a reputation of not delivering quality work at deadlines.

If you answer no to any one of these questions, you should think long and hard about whether the recommender is right for you.

## THE RECOMMENDATION TIME FACTOR

Timing is very important in selecting a brand champion to write your recommendation. Give yourself a year to eighteen months to begin cultivating relationships with key people who will become your brand champions.

I had a client who really understood the importance of having brand champions. He has actively identified people within and outside of his firm whom he respects and keeps in touch with regularly. He is known to put in a call or email when he needs advice on simple as well as major career decisions. Over time, these people have grown invested in him and have become accustomed to receiving updates from him that reinforce his brand. His ability to get the CEO of his billion-dollar private equity fund to write an insightful, humorous, and glowing recommendation represents the time and investment he made up front. And I would hazard a guess that this recommendation contributed in some measure to his admission to a top MBA program despite a lower than 600 GMAT score.

I have also witnessed firsthand how not having brand champions can threaten one's admission. Another client of mine did not have brand champions behind her when she began the application process. She had a boss who was not particularly supportive of her professional development, let alone her pursuit of an MBA. Further complicating matters, she had not kept in touch with previous supervisors with whom she had a great rapport. So when she began her application to business school, she felt awkward tracking these people down after four years had gone by to say, "Hey, remember me, we did great work a few years ago and I need a 'wow' recommendation from you." After serious scrambling and an aggressive recommendation strategy that involved a three-month accelerated relationship building, and after one recommender dropped out as a result of a car accident, she was able to eventually find recommenders who supported her application. The result was admission offers from three out of four top MBA programs.

Although she was lucky (or experienced divine intervention), I wouldn't recommend this approach because it brings undue strain to an already stressful process and the outcome could have been quite different.

## CHOOSING THE RIGHT MIX OF RECOMMENDERS

So you have developed close relationships with individuals who are invested in your success. How do you narrow it down to the two or three individuals who will write your letters of recommendation for business school? I address the different backgrounds of individuals who typically write recommendations for candidates. Ultimately, you will have to decide what the ideal recommendation mix is for you given your unique situation.

### Recommendations from Supervisors

One of your recommenders must be someone who has supervised your work and can speak to your leadership and managerial potential. If you cannot use your current supervisor (because you have worked at the firm for only a few months or because he is generally unsupportive about business school), then consider using a previous supervisor. However, know that the Admissions Board will be curious why you didn't use a direct supervisor. The additional information section of the application is a good place to address your choice of recommender.

The second recommendation ought to come from your professional life as well. It could be from the same firm or from a different firm. The important thing is to balance the perspective being offered to demonstrate the depth of your character as well as the breadth of experience and impact that you have had in the organization. For example, whereas one recommendation may stress your interaction with clients and your confidence, maturity, and performance outside the firm, your other recommendation may go into greater detail to show your work impact, analytical and quantitative acumen, and direct involvement on projects that resulted in success. There isn't one set formula. What's key is showing the different sides of who you are instead of a skewed, one-dimensional perspective.

I'm often asked about the specific examples the recommenders should use. Make sure that the recommenders do not use the exact four examples that you described in your essays. Not only will this make for a boring and redundant recommendation, it will raise flags that you have limited experience. You should have some of the recommenders reinforce stories you have highlighted in your essays, but they can add greater "color" and detail to the story. They should also provide fresh examples that you have not covered in your essays (which reinforce your personal brand) to present a rich and convincing recommendation instead of a regurgitation of your essays.

## Recommendations from Alumni of the MBA Program

I'm often asked whether alumni recommendations are important. The simple answer is yes and no. Yes, if they know your work from a close vantage point and can attest to the significant impact that you have had. The other situation in which alumni recommendations are preferred is when candidates come from companies where little is known about them. In such instances, it is helpful to have a recommendation from an alumnus of the MBA program who can attest to the rigor and quality of the candidate's experience.

But this is not a license to hunt down alumni from top MBA programs for the sole purpose of writing a recommendation if you have not worked with them in the past. If you use alumni recommenders, opt for those who know your work the best and can back up any assertions they make about your candidacy with detailed examples. If the alumnus doesn't know you very well, then it is not worth using him for a recommendation.

## Recommendations from Community Service (Outside of Work)

Equally important is your extracurricular involvement, especially if you have a strong track record of leadership and service. As discussed earlier, MBA Boards judge leadership not only in terms of college and career experiences but also in terms of community involvement. For example, if you serve on the board of directors of a nonprofit group and you have managed to develop a strong relationship with your chairperson, you may be better off having him write a recommendation for you instead of using three recommendations from the same job or from your professional life. Also, if you played a varsity sport during college and held leadership positions on the team, consider asking your coach to write a recommendation letter on your behalf. This is especially meaningful if you use this third recommendation as a supporting letter that provides another perspective of your leadership and personal characteristics. Many schools like Wharton, which requires two recommendations, are amenable to a third "supporting" recommendation if it truly adds another dimension to your story.

## Recommendations from Professors and College Administrators

I'm not usually a fan of professor recommendations, especially if the only point they can make is discussing your intelligence. Unless you did something unique with large impact while you were a student, you should shy away from professor recommendations. Of course, early career candidates are the exception to this. Even in such cases, however, professor recommendations should speak to your leadership, how you have taken initiative, and your maturity. Your transcript and GMAT score are enough data points to reinforce how smart you are. The Admissions Board wants to learn more about who you are as a future business leader, so the professor or college administrator should provide information that reinforces this point. Examples that can attest to your leadership potential are your involvement in starting a student organization or in transforming the experience of the student body by lobbying for and changing a campus-wide policy.

## Recommendations from Clients or Business Associates

Individuals who work in family businesses or who are founders of their own company will have some unique challenges when deciding on who to use for their recommendations. It isn't ideal to use your dad or a family member if you can avoid it. In any case, if you find yourself in the entrepreneurial situation where either you are the boss or a family member is in charge, you should use individuals who are familiar with your leadership, management experience, and impact. These individuals often can be clients or business associates such as your banker, attorney, or accountant. It will be important to manage the process carefully because they may not have extensive experience writing recommendation letters for business school.

Regardless of who you select to write your recommendations, the goal always is to make sure they reinforce your brand by showing the scope and impact of your experiences. One sure way to differentiate yourself from the pack is to demonstrate not only your ambition and commitment to your career but also your investment in others' success. The MBA Board is looking for well-rounded candidates, and recommendations can reinforce the notion that you are multidimensional.

## THE APPLICANT BACKGROUND IN RELATION TO THE RECOMMENDATIONS

I've discussed the different types of individuals who can write recommendation letters. Now let's look at the different MBA candidate backgrounds and the potential barriers they face when it comes to the recommendations.

### The Consultant and the Investment Banker

Consultants and investment bankers applying to business school make up a significant portion of the applicant pool. This means that the competition for candidates with this background is particularly fierce. Individuals writing your recommendation will most likely be writing recommendations for others as well. To a large extent, the skill set that will be highlighted includes your intellectual horsepower and ability to quickly grasp complicated materials, analytical and quantitative skills, decision-making and problem-solving skills, judgment, verbal and written communication skills, and confidence.

Beyond confirming your intelligence and analytical skills, recommenders for consultants and investment bankers need to address your emotional intelligence and interpersonal skills, flexibility in dealing with ambiguity, team dynamics, confidence and maturity in dealing with clients and superiors, creativity, and so much more. It isn't enough to talk about how smart a candidate is because it is already a foregone conclusion, given a solid academic track record, GMAT score, and blue chip firm. The focus should be on your personal characteristics and the impact you have had that is beyond your job description. Given that most recommenders will have good things to say about their candidates, it becomes even more important to describe not only the "what" of your background but the "how" of what you have done.

As far as recommenders for investment bankers, I recommend using vice presidents (VPs) and higher. It is not that associates can't speak to the quality of your work and accomplishments, but they are too close in position to you. All things being equal, with two analysts with strong recommendations, one from an associate and the other from a VP, the MBA Board would likely tip the scale for the VP recommendation over the associate. The caveat to this is that the VP needs to know your work very well and should be a brand champion. At the end of the day, a lackluster VP recommendation is worse than a stellar associate recommendation.

If you are a consultant, you should consider a supervisor and a senior-titled client who have worked with you extensively. A recommendation from a partner who knows you well because of leadership initiatives you have taken on a project or across the firm would be of value in setting you apart from your competition. The operative phrase is one "who knows you well." It isn't useful to have recommendations from highly ranked individuals if they don't know you well.

## The Engineer

Engineers are attractive to business schools because they often have project management and hands-on managerial experience supervising employees. This is particularly the case for those who have been line managers. The challenge for engineers is that their recommenders may not always be as savvy as those coming from consulting or investment banking industries. Therefore, to be on the safe side, candidates from engineering backgrounds have to vet the writing skills of their recommenders. Although I never promote writing your own recommendation letters, unlike consultants and banking professionals, who are adept in the nuances of the recommendation letters, it is important to sit down with the engineer recommender and provide key information about your achievements and your brand.

## The Nontraditional Candidate

Like engineers, applicants from nonprofit organizations, military, government, and artistic backgrounds need to be proactive to ensure that their recommenders understand what is expected of them and the purpose of the recommendation letters. For many applicants from this category, this may be the first recommendation letter for business school that your recommender is writing, so give your recommenders enough information about you, your accomplishments, and most important, why you want the MBA to ensure that they understand your brand and, in turn, write a glowing letter of recommendation. Similar to engineer recommendations, those coming from the nontraditional backgrounds require special care. Make sure to invest enough time setting the expectations and vetting the positioning and information your recommender intends to use for your defense.

So far, I have focused the first part of this chapter on macro issues facing the recommendations. In the next section, I'll examine the actual recommendation, including the actual recommendation rating (grid) and questions. I'll also provide insights into what the MBA Board is truly looking for in each of the questions covered. And of course before wrapping up I'll go through the common recommendation mistakes applicants to business school should avoid.

# TACKLING THE RECOMMENDATION QUESTIONS

It goes without saying, but recommenders should make sure they answer every question that is asked in the recommendation form. There is no room for cutting corners by writing one letter of recommendation and using it for different schools. Because each school words their questions differently and the specific information being asked varies, it is important to make sure your recommender fully answers each question while citing vivid examples to illustrate the point. Quantifying the impact the applicant had is more important than using superlative descriptors that come off as trite. Make sure you refresh your recommender's memory by providing him with concrete examples of your leadership and impact at your firm.

Be mindful of the recommender's time. It is unrealistic to ask recommenders to write more than five recommendation letters. Think of the law of diminishing returns. If you over-burden your recommenders, they are more inclined to write generic letters that they tailor to the different schools instead of spending a significant amount of time on each recommendation. To be safe, if you must apply to more than five schools, you may want to target a couple of additional individuals to write recommendations for you. This would allow you to focus your star recommenders on the MBA programs that you care the most about.

Recommendation forms typically have a set of questions that ask recommenders to rate the candidate. This grid is an important part of the recommendation and recommenders should give it adequate consideration when completing it. Your recommenders should give a realistic evaluation of you. But it should also be tempered with sound judgment. A balanced rating is essential. What do I mean by that? Certainly high-lighting a candidate's excellent qualities is important. However, recommenders should be able to also identify areas where the candidate can improve.

The reverse can also be a problem. In the course of my time in the admissions business I have seen too many recommenders hurt a candidate's chance of admission by going to the other extreme and "underselling" the candidate. Recommenders should not view recommendations as performance reviews. Unlike performance reviews that tend to be more critical and have more of an improvement focus, recommenders should not lose sight that the recommendation should be a tool to "sell" a candidate, not hurt him in the application process.

I'm often asked by applicants how the grid is interpreted by the Admissions Board. The MBA Board is likely to be skeptical if the candidate is ranked in the highest category across every single characteristic. The view is "if the candidate is truly that exceptional, does she need an MBA?" On the other hand, rankings that are below average can raise red flags. Therefore, the right approach when filling out the grid is to take a measured stance. If the candidate is truly exceptional, the recommender should rate the applicant in the very top of the grid for characteristics where he or she shines and lower in areas that need improvement. Some international recommendations can be conservative when ranking a candidate. The same goes for some industries. The good news is that the Admissions Board recognizes these types of differences.

Following is an example of a recommendation grid. This example is only an illustration to show how someone can be rated from "good" to "outstanding," reflecting where the candidate is strong and where improvement is needed. Candidates who are ranked average in some areas but outstanding in other areas can be admitted to top schools. The more important questions are what areas they received an average rating in, why, and what they are doing to address their developmental needs. In the end, there isn't a set formula.

# SAMPLE RECOMMENDATION RATING GRID

|  | No Information | Below Average | Average | Good | Excellent | Outstanding |
|---|---|---|---|---|---|---|
| Leadership Track Record |  |  |  |  |  | X |
| Motivation |  |  |  |  | X |  |
| Maturity |  |  |  |  | X |  |
| Teamwork |  |  |  |  |  | X |
| Oral Communication |  |  |  |  | X |  |
| Written Communication |  |  |  | X |  |  |
| Self-Awareness |  |  |  |  |  | X |
| Global Perspective |  |  |  |  | X |  |
| Interpersonal Dynamics |  |  |  |  | X |  |
| Intelligence |  |  |  |  | X |  |
| Analytical Skills |  |  |  |  | X |  |
| Quantitative Skills |  |  |  |  | X |  |
| Innovation and Creativity |  |  |  | X |  |  |
| Sense of Humor |  |  |  | X |  |  |

## Common Recommendation Questions and Admissions Insights

Each recommendation question is designed to reveal a candidate's professional experience and character. The admissions goal, ultimately, is to understand who the person is in a fully dimensional way.

I've categorized the recommendation questions into the "usual suspect" categories and identified the insight the MBA Board is interested in gleaning from each question.

# RECOMMENDATION QUESTIONS

| Recommendation Questions | Admissions Insights |
|---|---|
| Relationship with Candidate | The point of this question is to assess: How well you really know the candidate and whether you have enough interaction to provide an objective opinion<br><br>The length of time and the capacity in which you have worked together (for example, direct supervisor, mentor)<br><br>The typical interaction you have had with the candidate and how the candidate compares with his or her peers<br><br>Highlights of distinction and achievements, such as career growth and promotions |
| Leadership, Teamwork, and Interpersonal Dynamics | Addressing team dynamics of the candidate: Is the candidate an individual contributor, or does he or she thrive in team situations?<br><br>Does the candidate work well with others (including peers, superiors, and subordinates)? |

| Recommendation Questions | Admissions Insights |
|---|---|
| | Does the applicant focus only on how to get ahead? Does the candidate manage peer or subordinate relationships well? What type of a leader is the applicant? Is this someone who motivates and inspires others? Is this someone who has the ability to drive the vision of an organization or project? Does the candidate have natural leadership abilities? How so? Is the candidate comfortable leading from behind, or is he or she always pushing to be in front? Is this a respected leader? Is the candidate evolving from being a member of a team to stepping up to more leadership roles? Is the applicant becoming the "go to person" on his or her team? How well does the candidate handle conflict? Does the candidate think and act quickly on his or her feet? |
| Unique Personal Characteristics | This is the "why should we admit this candidate" question. The MBA Board is looking for the unique or special attributes that the candidate will bring to the class. |

| Recommendation Questions | Admissions Insights |
|---|---|
|  | It is important to address why a particular school should admit this candidate. Given what you know about the candidate, how would he or she fit with the MBA program? Does this applicant have a clear career focus and a natural curiosity to learn and stretch himself or herself for the next level?<br><br>Are there specific personal characteristics that the candidate has that are extraordinary? What specific examples back them up? Ultimately, the MBA Board wants candidates who can help shape the MBA program for the better. |
| Candidate's Strengths | This section offers a great opportunity to discuss two or three main attributes/strengths that the candidate has. It should support the attributes that the candidate has identified in the essays.<br><br>This third-party endorsement is very powerful in conveying what makes the candidate special and why the MBA Board should admit him or her. The MBA Board is looking for specific examples to back up the core strengths you highlight. It is critical! The examples should be in sync with the school and the candidate's personal brand. |

| Recommendation Questions | Admissions Insights |
|---|---|
| Candidate's Weaknesses | To remain credible, these need to be real weaknesses. A candidate is not perfect, and the MBA Board wants to know that there are areas being developed. Weaknesses that are flag raisers are major interpersonal skills issues, such as arrogance, shyness, insensitivity to others, "does not suffer fools," team dynamics issues, and communication weaknesses. MBA Boards are loathe to see strengths disguised as weaknesses or clichéd answers. Recommenders should always provide specific examples and indicate whether the candidate is open to feedback/criticism. |
| Intellectual Ability | The MBA Board is looking to understand the candidate's ability to handle a rigorous curriculum. They have reviewed the candidate's GMAT, GPA, and transcripts with a fine-tooth comb but will rely heavily on your feedback on the candidate's intellectual abilities, particularly if you can provide specific examples of the applicant's intellectual horsepower and quantitative contributions at the firm. |

| Recommendation Questions | Admissions Insights |
|---|---|
| | The Admissions Board wants to understand the rigors of the professional context where the candidate has worked. It is important to provide specific examples to showcase how the candidate demonstrated superior analysis or provided an innovative solution to a challenging business problem. Relevant skills include natural curiosity and an ability to think outside the box, adeptness with quantitative and analytical projects, and thought leadership (which also shows intelligence and intellectual curiosity). |
| Ethical Issues | Given the corporate scandals of the past few years and the public's skepticism of business, many MBA programs are concerned about the level of integrity and ethics that their candidates bring to their programs. As such, there is a strong focus on candidates' ethical behavior and trustworthiness. Be ready to comment on instances or examples that illustrate that the candidate has a very high moral code of ethics. Always use specific examples to illustrate your point. |

Feel free to share this "cheat sheet" with your recommenders once you have them on board to write recommendations for you. It will help them to glean some understanding of what is expected of them and the ulterior motives behind the set of recommendation questions they have to address.

I end this chapter with the major mistakes applicants make when it comes to the recommendations. Knowing what the landmines are and avoiding them will bring you a step closer to your MBA goals of acceptance to an elite institution.

# COMMON RECOMMENDATION MISTAKES TO AVOID

## Show Don't Tell

Often recommendations are too general and full of fluff. They tell you that the candidate is brilliant and use a lot of adjectives but have very little substance to back up the assertions. If, for example, the recommender says that John is an exceptional leader, it is critical to describe instances when John has stepped up to lead, how he has led, and what impact he has had on his team and the organization. The rule here is to show and not simply to tell. A good way to assess if the point is worth making is to add the phrases, "for example" or "in the following instance." If a vivid example does not come to mind to back up the point, or if the example that comes to mind doesn't strongly reinforce the message being communicated, it should be discarded.

## Beware the Contradiction Factor

The recommendation is an authentic yardstick by which an applicant's story is measured. So consider what happens in the mind of the MBA Board when an applicant positions herself as someone who will start and run a business and the recommender states that the applicant is comfortable only in established organizations. Other examples have to do with industry consistency. It doesn't help a candidate's case when he says that he is passionate about the health care industry and his recommender says that he will likely end up in a real estate industry as a developer or in some other industry that has nothing to do with the story the applicant has told about himself. This is a popular mistake that I observed while on the MBA Admissions Board at Harvard. Mistakes like these could have been avoided had the candidate spent the time necessary to educate his recommender on exactly what his position was. Take the time to make sure your recommenders understand your goals and are supportive of them.

## Recommendation Bias

Recommendations vary according to region and industry. For example, recommenders from certain countries tend to be by-the-book, blunt, and straight to the point. Their evaluation may be more focused on the areas of improvement and therefore may sometimes miss an opportunity to highlight the positives that the candidate brings. Sitting down with your recommender prior to his writing a recommendation for you and discussing any concerns you have as well as what you believe sets you apart will help ensure that your recommendation is balanced. The industry background of recommenders can sometimes influence the recommendation. If you happen to have a nontraditional background and your recommender has little experience writing an MBA recommendation, it is worth sitting down with him beforehand.

## Beware the Bland Recommendation

Bland recommendations lack spontaneity and seem too molded and coached. A quick way for recommenders to check if the recommendation is bland is to ask themselves, "If I remove the candidate's name from the recommendation, could this recommendation apply to any other person?" If so, your recommendation could very well lack distinction and will do little to endear you to the MBA Board. Ultimately, knowing the brand of the candidate will enable the recommender to move beyond the typical vanilla recommendation and produce a wow recommendation that supports your brand.

## Recommendation Ownership

Don't fall into the trap of writing your own recommendation. I know this is a common request from recommenders who either are too busy or are uncomfortable writing a recommendation. It is unethical to write your own recommendation, and the Admissions Board can tell that you did so because it will be similar to your essays. Even putting one recommendation next to the other will be obvious that they were written by the same person. Don't risk it.

If your recommender asks you to write the recommendation and they will sign it, as tempting as that may sound, I strongly suggest you decline tactfully. Point out to them that you will make the process as easy and streamlined as possible by providing content to remind them of the detailed projects and impact you had. You can even sit down with them to flesh out your story and the positioning of your recommendations. If they still insist that you should write the recommendation yourself, you should take this as evidence that they are not invested in you. You may have to find a different person if your recommender absolutely refuses to write the recommendation. A practical way to avoid this situation is to give your recommenders enough of a head start that they can devote the necessary time to your recommendation. Also, selecting the right people who are invested in your success and not overburdening them by having them support your eight applications will make it more manageable for them.

## Damning Recommendations

There are many ways a recommendation can have a damning effect on the candidate. The most popular is the recommendation that is too short, lacks examples, and is poorly written. For whatever reason (be it a lack of writing ability or lackluster commitment to the candidate), these recommendations call into question the candidate's judgment.

Rushed recommendations also have detrimental consequences because they tend to have spelling and grammatical errors, and in some instances, the wrong school name. And then there is the recommendation that offers back-handed compliments. These also have a negative impact on the admission outcome. Examples such as, "Wesley is very driven and likes to get things done effectively, but this means that he may sometimes step on the toes of individuals who operate at a slower pace" will absolutely mark him as a selfish and impatient person.

Finally, there is the recommendation that intentionally sabotages the candidate's admission chances. "Jaime is extremely intelligent but has difficulty expressing his thoughts in an articulate and clear manner making it difficult for those who work with him to benefit from his intellect. I have given him feedback to take communication classes and expect he will improve after he does so." Why is this a huge no-no? For starters, business school in general and leadership in particular demand that individuals communicate in a reasonable way in order to lead or manage a project or people. Saying up front that the candidate is a lousy communicator raises an alarm in the mind of the board member evaluating the application. At the end of the day, MBA programs want to admit individuals who can engage in meaningful discussions with their classmates.

Applicants should also beware of that friend who is too eager to write your recommendation. You may assume "it's in the bag" and may not manage the recommendation as closely and effectively as you would if the writer were not your friend. But it is precisely this hands-off approach that may come back to haunt you. Make sure the recommender is not jealous of your aspirations and achievements.

## TOP FIVE THINGS A RECOMMENDER SAYS THAT SHOULD MAKE YOU DITCH HIM OR HER

I don't think you should go for an MBA.

I'm kind of busy at this time.

Don't you think you are reaching too high?

Why don't you write the recommendation?

I don't need any input from you; I'm an expert at this.

This chapter has examined the role recommendation letters have in the admission evaluation. Select your recommenders carefully because the person you choose can determine the outcome of your admission. Take the time to think carefully about whom to select for this critical role. Chicago GSB puts it aptly when it states that: "Whomever you choose to write your recommendation make sure they know you well and can offer specific examples of your performance and contributions to the organization. Avoid choosing people simply based on their title or status. We are more concerned with content and substance than reputation." Take the time to begin to develop the relationships with individuals in your profession and community to win them over as brand champions. And it isn't too late to start today.

# CHAPTER TEN

## MBA Applicants' Backgrounds

EACH APPLICANT TO BUSINESS school is evaluated on his or her academic ability, leadership track record, and uniqueness. Keep in mind that each candidate represents a unique background. As a candidate, you should consider whether you are a rare gem in the applicant pool (former Eskimo school teacher) or whether you easily fall into a "usual suspect" category. Also bear in mind that each applicant has strengths and biases he or she will encounter in the application process. Being aware of this ahead of time can help you strategize and decide on what points to emphasize in your application. At the end of the day, you should always be thinking of additional insight or differentiation you can bring to your story to stand out. This section reviews the perceptions associated with different candidates' professional backgrounds and offers suggestions of what they can do to turn it to their advantage.

## THE USUAL SUSPECTS

Applicants considered usual suspects are primarily consultants, bankers, accountants, and engineers. These applicants are heavily represented in the applicant pool.

## 1. The Consultant

Consultants come with different types of experience, with strategy consulting as one of the more popular areas. Also, some consultants specialize in industry (financial, retail, or information technology [IT] consulting, for example). Some examples of firms from which candidates with a consulting background apply are: McKinsey, Bain, BCG, Booz Allen Hamilton, Accenture, and Cap Gemini. There are also consultants who have worked for financial services companies as well as *Fortune* 500 companies (such as American Express and GE) in an internal consulting role.

*Valuable Consultant Skill Set*
Consultants are credited for having the following skill set:

- Business savvy
- Strategic thinking
- Analytical thinking
- Excellent communication skills
- Problem-solving skills
- Emotional intelligence and interpersonal skills
- Project management skills

*Consultant Detractors*
The large number of consultants in the pool increases the competition because they are, in a way, competing against each other. Here are the detractors associated with candidates from consulting backgrounds:

- Talkative and can be seen as arrogant
- Viewed as idea people but sometimes lack operational and implementation skills
- Question whether they are the ones driving their career vision instead of simply following a well-laid plan

- Skepticism as to whether they need an MBA. (If you are planning to remain in consulting, the MBA Board may question why you want the MBA. Are you simply getting your ticket punched?)

*What to Do*

- Demonstrate your comfort level taking a path less traveled. It could be a decision you made professionally that wasn't popular or something you did in your community or in college. The important thing is to show the breadth and "richness" of who you are beyond being a smart, savvy professional who is great at analyzing and creating business solutions for clients.
- Show that you can go beyond developing great ideas; speak to experiences you've had in which you were able to manage people to implement an idea.
- Show that you are the one driving your future and decisions rather than sitting back on your laurels.
- Similar to the previous point, consultants need to show that they have a clear rationale for why they want an MBA and not because all their partners have one or because everyone around them gets one after a few years of experience.

## 2. The Banker

I'm being very broad in applying the "banker" label to include applicants working in investment management, private equity, venture capital, research, sales and trading, and investment banking. In any case, these candidates are overrepresented in the applicant pool at elite MBA programs.

*Valuable Banker Skill Set*

- Analytical sharpness
- Quantitative strength
- Savvy and polish
- Adept at working on challenging projects

*Banker Detractors*

- Type A and impatient
- Too self-motivated, not necessarily team players
- Limited management experience
- Number crunchers who execute but may not understand the business decisions behind the numbers
- Worker bee
- Not balanced—no life outside work

*What to Do*

- Show team mind-set: balance showing your individual involvement and impact with working behind the scenes and helping others become successful. It is important that your story is mixed with "we" and "I" instead of only your own involvement.
- Be sure to convey how your impact at work transcends the financial analysis that you did.
- Don't underestimate the power of initiative and coming up with creative ideas and seeing them to fruition.
- Seek opportunities to lead recruiting and training initiatives.
- Step up to fill a void when the opportunity presents itself. (Don't simply get your job done.)

## 3. The Accountant

Accountants are also seen as "usual suspect" candidates to business school. They are often represented in large numbers in the application pool.

*Valuable Accountant Skill Set*

- Great with numbers
- Highly detailed
- Organized
- Dependable

*Accountant Detractors*

- Tactical (not strategic)
- Not engaging, with nonstellar interpersonal skills
- Work can be boring
- Narrow skill set
- Lack creativity
- Executor, not driver of vision

*What to Do*

- Show an understanding and interest in the bigger picture.
- Demonstrate that you understand business decisions beyond the spreadsheets (how the numbers drive the decisions a business is making).
- Show your understanding of other functional areas; seek cross-functional projects to broaden perspective and skill set.
- Tell engaging stories. Make sure that all your essays are not simply describing financial reviews and reconciling monthly statements.
- Show your personality with appropriate humor and flair.

## 4. The Engineer

There are a lot of engineers in the applicant pool. They are viewed as a close cousin to accountants. Their roles are often technical. However, many of them are represented in varied industries. As a result, it is not unusual to see engineering candidates from pharmaceuticals, start-up ventures, technology companies, and even NASA.

*Valuable Engineer Skill Set*

- Strong with numbers
- Technically advanced
- Project management exposure
- Doers: implementation experience

*Engineer Detractors*

- Poor communication skills
- Rigid
- Executors, not strategic or big-picture thinkers
- Poor interpersonal skills

*What to Do*

- Demonstrate that you have vision and that you can come up with an idea, sell it to people, and rally people behind a goal.
- Show personality besides being smart and great at your job. Show that you have a life outside work that is dynamic and interesting.
- Show that you are flexible, can go with the flow, and are not limited by only one approach or idea.
- Make sure you demonstrate your real need for the MBA to get you closer to your career goals.
- Stress your interpersonal and people-related skills and experience.

# NONTRADITIONAL CANDIDATES

A growing number of nontraditional candidates (NTCs) are recognizing the value of an MBA. Individuals from nonprofit organizations, military personnel, artists, government workers, and early career applicants fall in the NTC category. NTCs are sought by top MBA programs because of the diversity of rich experiences and perspectives they offer in the class. Admitted candidates from this background usually have three qualities in common: (1) they have an exceptional leadership track record, (2) they have done an outstanding job building a strong case for why they need an MBA, and (3) they typically have a lot of passion for the work they do. But despite the strengths that they bring, NTCs have major hurdles in the application process: they need to convince the MBA Board that they have a rigorous background and relevant or transferable skills and that the MBA makes sense given their long-term goals.

## 1. The Nonprofit Manager

One typically does not associate people who "do good" with signing up for the MBA. However, this is a growing phenomenon as more individuals from socially responsible backgrounds recognize that the practical skills taught in business schools are tools that can galvanize their nonprofit organizations. I anticipate that this trend will continue as the lines between sectors blur. Applicants from nonprofit backgrounds provide a different perspective that can enrich the diversity of the student body. But before landing that coveted admission, they will need to show that they have a clearly mapped-out plan for which an MBA is an integral bridge to its accomplishment. Showing intellectual strength and solid managerial accomplishment will help nonprofit candidates mitigate any concerns the MBA Board may have about their candidacy.

*Valuable Nonprofit Skill Set*

- A history of operational experience
- Very passionate about industry
- Strong interpersonal skills
- Strong communicator

*Nonprofit Detractors*

- Weak quantitative skills
- Weak analytical skills
- Question the rigor of their work experience
- Question why they want an MBA

*What to Do*

- Make sure your academic (GMAT and GPA) data points are sound. Take a class or two in finance or accounting and earn strong grades. Aim for a GMAT score north of 700 to make academics a non-issue.
- Present a crystal-clear vision of your goals and outline how the MBA will help you achieve them.
- Don't assume the MBA Board can see the connections and relevance of your work experience and your business school goals. Be proactive in marketing the transferable skills you have.
- Demonstrate that your work experience is rigorous and that you can keep up intellectually with your classmates who come from more traditional backgrounds.

## 2. The Military Candidate

A conversation between two Harvard students captures the perception of military students. Mike: "I'm concerned about how I will do in this class. It's not easy jumping in to make my point in section. I worry about making intelligent comments on the case." Sam: "I know what you mean. Can you imagine what Joe, the Navy SEAL in our class, thinks when he's in class—*This is a piece of cake. I'll take many cold calls in section over another mission in Fallujah!*" Military candidates have been in remarkably challenging situations and have had their leadership abilities tested numerous times. The challenge for them isn't showing that they have leadership experience but that they can adapt to a nonmilitary environment.

## Valuable Military Skill Set

- Excellent leadership track record
- Excellent team experience
- Strong communication skills
- Solid interpersonal skills

## Military Detractors

- Can be rigid and hierarchical
- Tough time adapting to civilian world
- Disconnect between goals and experience
- Unclear that the MBA is vital for the career goal

## What to Do

- Show that you can be flexible.
- Pick essay topics that show different aspects of who you are beyond your experience in the military.
- Demonstrate awareness and understanding of the civilian business environment.
- Nail the rationale for why you want an MBA and what it will help you achieve professionally. An example can be

tying your reconstruction work in war-torn regions with your interest in running an infrastructure development company in the emerging markets. Drawing parallels with your current experience and your future goals can help you create credibility.

- Share stories that show the lighter, softer side of your personality.

## 3. The Artist

Artists can be performers or managers of artist organizations. They may want to empower future artists by growing the arts lobby organization they started from a regional business to a national one. They may also be performers in a music conservatory but would like to transition to the business side of managing one. Perhaps they are recording artists with some recording success but want to manage other artists and want to start their own label. Even those in the business side of the arts can make a compelling case for why they need an MBA. A case in point is someone who works for Christie's managing their South Asian auctions, and plans to create his own business targeting the region. Whatever the case, artists will need to show that they have a clear career plan and that there is a business opportunity on which they plan to capitalize. As an artist, even if you are a career changer and want to enter a new industry, it is critical to show that you have achieved some success in your current career.

*Valuable Artist Skill Set*

- Passionate
- Creative
- Interesting and different perspective
- Engaging and dynamic

*Artist Detractors*

- Question whether the MBA is necessary for their goals
- Skepticism about transitioning to new career (if career changer)
- Weak quantitative skills
- Weak analytical skills
- Question rigor of their experience

*What to Do*

- Take the GMAT early and nail a very strong score (higher than 700, ideally). Take business courses and earn As in them.
- Make sure your vision is clear and map out exactly the steps you plan to take to achieve your career goals.
- Demonstrate that you need the MBA given your goals.
- Share stories from your experiences that show awareness of the business environment and connect the dots from your track record to show compelling impact.
- Show that you are more than an interesting and passionate candidate. It is important to show your serious side and demonstrate clarity of vision for your future.

## 4. The Public Sector (Government) Candidate

Talented individuals who work in the public sector and want to find innovative strategies to tackle public issues can make a strong case for their need of a business education. Stanford Graduate School of Business has been at the forefront of providing leadership to individuals from the public sector through its Certificate in Public Management and the Public Management Program. But Stanford isn't alone in this commitment. Many top MBA programs look to attract public sector candidates to their programs. Whether you work for the Environmental Protection Agency or serve as the assistant to the prime minister of a country, you can make a cogent argument that developing business skills through an MBA will help you be more successful in your public sector role. Because many issues have a private and public sector connection, you should highlight your awareness of the complexity of business issues facing the public sector today and how global business training can help equip you with the requisite skills to handle them.

*Valuable Government Skill Set*

- Different perspective
- Insights into the interplay between business and politics
- Management experience
- Great team dynamics and experience

*Government Detractors*

- Experience may not be seen as rigorous enough
- Perspective may be too narrowly defined and may lack broader business insights
- May not have solid quantitative background
- Unclear whether the MBA is a fit given background

*What to Do*

- Don't assume the MBA Board will connect all the dots of your story. Take the time to connect the dots for them. Focus on the relevant skills you have and how they translate to business.
- Demonstrate that you have a rigorous background (whether through your academic preparation or work experience).

- You will need to pay particular attention to your justification for why you need an MBA. Make sure that your rationale justifies why you need an MBA in the first place.

## 5. The Early Career Candidate

Twelve years ago you would be hard-pressed to find many college seniors in an MBA class, let alone MBA programs boldly declaring that they are seeking candidates who are early in their career (less than two years of work experience). For the past few years, many MBA programs have begun to court candidates who are very early in their career. Harvard and Stanford's MBA programs were two of the first to take this position. Many other programs have also expanded their marketing to college seniors and individuals who have less than two years of professional experience. Even as I write this book, Harvard Business School has announced the launch of its 2+2 program (admitting college juniors who then work for two years after earning their undergraduate degrees before taking up their admission offer). Employers haven't been shy about coming on board with this program either.

Although many schools have become open to younger applicants, the reality is that only a portion of the class will be represented in this demographic group. The average age of an MBA entering class at most top MBA programs will likely remain between twenty-six and twenty-eight years old.

The important message is that early career (EC) applicants who are great leaders, have an excellent track record of making an impact, and demonstrate professional and personal maturity should consider applying to business school whenever they feel ready.

EC candidates, like every other applicant to business school, have to make a compelling case for why they need the MBA. For EC candidates, there is even greater pressure to make this case. The questions every MBA Board member will have are, "Why you are applying now? What is the hurry?" Therefore, if you happen to fall in this category, you do need to demonstrate that you have thoroughly reviewed your career goals, have enough meaningful experience to bring to the classroom, and can show that the MBA is a critical next step for you to achieve your career success.

*Valuable Early Career Skill Set*

- Clarity of career focus
- Excellent leadership background
- Driven
- Push the status quo, innovative
- Inquisitive and naturally curious

*Early Career Detractors*

- Too much in a hurry
- Overly confident
- Lack of relevant experience
- Emotional intelligence and maturity can be a problem

*What to Do*

- Take the GMAT and have very strong scores (at least within the range of the program's median score).
- Have an excellent academic track record, which includes a strong GPA as well as some business courses.
- Demonstrate exceptional evidence of leadership in college. The laundry list of club membership absolutely will not cut it. Because you will have limited work experience, you should be able to demonstrate that you are a "natural" leader with real involvement and results you can point to.

If you have managed classmates on projects or worked in roles in which you have been given managerial responsibility, then highlight that experience. For instance, if you managed the student union at your college, this example can showcase your managerial potential.

- Maturity is an important trait for all candidates, but is even more critical for an EC candidate because you need to be able to fit in among classmates who are much older and have more work experience.
- Show laser-like focus when it comes to career goals. Career goals that are ambiguous or general will not cut it. Avoid this by making sure that you leave the board member with an iron-clad perception that you are grounded and have a clear but obtainable goal that absolutely warrants an MBA degree.
- Select your recommenders wisely. Although you can likely get away with one recommendation from one professor, having all academic recommendations that stress how smart you are will not work. You need to show your business potential, so look for a recommender who has observed you in a professional situation, whether in an internship or a nonacademic leadership capacity. Student deans can offer strong recommendations if they can talk about how you have impacted the institution through your student leadership roles.

## 6. The Entrepreneurial Candidate

Entrepreneurs are attracted to the MBA for the practical skills they can gain, access to a broader network, and the opportunity to refine and develop their business ideas. MBA programs in turn are attracted to entrepreneurs for the interesting business experience they add to the class as well as their natural tendency to think outside the box when tackling business issues. If you are running your own business or working for a family business and wish to pursue an MBA, you should take a few moments to glean how your profile is viewed by the MBA Board.

*Valuable Entrepreneur Skill Set*

- Highly creative
- Passionate
- Dogged commitment to their business
- Interesting entrepreneurial work experience and lessons learned

*Entrepreneur Detractors*

- Quantitative and analytical gaps
- Question whether they can sit through an entire MBA program
- Question whether the MBA is necessary for their career goals
- Question whether the MBA is an escape plan in the face of a failed venture

*What to Do*

- Show that the MBA isn't a passing fancy, that it is a calculated decision that will help you grow your business or start another business in the future.
- Select the right program so there isn't any question about fit. There are MBA programs that are more inclined towards entrepreneurship (for example, MIT Sloan) and entrepreneurs should select programs that embrace entrepreneurs. You may also opt for programs that are accelerated or begin in January instead of the usual fall start as they are more geared toward entrepreneurs.

- Demonstrate that the business you started was substantial so the MBA Board takes you seriously. Starting a t-shirt business in high school and selling a handful doesn't brand you as an entrepreneur.
- Even if the venture failed, it is important to share lessons learned, what you would do differently, and articulate how a formal background in business can help you launch a successful enterprise in the future.

---

## JOINT OR DUAL DEGREE PROGRAMS

When it comes to dual degree programs, confusion has existed for a long time regarding the application process, requirements, and deadlines. Fortunately, most MBA programs have stream-lined their dual degree processes and have created more clarity and information about them. When applying to a joint or dual degree program, it is your responsibility to convince the Admissions Boards for both programs that you truly require both degrees and have the background to enrich their programs. If you decide to apply to a joint or dual degree program, here are a few items to keep in mind:

1. Be clear on exactly why you need both degrees. Why is the degree necessary for your career? Address why taking a few classes from the second program isn't enough to meet your goals.
2. Recognize that every program is different. Know both programs very well and invest in the applications; don't assume one or the other is "in the bag."
3. Make sure you meet the deadlines of each program. It is usually the case that you will need to apply to both programs separately as well as submit a dual degree application, which often entails additional essays.

## FINAL THOUGHTS

There is no such thing as a perfect profile. Every candidate has to overcome potential detractors, and it is to their advantage to understand how the Admissions Board views their profile in order to strategically overcome any hidden bias to their story. Becoming aware of the hidden biases to your profile empowers you to proactively address them so that you cast your application in the most powerful light possible.

# CHAPTER ELEVEN

## More MBA Applicants' Backgrounds

THIS CHAPTER COVERS WOMEN, minorities, and international candidates. You may be wondering why there is a separate chapter devoted to these three groups. As I grappled with this question, I kept returning to my observations of the unique issues some individuals in these three groups face. As a result, I have attempted to provide some useful perspectives for candidates who fall in one of these three categories.

### WOMEN

Women at top MBA programs make up only 30 to 39 percent of the class compared with the nation's leading medical and law schools, which are usually composed of nearly 50 percent female students. MBA programs such as Stanford Graduate School of Business and Wharton have some of the highest percentages of female students (38 and 37 percent for the class of 2009, respectively). The reasons fewer women apply to business schools vary. Here are some of the common reasons given for why fewer women apply and enroll at leading MBA programs:

1. Lack of enough female role models in business
2. The perception that MBA programs and business in general are cutthroat and Machiavellian

3. Concerns about quantitative skills

4. Skepticism surrounding the value of the MBA, especially when considering balancing professional and personal life goals

5. The age factor: unlike other graduate programs where female candidates typically enroll right after college, most applicants to business school apply after working a few years. This may create friction between choosing a career and deciding to begin a family. (Choosing the latter option may keep many would-be female candidates from applying.)

The dearth of female MBAs has been a topic of recent discussions and concern among deans at top MBA programs. As a result, many of these programs are embarking on more aggressive marketing efforts to attract a greater number of women to their programs. It is indeed this same issue that has partly affected the push for early career initiatives at some leading business schools with hopes of "reaching" more bright female candidates.

Catalyst, a research and advisory organization, authored a landmark paper, "Women and the MBA: Gateway to Opportunity," in 2002 that revealed a disproportionate number of women were pursuing graduate business education. Organizations such as the Forté Foundation (www.fortefoundation.org) are filling this need. The mission of the Forté Foundation is to "increase the number of women business owners and business leaders and to support their careers through business education and networks." The Forté Foundation, created in November 2001, has members that include individual women, business schools, nonprofit organizations, and large corporations. Today, top MBA programs partner with the Forté Foundation to market their programs to prospective female candidates. I highly recommend the Forté Foundation to female candidates because it offers unparalleled information about business schools from a woman's perspective. The endless resources—a network of talented women, thoughtful leadership articles, female mentors, podcasts featuring accomplished women who provide career advice, admissions events, and, not least, financial support—empower female candidates and help alleviate worries and obstacles that make applying to business school a challenge for them.

The MBA has become much more diverse today. Gone are the days when MBAs were perceived as hard-charging men in pinstripe suits whose sole goal in life was to close the next financial deal. More recently, the message is getting out that MBAs can be socially conscious entrepreneurs or individuals who are transforming the way government operates. In addition, the increasing push for diversity at MBA programs, more active female alumni networks, and growing sensitivity in corporate America regarding work–life balance and telecommuting options make this a great time for anyone to pursue an MBA, especially women.

Harvard Business School has even created a weeklong executive development program known as "A New Path: Setting New Professional Directions" to help women wishing to return to the workforce update their business skills and reassess their career path (www.exed.hbs.edu/programs/path/objectives.html).

MBA Boards across top business schools have responded to this scarcity of female applicants by adopting more aggressive recruiting and marketing efforts to attract female candidates to apply. A few examples of such efforts are open house marketing events held by the MBA Boards that target women applicants. At these events, female alumni and students serve on panels and address candidates' questions while sharing their experiences and perspectives as women and the value of the MBA on their career. Female student associations at top MBA programs tend to be active and often partner with MBA Boards on marketing initiatives and planning admitted students' weekends to strengthen the yield of admitted female students. I strongly encourage all female candidates to participate in these open house events as well as attend the Forté Foundation events. They are excellent opportunities to learn about the MBA program from a woman's perspective, but more than that, it gives you a chance to make connections with individuals who are closest to the programs.

## MINORITIES

Minority students represent between 10 and 25 percent of the enrolled students at top MBA programs. Expanding the ethnic diversity of their program is important to most MBA programs. And like the female-only open house marketing events that target women candidates, MBA Boards offer minority open house events to provide a forum for candidates from minority backgrounds to learn about their programs.

Current students and alumni from minority backgrounds also partner with the MBA Board on their recruitment and yield events. In many of these programs, annual alumni conferences attract a significant amount of prospective minority students who use this opportunity to assess whether the program is a fit for them. For prospective minority students on the fence, these conferences can be instrumental in their decision to apply to the MBA in general and the business school program in particular. Wharton's Whitney Young Conference (www.wmyconference.com) and Harvard's Naylor Fitzhugh Conference (www.hbsaasu.com) are two examples of the largest minority conferences at top business schools.

There are also organizations that provide resources and support to minority candidates. The Diversity Pipeline Alliance, the MBA Consortium, and Management Leadership for Tomorrow are a few examples of such programs.

*Diversity Pipeline Alliance:* The Diversity Pipeline Alliance (the "Pipeline") is a network of national organizations that share the common goal of preparing students and professionals of color for leadership and management in the twenty-first century workforce.

*The MBA Consortium:* The Consortium for Graduate Study in Management is a leading organization for promoting diversity in American business. Started in the mid-1960s, it provides an annual competition that awards merit-based, full-tuition fellowships to America's best and brightest diverse candidates. With more than 5000 alumni, fellowship recipients are given access to a robust network.

*Management Leadership for Tomorrow:* MLT (www.ml4t.org) is another great resource for prospective applicants. Started by a Harvard MBA, John Rice, MLT focuses on introducing minorities to business careers and education by providing one-on-one mentoring, boot camps, and a network from the application process to post graduation career support.

Another good support group for minorities is the Robert Toigo Foundation (RTF) (www.toigofoundation.org), which provides a combination of scholarship, mentorship, and training as well as a robust career network for minorities interested in the financial services industry.

## INTERNATIONALS

International students make up 20 to 40 percent of MBA programs in the United States, and as many as seventy countries are represented in many instances. International candidates clearly add to the diversity of MBA programs, and no area has seen as much activity as the international recruitment efforts launched by admissions offices at many top MBA programs.

Today, reviewing the MBA websites, it is quite common to see an extensive list of countries on the admissions' travel schedule. Not only are MBA Boards visiting a variety of countries to "sell" their brand to prospective candidates, they are also adding interview schedules instead of relying only on alumni. New York University Stern Business School is one such program that sends MBA Board members to China and other countries to interview prospective candidates. Wharton and Kellogg have been leaders in recruiting prospective candidates in Africa in addition to other regions across the globe.

International centers are also becoming quite popular as offshoots of the MBA program, enabling schools to establish infrastructure abroad to develop intellectual capital for faculty as well as to establish relationships and partnerships in strategic countries.

Alumni returning to their home countries are proving a powerful force in providing networking opportunities for each other and admissions support for MBA candidates. Alumni clubs exist in a variety of countries around the world. If you find that candidates from your country are underrepresented or that there is no alumni association there, this could be one initiative you can help bring attention to after you are admitted.

Despite the focus international candidates are receiving from MBA Boards at leading business schools, international candidates face several challenges worth exploring. Topping this list is the visa issue facing internationals who reside outside the United States. Post-September 2001, U.S. immigration laws have tightened, making it more challenging for international students to receive visas in a short time frame. Therefore, international candidates are encouraged to apply in the earlier rounds to ensure that they have enough time to obtain the visa. Most visa consulate offices require evidence that the candidate can fund his or her education. Before going in for your visa interview, you should make sure you are armed with all supporting materials to minimize the chance of your visa application being denied.

Beyond the visa issue, another concern that international candidates face is securing work permits for employment in the

United States. International students are entitled to one year of practical training in their area of study. Most international students take advantage of this option after graduating. During their year-long "practical training" they are able to have their company file for their H-1 B working permits.

The economic downturn of the early 2000s has posed some challenges for securing employment after business school. Recent international MBAs have not been exempt from the struggles that the classes of 2001–2003 faced. In some cases companies that were open to hiring international students hired fewer graduates, making it difficult for internationals to secure employment in the United States. This trend has led some international candidates to opt for MBA programs outside the United States because of the greater flexibility they offer: shorter program length (one year to eighteen months) and open policies for granting work permits. Popular MBA programs such as INSEAD, IMD, and London Business School draw the largest numbers of internationals abroad. U.S. MBA programs will continue to compete with international MBA programs, which often offer language components that make them attractive to international applicants. MBA Boards will have to continue to aggressively market to international talent through proactive marketing and bringing the admissions information to international students' home countries.

While MBA programs continue to be challenged in attracting top international talent to the United States, it isn't an invitation to international applicants to become complacent when applying to business school. As of October 2007, the Graduate Management Admissions Council reported a significant increase (22.84 percent) in the number of test takers outside the United States compared with those who took the test in October 2006. These data suggest that more applicants, particularly internationals, are taking the GMAT and this increase will likely result in steeper competition this admission cycle.

On the evaluation front, many questions have been asked about how MBA Boards view international candidates in the application process. A common misconception is that MBA Boards have different admissions criteria for international candidates compared with U.S. citizens. This is far from the truth. Both groups of candidates are evaluated based on the same admissions criteria described in earlier chapters. That said, an area where I have observed a slight gap among international candidates is related to extracurricular involvement. In the United States, there is a strong culture of community service and extracurricular activities. Take the college application, for instance. High school students in the United States learn early that they need more than a perfect SAT score and GPA to be admitted to their top schools. Hence, they become savvy about building their extracurricular activities and a track record of leadership. Furthermore, American colleges offer ample opportunities to do internships and participate in student leadership and community service. With an emphasis on being well-rounded individuals, the average candidate in America has extensive opportunities to develop a strong leadership and community service track record.

This is not to suggest that these opportunities are nonexistent for internationals. However, international candidates have to be more aggressive when identifying opportunities to impact and lead in their communities. In situations in which the opportunities are absent, you should look into creating an organization from scratch, giving you a great opportunity to showcase your entrepreneurial leadership. I once worked with an international candidate who was reapplying to business school. He had created a brand-new community organization to help university students get placed for internships in his home country. I suspect that this leadership involvement is partly why he was admitted to a top MBA program the second time around.

Obtaining recommendation letters is another area in which international candidates should pay careful attention. I've noticed that international recommenders are not always as knowledgeable about how to "market" candidates. You should pay careful attention to selecting the right recommender if you are an international candidate. Make sure the writing ability of your recommender is up to par and that he or she has a good command of the English language. Remember, you are being assessed on your management potential and leadership, so remind your recommenders to stress these points and not simply state that you are a hard worker and extremely intelligent.

Finally, funding the education is an issue that international students grapple with. Unlike many graduate programs, which do not offer loans to international students, many of the U.S. MBA programs have relationships with lending institutions, making it possible for international candidates to qualify for loans. CitiAssist (www.citiassist.com) or comparable lending agencies offer international candidates loans to cover their business school expenses. I cover more on financial aid in the chapter on funding the MBA.

# CHAPTER TWELVE

## Admissions Decisions

A FTER MANY MONTHS INVESTING in the application, the long-awaited decision day has arrived. Decision day, or aptly, D day, is a day that is full of angst for MBA candidates. The wait has been long and candidates have given everything they can to earn a spot at their dream school. Rumors have not been in short supply in popular online chat rooms, either. This day is particularly abuzz with final salutations and last-minute encouragements. The clock strikes at the prescribed time and the results pour in.

For about 10 to 20 percent of applicants, the news is positive. Congratulatory phone calls from MBA admissions directors such as Derrick Bolton, Rosemarie Martinelli, and Dee Leopold bring good news to anxious candidates. For many, however, the admission outcome is disappointing. These applicants receive the conciliatory email informing them that they are great candidates but an overly competitive year and exceptional applicant pool made it impossible to admit them. I will use this chapter to discuss the different admission decision outcomes and offer suggestions on how to manage each situation.

## ADMITTED, NOW WHAT?

Once the euphoria of the good news has cleared, you will have some practical tasks to attend to in preparation for this new chapter of your life.

The first order of business is to follow up with your brand champions (recommenders) to inform them of the admission decision and to thank them for their role in making your application successful. (You should have already sent a thank you gift after completing your application.)

After you have visited the schools, it is a good idea to pick up program paraphernalia such as t-shirts or baseball hats as a small token of thanks to your recommenders. On the other hand, you may prefer to simply take them out to lunch or for drinks to celebrate. The important message here is to convey your gratitude for their time and commitment to your success.

It is important to maintain a long-term outlook on your relationship with these brand champions. Staying in touch with them while you are in business school and beyond is to your advantage. After all, you may need them again in the future.

Deciding on which MBA program to enroll in requires thoughtful analysis and research. Often friends and family have strong and conflicting opinions of where you should enroll. But the decision is ultimately yours (unless you have a partner, in which case both of you will need to make the decision together).

As a first step in deciding which MBA program you will attend, jot down the pros and cons of each program. Then visit the programs you are considering for their admitted students' weekend events.

One note of caution about these events is that all the schools are going to have their best face on and will have a full-court press to impress and sell you on their program. Therefore, you will need to dig a bit deeper to make sure that your questions are answered and that the program really offers what it says it does.

## SOME TOPICS TO EXPLORE DURING ADMITTED STUDENTS' WEEKEND

How comfortable are you with the teaching method at the school? Attending multiple classes during your visit will give you perspective that should confirm or raise flags regarding whether the teaching method is appropriate for you. The current students can also attest to the value and detractors of the teaching method. The faculty can contribute to the quality of your education, so do not hesitate to find out whether the faculty are accessible to the students and if opportunities exist to work with them on cases and projects outside the classroom. Social life is very important. Take your significant other if you have one to explore the culture of the program outside the classroom. How integrated are partners in the overall fabric of the social life? What are things that could be improved upon in this area, and what is currently being done? What social activities do students participate in, and do they appeal to you?

Career services and support have become more important as the economy has gone through downturns in the recent years. Research the level of commitment the career services team gives to students. Talking to students and the career services staff will give you some perspective in this area. Pay close attention to employment statistics of recent graduates. This information is accessible from the career services office.

Once you have made your decision and have paid your deposit, you are ready to tackle the prematriculation process. You will likely be inundated with emails and packets that can quickly become overwhelming. Although it can be tempting to put off going through the materials you receive, take the time to review them carefully to avoid missing any key deadlines. I have identified the major prematriculation topics, although this list is certainly not exhaustive and there may be other issues that you need to address based on your particular situation.

## Prematriculation Preparation

The prematriculation process can last for several months until your program begins. Devote the time to ensure that you attend to all matters dealing with this process.

### Financial Aid

Make sure you have all the required financial aid forms completed and submitted on time. Now that you are an "insider," you may also be able to identify additional funding opportunities that were not advertised on the program's website. Do not be bashful about contacting the financial aid staff to inquire about further opportunities for scholarships. If you do this, however, it is important to do so tastefully without being annoying. The next chapter covers financial aid information in greater detail.

### Housing

Where you will live can have a tremendous impact on your MBA experience, so choose wisely. Is your program a residential campus? If not, how important is it for you to live close to campus? What about roommates? The MBA experience is not solely in the classroom. In fact, many of the exciting and interesting experiences will take place after classes. Do enough introspection to decide what matters to you and what kind of experience you wish to have before you select your housing. Since my husband attended business school and we lived both on campus and off, I can offer my personal opinion based on both experiences. On-campus is all about convenience, and you are truly in the mix of things. Off-campus gives you a bit more space (if that is what you seek) and can mean that your experience is expanded to the broader community instead of focused on the MBA nucleus of your program. In either case, be proactive. Finding great accommodations is challenging at best and near impossible if you are in a metropolitan city, so start early to sort out your housing situation. Many programs provide on-campus housing based on a lottery system, so plan to take care of your housing as soon as you can and don't leave it to the last minute because you can lose out on your lottery if you miss the deadline. Roommates can also pose their set of problems if you don't select carefully. Some friendships do not survive after the friends have lived together: just because you get along with your friend doesn't always mean you will enjoy living with him or her. If your friend is a certified slob and you can't stand to see a plate in the kitchen sink, you may want to think twice before rooming together. It is not unusual to see two friends who came to business school as best friends graduate and end up not speaking to each other after living together. Whatever you decide to do with your housing decision, think long and hard about what your options are and what works for you to ensure a pleasant living experience.

## Academic Preparation

Regardless of whether your admission is conditional on academic study, it is to your advantage to brush up on your quantitative and analytical skills by taking a course or at the very least reading through a well-written text on statistics, accounting, and financial analysis. This is particularly useful for individuals who have been out of school for more than five years. Many MBA programs require incoming students to complete a prematriculation "mini course" offered by the program. These can be in the form of math boot camps or intensive English language programs. The advantage of these programs is that you will have a chance to get to know a small group of your classmates before the semester starts. Many MBA programs also require their entering class to complete a series of analytic and career assessments. These are required and can take time to complete, so although you may be inclined to procrastinate, set aside enough time so that you don't jeopardize your admission by not completing the assessment.

### Career Preparation

Everyone, particularly career changers, should consider spending some time thinking about what it is they wish to study and their career goals. Many MBA programs use Career Leader, a great tool for self-assessment and career guidance. You may also choose to arrange informational meetings with alumni from your MBA program or professionals in the industry in which you wish to work. Consider spending a couple of months during the summer before you start business school working in the role or industry you plan to move into after the MBA. A former client of mine who was a banker but wanted to explore consulting left his job to work for a consulting company in a new geographic location. It was a six-month stint, but it gave him exposure to a new industry beyond the summer internship and also allowed him to explore a new region (which he discovered he loved). This experience allowed him to confirm that consulting was the right career for him even before he began his MBA. Investing in working in a new career for a couple of months before you begin business school can give you a bit of a boost when it comes to securing a job. Such positions may be unpaid but will pay dividends when you begin your job search. Besides, you can't underestimate the value of hitting the ground running. Regardless of your decision, be sensitive to how you exit from your firm. If you plan to explore another career opportunity before starting your MBA, do give your employer ample notice before you leave your job. And please, aim to wrap up all outstanding projects to the best of your ability. It is always wise to leave your bridges intact for the future.

## Securing a Visa

For international students outside the United States, begin your visa application process as early as possible (once you receive your admission notice), as the process has become more complicated and involves more time. Even before you receive your admission offer, you should have all documents ready for the embassy or consulate office.

## Have Fun!

Finally, allow time to relax. You may wish to travel to see friends and family or to spend some time on a passion that you have been neglecting. Also, there is ample opportunity to meet your soon-to-be classmates through the prematriculation sites and informal get-togethers in your city of residence. Some of your closest friendships may be established during one of these trips before the program formally begins. An applicant I know used the summer before starting his MBA to finally earn his pilot's license.

# CONDITIONAL ADMISSION

What if you are admitted conditionally? Conditional admission typically has two stipulations: (1) improving quantitative background and (2) developing English language skills.

Some MBA programs provide summer or prematriculation programs. These programs often cover English language development and analytical and quantitative preparation. In other cases, the admission is conditional on the student taking courses from a university in his or her home city.

Whatever the case, it is important to view this admission positively. After all, the MBA Board would not have admitted you if it did not think you had the ability to handle its program. The additional coursework is to provide you with an opportunity to strengthen any gaps and to empower you to succeed when the program begins. Interestingly enough, much of the feedback I have received on this, especially programs sponsored by the MBA, has been good. To paraphrase one student's view, "The prematriculation program was wonderful as it gave me a chance to meet many of my classmates and form a close bond with them before classes began. It was like starting a program with more than twenty friends."

One point to underscore regarding conditional admission is to make sure that you have read the fine print on your admission letter. The responsibility is on you to fulfill the conditions on which your admission is made. You don't want an oversight to cost you a spot at your dream school.

## DEFERRED ADMISSION

Most top MBA programs prefer that candidates apply only when they are ready, and the majority of them do not grant deferrals except under extenuating circumstances. Contact each of the MBA programs to find out exactly what their policy is on deferred admission. Some examples of what the MBA Board considers extenuating circumstances include:

- When an illness precludes you from enrolling (you will need medical records from your doctor to attest to this)
- When you are the primary caretaker of an immediate family member who is struggling with a serious health problem
- When you are in the military and have been deployed to combat or assignment
- When you are a college senior whom the MBA Board feels will be better served if you gained professional experience

Unfortunately, at many programs, once-in-a-lifetime career opportunities, although noteworthy achievements, are rarely deemed acceptable reasons to grant a deferral. Be aware that the MBA Board reserves the right to make the final call on who they will offer deferred admission to. If your request for a deferral is declined and you choose to reapply in the future, you need to be aware that having been admitted previously does not guarantee you will be readmitted in the future. Admission is always based on the makeup of the class and the rigor of the applicant pool. So, if a deferral is not granted, think through your decision carefully before passing up your admission offer. Be sure that the new opportunity is worth it! I have firsthand experience during my time on Harvard's Admissions Board seeing candidates who did not get in the second time around (even though they were admitted in the past).

## WAIT LIST

We have all heard of the wait list wasteland and the many myths swirling around this application outcome. I suspect that to some degree, the myths that surround the wait list are a result of the heterogeneity of MBA programs' policies. Each MBA program deals with their wait lists differently, so it is critical to find out the specifics of each program's policy. Contact the MBA program and maintain communication with the MBA Board member designated to manage the wait list.

I dealt with the wait list during my time at Harvard, and I saw up close the angst and stress candidates experience while awaiting their admission outcome. The truth with the wait list is that it is hard to crack exactly why you were placed on that list. After all, your application was seen as certainly "admissible" but there is something that didn't quite push it into the admitted pile. A major reason is the sheer quality of the applicant pool. With so many talented candidates applying to business school, sometimes strong is not considered strong enough given the competition. In other cases, you may have applied in a year when many people with nearly identical backgrounds applied. It can also be a result of numbers, be it a GPA or GMAT score. An applicant I know was placed on the wait list of a top MBA program and after I read her application, which was very strong, it occurred to me that her Achilles heel was her GMAT score. It was several standard deviations from the norm. She had retaken the exam and had done quite well but unfortunately the new score was not taken into consideration because the MBA program did not accept additional information after the deadline. Her application was ultimately rejected. It is therefore important to apply to MBA programs when you have the absolute strongest application you possibly can assemble.

If you find yourself in the unenviable position of being wait-listed, here are some practical steps you can take to manage the process:

1. Immediately express your interest in remaining on the wait list via an email to the wait list manager.
2. Inquire about the policy, size of the wait list, and timing for the decisions (if this has not been clarified by the wait list manager).
3. For programs open to receiving additional information, consider sending new and relevant information to bolster your case. A higher GMAT score, a promotion at work with additional management responsibility, and an award in your community for your volunteer involvement are all good examples of valid information that you can send to the MBA Board. The challenge, however, is that each MBA program has a different wait list policy, so make sure you know precisely what's acceptable and what's not.

> For instance, Wharton explicitly requests that you
> do not send additional information, whereas you can
> send compelling new information to Kellogg. These
> policies can change from one year to the next, so call
> to confirm the program's current wait list policy.

Unfortunately, the percentage of applicants admitted from the wait list is low, so it is in your best interest to keep your other options open. The bird in hand theory applies here. It is not unusual to see situations in which fewer than ten people are admitted from a 200-plus wait list. Do you accept the offer of admission while you wait to hear back from your preferred program where you are wait-listed? It is a delicate balancing act. Ideally, you should try to get an extension before you make your decision. In the meantime, you should find out whether there is anything else you can offer to bolster your case where you are wait-listed. Obviously, if it is May and you have been on the wait list for a while, you may have to accept that it is highly unlikely that you will get off the wait list.

If this is the only MBA program to which you applied, or if all your results from other programs were unfavorable, make it clear to the MBA Board that its program is your top choice and that you are willing to remain on the wait list to the last day and will enroll at the last minute if an admission offer is extended to you.

What happens if you are denied admission after being on the wait list? The next section will provide you with some options you may want to consider.

## DENIED ADMISSION

First of all, if the admission decision is a denial, it is important to keep in mind that this is not the end of the world. After you have gotten over the initial disappointment, you should examine what your application lacked. There are a variety of reasons a candidate does not gain admission. The key ones are:

1. The candidate did not apply to realistic programs, but rather applied only to schools in which he or she had very little chance of gaining admission.
2. The candidate applied too early or too late in his or her career.
3. The candidate was not a fit for the program to which he or she applied.
4. The candidate was strong, *but* the overall application pool happened to have exceptionally strong candidates, raising the admission stake.
5. The candidate's brand was unclear or lacked focus.
6. The candidate failed to make a compelling case for why he or she needs the MBA.
7. The candidate's application lacked self-awareness.
8. The candidate's application had fundamental flags around judgment or interpersonal issues.
9. The candidate's application lacked strong evidence of leadership or community involvement.
10. The candidate's application raised concerns regarding academic preparation and intellectual strength.
11. The candidate's recommendations had a damning effect.
12. The candidate rushed the application and did not spend enough time on it.
13. The candidate bombed the interview.

Take a step back and evaluate your application in its entirety. Better yet, have someone you respect and who knows you very well review your application and provide you with feedback. Current students or alumni of the program are usually effective in giving useful feedback.

Understanding what went wrong with the application can come from feedback from the MBA Board. MBA programs vary in their policies on providing feedback. For instance, whereas Harvard Business School offers feedback only to college seniors programs such as Tuck, Wharton, and Anderson offer feedback and even encourage applicants to apply again in the future.

Feedback sessions are typically offered at the end of the admissions cycle, during the summer. Given the volume of reapplicants, I recommend that you sign up as soon as feedback spots become available since they fill up quickly. Also, because the feedback from the MBA Board can be particularly helpful, taking this extra step can play a major role in your reapplication should you choose to reapply. There are many programs that do not provide feedback to applicants whose applications were denied, so you may also wish to have an independent consultant evaluate your old application and provide you with strategic steps you can pursue to increase your admission outcome in the future.

## REAPPLICATION

After reassessing your application (whether through MBA Board feedback, admissions consulting evaluation, or self-reflection), you will be in a better position to decide whether you should reapply in the future.

The chance of a different admission outcome the next time around depends on what the issue was the first time. Academic gaps are much easier to address by retaking the GMAT and earning excellent grades in quantitative business courses. Weak leadership or community involvement can be addressed by spending a couple of years building a track record in this area before reapplying. However, issues of fit are more challenging because they reflect incongruity between your brand and that of the MBA program.

MBA programs do not publish percentages of reapplicants accepted, but anecdotal evidence indicates that several reapplicants gain admission the second time around. That said, applying more than two times to an MBA program is overdoing it. The second declined admission may suggest that there isn't a fit between you and the MBA program— your academic numbers may be too low compared with your competition or you are looking to pursue a health care career and the program doesn't have health care offerings. There are many other MBA programs where you will be successful, and it is worth expanding the list of MBA programs to give yourself the best shot at being admitted.

## PRACTICAL STEPS FOR REAPPLICANTS TO TAKE TO IMPROVE THEIR APPLICATION

Do your homework and make sure you know the MBA program inside out. Don't apply without visiting the program and attending a class. (This is a common mistake applicants make.)

Be very specific when discussing why you want to be accepted to a particular MBA program and how it will enhance your career trajectory. Demonstrate a clear fit between you and the MBA program.

Beef up your career and community leadership and make sure you have tangible examples of the impact you have made since your previous application.

Simply reapplying with the same "goods" will likely yield an unfavorable outcome. Be willing to take major action. It may mean changing your job, taking on significant responsibility at work, or doing an international project.

Increase your GMAT score significantly by taking a class if necessary and make sure your score is at least within the median score of admitted students. Take business or quantitative classes and earn As in them to show your intellectual aptitude. Good options are introduction courses in finance, microeconomics and macroeconomics, statistics, and accounting.

Cultivate relationships with individuals who will become your brand champions and make sure that they are on board and committed to writing glowing recommendation letters for you. Tactfully request to see your recommendations from previous recommenders if they are open to sharing them with you.

Invest time in clarifying your brand and be proactive to make sure your application reflects a powerful brand that is in sync with the MBA program.

Apply early to avoid running into a situation in which few admission spots remain.

This can't be overstressed: visit the campus and attend different open house events and information sessions given by the school to make sure you fully understand the program and its brand.

A reapplication is not an invitation to suspend your judgment. Some application situations are lost causes. If after retaking the GMAT your score remains below 500, you may have to rethink your school list. Just because a candidate believes he or she belongs to a particular program does not mean he or she will be admitted. I know of a candidate who applied four times to a top MBA program and even after his fourth rejection remained optimistic that he would eventually gain admission. This is clearly delusional and not a good example of persistence. I don't think there is anything wrong with reapplying once to your dream school, especially if you didn't spend much time on your application the first time through.

At the same time, I've evaluated applications where it was apparent that there wasn't anything the candidate could do to change the admission outcome. It may be a fundamental fit issue. Or it could come down to being overqualified for the

MBA. Therefore, objective evaluation and honest introspection will help you ascertain whether a reapplication is worth the trouble. The following example illustrates this point. I got a call from a business associate who wanted me to evaluate a friend's application. He was an Asian male with exceptional academic and GMAT scores, he had great evidence of leadership, and he had worked at three blue chip firms. After reading his essays (he happened to be a very good writer) and entire application, it was clear to me that he was in that category of applicants that had all the "goods" but couldn't make a convincing case for why he needed the MBA. His application was strong enough that he was interviewed by Harvard, Stanford, and Wharton, and all three schools rejected his application. This is one of the hardest situations to overcome as a reapplicant. In his case he couldn't improve his GMAT score or change jobs to get more leadership experience. He already had met these requirements. It simply came down to whether the MBA Board believed that he needed the MBA or whether he was simply getting his ticket stamped. Waiting too long to apply to business school can result in a rejected application.

## FINAL THOUGHTS

Hopefully by the time you have made it to this point of the book, you have already gleaned enough insights to ensure that you avoid the landmines that surround the entire application process. I've touched on the less-favorable potential outcomes as well to help applicants navigate effectively should they find themselves in an unenviable situation of a wait list or denied admission. Applying the suggestions I highlight in this section should help to increase their odds of a favorable outcome in the future. Once you are armed with an admission offer, another set of anxieties may take front stage: figuring out how to fund your education. I examine the subject of funding the MBA in the next chapter.

# CHAPTER THIRTEEN

## Funding the MBA

BUSINESS SCHOOLS BELIEVE IT is the responsibility of the applicant to meet the financial burden for their education. With that said, many MBA programs attempt to soften the financial blow to applicants by offering scholarships, loans, and loan forgiveness programs. There is no question that the MBA is an expensive investment. This large financial cost can dissuade many applicants from applying to business school. On the other hand, some applicants pay too little attention to how they will fund the MBA. Members of this latter group tend to focus primarily on the uphill application process with little attention to funding the MBA, at least until they have an admission offer in hand. A tardy response to the financing of the MBA may cost you tens of thousands of scholarship dollars.

This chapter attempts to make the funding process more transparent. Strong evidence exists to support the investment in the MBA. However, it is not a license to charge everything without limits. Funding your MBA requires practical planning and discipline to achieve your education dreams. I will discuss the overall cost of the MBA and funding sources. I'll also provide suggestions of how candidates should go about preparing themselves to fund their MBA.

## THE MBA COST

Two years in business school will cost you a hefty amount of money. You will need to cover the cost of tuition, room, board, transportation, books, medical insurance, special trips, and other miscellaneous fees associated with a business education. A few years ago, an MBA at Harvard Business School would cost you about $110,000 for room, board, fees, and tuition. Today, the cost is upward of $146,000 for a single student and $185,200 for a married student with a child. The total cost of the MBA for a single student residing on campus at Stanford Graduate School of Business (GSB) is $143,898. These numbers, although staggering, are consistent across top MBA programs in the United States.

Schools in large cities are not the only ones that have to deal with the high MBA cost. Even programs in small towns, such as Tuck, Cornell, and Darden, have an equally high price tag for their business school. Tuck's sample MBA fees illustrate this point.

## TUITION AND COSTS

| Tuition and Costs for Academic Year 2007–2008 | | |
|---|---|---|
| | T'07 | T'08 |
| Tuition: | $42,990 | $42,990 |
| Books and supplies: | $3,200 | $3,200 |
| Room and board: | $11,100 | $9,725 |
| Miscellaneous and health expenses: | $12,910 | $10,350 |
| Technology fee and notebook computer: | N/A | $2,535 |
| Total: | $70,200 | $68,800 |

The MBA costs can increase significantly for students who do not create and live within their budget. Some students feel that the MBA is a once-in-a-lifetime experience and use this rationale to justify why they need to participate in every trek (fun trip) around the world with their classmates. The cost of these exotic jaunts can be more than $20,000, adding to the debt students take on when they graduate from their MBA programs.

At a glance the tab for an MBA will leave many applicants with their heads spinning. The good news is that the MBA is an investment in one's career for the long term. In 2005, the median starting salary at Stanford was $100,000 post business school. These high salaries are not unique to Stanford. Tuck, for instance, cites its median and mean starting salary as $100,000 in 2006. These career statistics demonstrate that the return on the MBA investment does pay for itself over time.

## FUNDING SOURCES

There are five main ways to fund the MBA. Many candidates rely on several combinations of these.

### Company Sponsorships

Some companies offer to cover their employees' education. In exchange the employees return to the firm to work for a few years after their MBA. This offer is usually extended to star employees who a company wishes to retain. Some consulting companies are amenable to company sponsorships. Even if your firm doesn't typically offer sponsorship opportunities, if you have consistently received top evaluations and have brand champions at your firm, don't be shy about proposing this option if you intend to return to your industry.

### Loans

Loans are the most common option for funding the MBA. You will need to know what your credit score is because the loan interest rate will be based on your credit score and history. Lenders determine loan rates based on the three different credit scores: Equifax, TransUnion, and Experian. It is important to know what your score is for all three. Fair Isaac and Co (FICO) tracks credit histories and scores of all three agencies. Applicants should order a copy of all three scores by going to www.myfico.com. Lending agencies use payment history, how much you owe, how long you have had the credit, how much new debt you have taken on, and the types of credit you have to determine your credit score. You can save a lot of money by cleaning up your credit prior to applying for a loan to fund your MBA.

There are different types of loans available to MBA candidates.

1.  The Federal Loan Programs (Stafford and Perkins Loans) are available only to U.S. citizens and permanent residents. The Stafford Loan (www.stafford-loan.com) provides the best rates to students. There are two types of Stafford Loans: subsidized (need-based awards that defer payment until you complete your program) and unsubsidized (non-need-based with payments required while you attend business school). The Perkins Loan (www.perkinsloans.com) provides low-interest loans to offset the cost of graduate education. Another popular loan program is the Graduate Plus Loan (www.gradloans.com), which is a federally sponsored program available to U.S. and permanent residents and eligible non-citizens with a good credit history.

2.  Private MBA loan programs are open to international candidates. These loans are designed by the MBA programs and the bank with the candidate in mind. Two popular ones are the CitiAssist Loans offered at programs such as Harvard Business School, Columbia, and Cornell and the National Education

Loan Network (Nelnet) offered at programs such as Stanford GSB.

3. Loan forgiveness programs: MBA programs have created loan forgiveness programs to reduce the financial burden of the MBA on applicants who pursue careers in the nonprofit or public sectors. MBA programs such as Harvard Business School have created a loan forgiveness program for graduates in social enterprise. Stanford GSB is piloting a program for internationals who choose to work in developing countries after business school. Fuqua has a generous loan assistance program that offers financial awards to alumni who work in nonprofit and government organizations. Other top MBA programs offer similar loan forgiveness programs, so take the time to research what each specific program offers.

## University Awards

These scholarships are often merit-based but can be need-based as well. Many top programs offer awards to students to help offset the cost of the MBA education. Stanford GSB, for instance, offers five students $25,000 each in the form of Siebel Scholarships after their first year based on exceptional leadership and academic achievements. In the case of Chicago GSB, awards are given to students through scholarships that range between $15,000 and $25,000 each year. Tuck offers scholarships that start as little as $3000 and go up to a full scholarship for applicants based on merit and need. Cornell's Park Fellowship is usually in the tens of thousands of dollars. All top MBA programs have some form of award available to incoming students, so take the time to find out what your target programs offer, the requirements, and the deadlines so that you can apply in time for them.

## Special Target Awards

These are scholarships that are offered to particular demographic groups. Some MBA programs offer a limited number of Forté Fellowships to women applicants. The Toigo Foundation offers scholarships to minority candidates studying at Toigo partner schools. Another popular fellowship is the Consortium Fellowship, which is for underrepresented minority candidates applying to MBA programs that are members of the MBA Consortium. Specific companies are also involved in offering fellowships and scholarships to incoming business school students. Banks such as Goldman Sachs, JPMorgan, and CSFB provide fellowships to MBA candidates. Even *Fortune* 500 corporations offer scholarships to candidates with industry experience and interest. The point here is that while it is hard to find financial coverage for the MBA, investing in thorough research will help you identify resources that can make funding your MBA possible.

## Personal Savings

Applicants to business school have an expected family contribution (EFC) that they need to make toward covering the cost of their education. Applicants need to start a couple of years before applying to business school to save money and cut down on their expenses. MBA financial aid officers expect that you will contribute sizably to your MBA costs.

I can't stress enough the importance of hustling to find scholarships and financial sponsorship. Unfortunately, you can't always count on every single award being on the MBA program websites and catalogs. You will have to be a bit of a detective and will need to dig discretely to find out if there are other scholarships available that are under the radar.

---

## MATERIALS REQUIRED FOR
## FINANCIAL AID APPLICATION

An application to the MBA program submitted in time for the financial aid deadlines (verify each MBA program's deadline ahead of time)

A completed FAFSA (Free Application for Federal Student Aid) form (www.fafsa.com)

The financial aid forms for the MBA program

Your most recent federal tax returns

Evidence of salary (pay stubs)

Documentation of assets and bank statements

Confirm with the financial aid office at your MBA program as to whether they require other forms or documentation

---

# PREPARING YOURSELF FINANCIALLY TO FUND YOUR MBA

Applicants are expected to have some savings that they will use to offset the cost of their MBA. The reality for many candidates, however, is that this isn't always the case. If you are already in the application stage, then you will need to focus your strategy on finding as much "free" money as you can to help you bear the financial burden. But don't expect the financial aid office to throw loads of money at you. If, on the other hand, you are still thinking of applying in the future, there are steps you can take today to prepare you financially.

## KEY STEPS TO PREPARE FOR FUNDING YOUR MBA

Good Credit History: Your credit history drives the interest rates that you will receive on loans. Devote time to establishing good credit. If you have poor credit, take the time to clean up your credit history. Someone I know had a horrible credit history (560 credit score), and after devoting a couple of years to cleaning up his credit, his score jumped higher than 700. Strong credit scores can be the difference in tens of thousands of dollars saved on lower interest payments.

Build a Cash Reserve: Planning early gives you the opportunity to save money toward your MBA. Loans and scholarships are not the only way to fund your degree.

Establish Relationships with Co-Signers: This is particularly useful for international students whose interest rates can be reduced several percentage points when they have a co-signer for their loan rather than applying for the loan on their own.

Invest time up front to research private scholarships and fellowships. Many private organizations set aside awards that often go unused because people didn't apply for them.

Worrying about funding the MBA should not preclude you from applying to your dream school. It is an investment in your future and a worthwhile one at that. Getting in is the hardest part. Once you are admitted, you will find various outlets to explore to finance your MBA. Diligence, planning, and a little bit of ingenuity can go a long way in helping you secure financing to offset the cost of the business education.

# CHAPTER FOURTEEN

## Final Thoughts

I HOPE *THE BEST BUSINESS SCHOOLS' ADMISSIONS SECRETS* has dispelled your concerns about the application and has made the process more transparent and hopefully less stressful. I have given you a glimpse into how the Admissions Boards at top business schools perceive candidates. I've also shared with you specific and practical tips on how you can avoid making mistakes that can cost you admission into your desired MBA program. But most important, I have harped on the importance of seeing yourself as a brand and managing your brand successfully in the application process. Regardless of whether you decide to pursue an MBA or not, I encourage you to invest in your personal brand.

Practical takeaways from this book include the following:

1. You are a brand! Invest in conducting a brand audit and begin today to manage your personal brand. Not only will it help you land admission into a top business school, but it will also help you live your life in a meaningful, focused way. Don't forget to live your life with passion, guts, impact, and insight.
2. Know the brands of the MBA programs and research them to ensure a fit with the programs you end up selecting.

3. The essays are critical to gaining admission to elite business schools. Successful applications have well-executed essays that have the following six characteristics: compelling, captivating, consistent, credible, concise, and clear.

4. Brand champions can make or break an admission, so choose wisely and invest in cultivating recommenders who will become raving fans.

5. Don't underestimate the importance of the interview; it is your chance to make a strong impression on the Admissions Board. Preparation and practice will enable you to sell your brand successfully to the Admissions Board.

6. Understand the three admissions criteria: leadership, academics, and unique brand differentiation. Know what your strengths are and where you fall short. Commit to plugging the holes in your candidacy, whether it is gaining more leadership experience, taking business classes, retaking the GMAT, or simply developing your personal brand to become an appealing candidate.

The good news is that you don't have to be a rock star to get admitted to your dream school. Getting in involves doing your research, tailoring your story to fit the program's brand, and capitalizing on your unique brand differentiation. Embrace your brand, give yourself enough time to market your story, and do it right the first time. I wish all of you well as you brand your way to success!

# APPLICATION INSIGHTS

## NYU (Stern) MBA Perspective

### FERNANDO D'ALESSIO (STERN, 2006)

**Prior to MBA Career Path:**
Investment Banker (JPMorgan & HSBC).

**Post-MBA Career Path:**
Investment Banker (U.S. focused – advising family business and PE shops).

**How many years of work experience did you have prior to the MBA:**
Seven years.

**What was your greatest concern applying to business school and how did you address it:**
I had heard from friends who had attended business school that it is a race to get a job and that a good part of the experience is about recruiting. I was concerned about whether I had too much experience (I always felt the more years of experience, the more you can get out of the program but when visiting schools, I noticed I was on the older side). I realized that timing is a big deal and if I could do it all over again, I would have applied three years earlier.

## Why did you select your MBA program:

I applied to a few schools and my focus was on programs that were strong in general management and finance. I also wanted a program that had a good environment for student activities. Location was also important to me since I wanted to stay close to or remain in New York City. Most importantly, given my seven years' experience, I wanted to make the most out of graduate education by taking the majority of my second-year classes with part-time students, and NYU Stern is known to have one of the top part-time MBA programs in the country.

## What was the most interesting part of your MBA program:

At Stern, you have the choice to exempt out of classes and since my undergraduate degree was in Economics, I was able to exempt out of two required Economics courses and take a proficiency exam to exempt out of Statistics. I appreciated the fact that you could specialize in up to 3 majors and I pursued a Finance, Management, and Entrepreneurship major. But most importantly for me, I wanted a firm foundation in finance and entrepreneurship as well as interaction with experienced professionals, and I got a solid training in this area at Stern.

## How did you find the academic part of your program:

It was challenging. There were different teaching methodologies used and some professors used the case-based method and others relied on lectures or a combination. I liked having both since some courses were suited for cases while others were better for the lectures. I appreciated the diversity of teaching approaches at Stern.

## How did you find the social part of your program:

The social life at Stern was very active. But I kept a low profile since I was married and didn't party as hard as some of my classmates. Being in New York City is definitely a great advantage.

## What was your job search like:

I adopted a focused approach from the very beginning. I had done M&A for seven years so I wanted to complement my experience with new skills. I wanted a firm with strong restructuring background or financial sponsors exposure and I joined a firm that offered both after business school. In addition, I kept my options open and applied to a couple of consulting positions as well.

## How did the MBA prepare you for your career:

Stern has a great program that helps career switchers. Once you are admitted to Stern, you have a lot of support. For example, there are programs that prepare students for a new career by providing them access to professionals from the industry. The school offers various workshops and one-on-one preparation to help students prepare for cases and mock interviews. I was especially impressed with how collaborative students were with each other and it was common for second-year students to help first-year students.

## What advice do you have for applicants to maximize their application:

Know why you want the MBA. It is important to be well-prepared. Before you apply you should visit the schools and talk to students and alumni to make sure it is a fit. You should also study hard to make sure you nail the GMAT and get a solid score so you can check that box and move on to more challenging aspects of the application. If the GMAT is weak, you have already taken yourself out of the game before it starts.

# Stanford MBA Perspective

---

## RECY DUNN (STANFORD GSB, 2004)

### Prior to MBA Career Path:
I was an SEO intern at Merrill and worked at energy companies Texaco (Chevron) and Amoco (BP) as an analyst in sales and trading (energy); a year into it, I had an epiphany that I didn't want to be a trader. While interviewing for new opportunities, I had a layover in NYC, and in conversation with some friends, I joked about how it would be great to work at SEO (a nonprofit). I called and they said come in to interview. A few weeks later they offered me a job. I quit my trading job, sold my car on a Friday, flew to NYC Saturday, and began work Monday morning. It was a huge pay cut but I enjoyed the work: it brought joy and meaning to my life.

### Post-Career Path:
I did an internship at Wells Fargo after my first year in business school and realized I hated the big company experience. I accepted the fact that my passion was education. How do you make money doing what you love? I joined Platform Learning, a for-profit company with an education mission. Then I spent two years completing the Broad Residency at Urban Education

with a placement in DC Public Schools. I currently work in a general management role as an advisor to the Deputy Superintendent in Prince George's County, Maryland.

## How many years of work experience did you have prior to the MBA:

Five years.

## What was your greatest concern applying to business school:

How to tell my story in a way that would help me gain admission. I felt I didn't have functional knowledge in a particular business area plus I worried about my undergrad transcript. Since I didn't have the typical banker, consultant, or GM corporate exposure I knew I had to focus on pitching my story effectively.

## Why did you select your MBA program:

I chose Stanford GSB because of its reputation as an excellent general management program. I was also drawn to its program offerings and the truly collaborative environment where classmates committed to working together.

## What was the most interesting part of your MBA program:

The education was top notch. I was amazed at how much access we had to faculty, flexibility to work with them on new and interesting research. I also appreciated the exposure to the business executives who came to speak at the school. I found GSB to be flexible allowing me to pursue a joint degree program with a Masters in Education.

## What surprised you the most about your program:

I was impressed with the number of opportunities and clubs on campus; there was something for everybody. Being a part of rugby club, marketing club, and Black Business Student Association, I enjoyed the diversity of options that was available.

My takeaway was realizing that management is more than accounting and finance; I learned the importance of organizational behavior and the role of interpersonal dynamics and softer skills when leading with impact.

## What was your job search like:
The Director of Stanford Career Services was an alumnus which says a lot about the school's investment in its students' careers. My job search was more nontraditional since I was looking for an education position so I had to do a little more ground work. But Career Services gave me access to tons of alumni and training to prepare me for interviews. They even had consultants come in to help students who didn't know exactly what they wanted to do career-wise.

## What advice do you have for applicants:
Apply early, don't be afraid to let the Board know who you are. So many people just try to simply explain their resume. Be willing to let your guard down and definitely introspect. Focus on essays and paint a picture for the admissions committee so they get a sense of where you were, what you were doing, what you were feeling. And finally, have a clear vision of what you want to do in the future.

# MBA Admissions Board Perspective

JEVELYN BONNER-REED, Former Associate
Director of Admissions at Kellogg (HAAS, 1998)

## When should candidates begin planning their application for business school:

Their senior year in college: they should take the GMAT while they are still in studying mode (especially since their peers will be working on their LSAT/MCAT exams). The GMAT score is valid for five years, so taking it their senior year allows candidates to focus on the other aspects of their application once they are ready to apply to business school.

## What key qualities stand out in applicants who are admitted:

Balanced individuals who put energy into their academics, work, and extracurricular activities. A trend towards pushing yourself and not settling is important. If you are a history major, why didn't you challenge yourself by taking quantitative courses? If you start off as a member in clubs, what stopped you from moving into leadership roles? If you took the GMAT once and your score is okay, why did you not try to improve it? MBA Boards do not like to see candidates taking the GMAT twenty times but it is okay to retake the GMAT once or twice. These are the types of questions on the minds of MBA Boards.

## What is the most important part of the application:

The whole package is important but the essays are critical because the applicant has total control over them and can constantly revise them unlike other parts of the application. In a pool of similar looking candidates, they can be the differentiating factor that persuades the reader to admit you. Additionally, you can use them to explain gaps in your background (if you have low grades or employment gaps, you can address these issues in a mature manner).

## What steps can career changers take before applying to an MBA program:

They can do informational interviews for the new career to understand skills they will need and make sure it's a fit. They should also highlight skills they have that are transferable to the new career. Some admissions people may be uncomfortable if it's too big a career jump or if the candidate has unrealistic expectations of what it might take to successfully switch careers.

## What are the most common admissions mistakes you have seen applicants make:

Applicants worry too much about what the Admission Board wants to hear instead of representing themselves. Applying to too many schools can lead to application burnout. Another mistake is not doing the research before you apply, resulting in a missed opportunity to convey specifics about the school.

## What advice do you have about selecting recommenders:

Choose someone who knows your work very well: a manager or professional mentor who has worked at the company and knows you. You can also use a client. The first time they hear you are applying shouldn't be when you are sitting with them to ask for a recommendation letter.

## What characteristics are found in excellent recommendations:

They are succinct, yet detailed with real examples. If it is too long, you lose the reader's interest.

## How important is age and number of years of work experience:

Having two to three years is helpful (you can contribute to classroom discussion); but too much work experience makes it harder to switch careers. The bottom line is whenever you think you are ready for business school. You may have to determine whether a full-time, part-time, or executive MBA is most appropriate.

## How do Admissions Boards view reapplicants:

It depends on why you were denied admission in the first place. If it is anything but environmental fit, you have as good a shot as anyone else when you reapply. If it's a fit issue, there is nothing you can do about it. Candidates should consider fit not only in terms of the different two-year MBA programs but should assess whether they would be best served in a different type of program such as an executive or part-time MBA program. You should request feedback from the school about your candidacy when it's offered! Unfortunately, most schools do not offer this service.

## What should applicants do to address weak scores or GPA:

Whatever you do, you can't have both. The GMAT or the GPA has to be at least in the median ballpark for the school. If one is below average you can point to the other to show your academic competency. Also candidates can take specific courses at local colleges and universities to address any academic deficiency.

## What advice do you have for wait-listed candidates:

Find out how the program likes to handle wait-listed candidates and follow the requirements. Some schools allow for candidates to submit additional information about their candidacy while others want you to just wait.

## What should candidates do to nail the interview:

Practice!!! Some people have been at their jobs for a few years and haven't interviewed for a while. Practice and prepare as if you were going into a job interview. Share work and life experience examples and do your research on each school beforehand.

## What should rejected candidates do to improve their application next time:

Step back, evaluate why you didn't get in at all, do a feedback session if offered, and potentially reapply to the program. You should also expand your school choice list. Have something different to bring to the table (e.g. higher GMAT score, new course work with strong grades if your GPA is low, and earn a promotion or more responsibility at work if you were stagnating in your current role).

## You have an MBA. What did you value about your MBA:

Learning the language of business. My undergrad was in Engineering so the MBA opened my eyes to areas I knew little about (Marketing, Finance, etc.). I grew up in the Midwest with little to no international experience so I was most impressed with the level of international exposure I found in business school. From living in the International House with international students from all over the world, to trips around the world with classmates, to doing an exchange program at London Business School. My MBA was truly global and opened a whole new world to me.

# Columbia MBA Perspective

## FRED CHIMA (COLUMBIA GRADUATE SCHOOL OF BUSINESS, 2004)

### Prior to MBA Career Path:
Worked at PricewaterhouseCoopers in the Assurance and Business Advisory Group starting as Associate and later promoted to Manager.

### Post-MBA Career Path:
Spent my summer after my first year in business school in Banking at Citigroup (London). After graduating I joined Credit Suisse First Boston in NYC in the Investment Banking Group.

### How many years of work experience did you have prior to the MBA:
Four and a half years.

### What was your greatest concern applying to business school:
Experience wasn't a concern since I felt I had enough experience. I was concerned about financing the MBA. I felt it was a big investment. I also wondered whether the MBA would get me from point A to point B. After careful research, I felt

comfortable with the investment. Speaking to alumni who had gone to Columbia and made the jump to finance reassured me that my goal was realistic and feasible.

## Why did you select your MBA program:

I wanted a program that was recognized internationally since I was an international student. I also wanted a program with an excellent reputation in finance and technical depth. Furthermore, geographic location was important to me: I wasn't interested in being outside of the Northeast. For these reasons Columbia was a good fit.

## What was the most interesting part of your MBA program:

Coming into the program, I underestimated the depth of diversity of my class. I mean diversity in terms of experience/background, not just ethnicity. My class was incredibly diverse: former entertainers, a rancher, bankers, etc. And everyone has the same goal. You make friends with classmates from all over the world. The program puts you through quite a bit of change.

## How did you find the academic part of your program:

Coming from a solid accounting background, as a CPA, I felt that the first year wasn't as challenging. I could have exempted more classes but I wanted to take all the classes to make sure I wasn't missing out on anything. My second year was awesome. I got to pick the classes I was interested in: I like finance but my passion really is the intersection of politics and business so I took 3–4 classes from the School of International and Public Affairs (SIPA).

## How did you find the social part of your program:

It was at first challenging (international students go through this I believe). MBA programs attract certain personalities (mostly socially aggressive and type A personalities) and if you aren't like that it may be hard initially. Over time, however, everyone adapts. Business schools push you to adapt. Internationals may need a bit of adapting initially. After a semester you'll find your stride.

## What was your job search like:

I found it very distracting. I knew I wanted a career change. I was initially confused about how I would make my career transition from accounting to finance. I attended all the presentations in banking which by the way was a big mistake (you lose focus); I didn't know if I wanted to be in NYC or pursue an international role. As a career changer, I needed to pound the pavements, especially in a tough economy, where many analysts were returning to old firms/industry, making it more competitive. I got my internship from interviewing through the Career Services Office. For my full-time role, it was through a connection I made while in business school.

## How did the MBA prepare you for your career:

From a people/soft skills perspective it was invaluable. Banking has two legs: how good are you technically and how good are you in getting along with people. The softer stuff is what I learned a lot about, the intangibles, how a team works, managing up and down, and becoming comfortable being in unfamiliar environments. Technically, I felt it was a brush up of my skills instead of giving me new skills necessarily. I may have survived without an MBA my first year in an Associate role but would I have survived beyond the first year? Not necessarily. As you move into a more senior role, your responsibility goes beyond basic accounting and finance skills and focuses more on looking at business in a holistic way. This is a skill set I got from Columbia! The cases, projects tend to look at things from an overall perspective. You think back to cases you did, the challenges the protagonists faced and the solutions they came up with. Another benefit of the MBA is that it builds one's confidence. You have classmates with strong opinions. Even if you are quiet you learn how to defend your ideas and when in banking if you encounter people who are type A, you can hold your own. The MBA gives you credibility in your profession.

## What advice do you have for applicants to maximize their application:

First of all, think about what you want to get out of the program. It will help you focus on the schools to apply to. I don't believe you should apply to ten schools. Once you identify the programs, dig in, talk to the alumni and admissions people. It doesn't guarantee admission, but invest into them knowing you. Don't worry about financing the program. Get over the concerns about money. International students receive loans so you should view the MBA as an investment.

For career changers, you should talk to as many people in the career of interest. They will give you a lot of perspectives that will help you understand how to go about making the career switch. Even if you are an international student, don't be shy. You should assert yourself. Just because you are from another culture doesn't mean you can't speak up. Be introspective, and assess what you bring to the table. I had a CPA, experience from a top Accounting firm. I also knew what I wanted to do—M&A. I met with Associates and found out what they do in the M&A groups at their firms. By learning exactly what skills were needed and specifics of the role, I was able to effectively market myself by capitalizing on my experience and my understanding of the career I planned to follow after business school. It paid off.

# Harvard MBA Perspectives

---

## KHARY CUFFE (HBS, 2007) & SELENA CUFFE (HBS, 2003)

### Prior to MBA Career Path:
*Khary:* Analyst in Asset Backed Securities Group (Prudential); Investment Associate (Seedco)

*Selena:* Business Development (United Airlines)

### Post-MBA Career Path:
*Khary:* Baby Care Brand Management (P&G); Wine Importation (Heritage Link Brands)

*Selena:* Food & Beverage Brand Management (P&G), Council on International Educational Exchange (CIEE); Wine Importation (Heritage Link Brands)

### How many years of work experience did you have prior to the MBA:
*Khary & Selena:* Four years.

### Did you meet at business school:
*Khary:* I met my wife as a prospective student during one of my visits to Harvard.

## What was your greatest concern applying to business school:

*Khary:* Picking the right school and getting admitted.

*Selena:* Cost was a concern for me. I wondered whether it was a worthwhile investment financially. I also was concerned about how I would fund my education. Finally, I also wondered about the GMAT before taking it but it turned out not to be an issue.

## Why did you select your MBA program:

*Khary:* As a minority, I wanted a program that had good diversity and a strong brand reputation. Harvard had both. I was also attracted to the learning model at Harvard and found the entire academic experience engaging.

*Selena:* When I visited HBS, it immediately felt like a fit. During the class discussion, I found myself wanting to join in.

## What was the most interesting part of your MBA program:

*Khary:* For me it was the people I met, the variety of interests, and the opportunity to do a joint degree.

*Selena:* The Treks exposed me to places I may not have explored in my life. For example, meeting members of parliament in different countries and engaging in dialogue with them about the future of their country and how business fit into their vision was interesting. During a subsequent trip to South Africa, I learned that despite South Africa's $3 billion wine industry, blacks owned less than 2 percent. And there were no distribution channels for their wines to the U.S. Subsequently I began to explore how to bring their wine to the U.S. As a result, in 2007 we launched Heritage Link Brands in the U.S. market to do just that!

## What surprised you the most about your MBA program:

*Khary:* The caliber of classmates is remarkable. You can't help but wonder whether you can compete at that level. I certainly consider myself a confident person but surrounded by rock stars, it has you stepping up your game!

*Selena:* I was surprised by how easygoing and approachable the professors were. Interacting with Harvard professors felt like sitting down with a friend over coffee. This is the case even after business school. The relationship with your professors is long lasting.

## How did you find the academic part of your program:
*Khary:* I found it to be great. While it was challenging, I felt it was immediately applicable. I have been able to apply a lot of lessons I learned in business school to our company, Heritage Link Brands.

*Selena:* I found it to be challenging but not too stressful. I enjoyed it. It pushed my limits but I never felt I was out of my element.

## How did you find the social part of your program:
*Khary:* It was great. There were always a ton of activities to do. Student groups were very active and engaged.

*Selena:* It was very robust. There were more things to do than you could do in a day, week, or semester! It was complete fun and there is something for everyone regardless of your interests.

## How did the MBA prepare you for your career:
*Khary:* From a technical standpoint, I didn't feel the MBA was as relevant. From a professional network standpoint as well as developing soft skills, it was absolutely helpful.

*Selena:* Business School gave me courage to become an entrepreneur. Two classes, The Entrepreneurial Manager and Entrepreneurial Marketing, for instance, provided the frameworks for how to build a business from start to finish.

## What advice do you have for applicants to maximize their application:

*Khary:* Visit the school, not during prospective students' day but when there isn't a special event going on so you can get the "real" sense of the school. Once you decide you will apply, get help. Use a consultant or organization like Managing Leaders for Tomorrow (MLT). Talk to students from the school. And finally, with your app, be yourself.

*Selena:* I am a firm believer in getting students who are at the school to look over your application. They have insight into the culture of the program. Having said that, use judgment. I wouldn't share the application with everybody either.

---

## CHRIS RYAN (FUQUA [DUKE], 2000)

**Prior to MBA Career Path:**
High-school Teacher

**Post-MBA Career Path:**
Consultant, Education Company Executive, Independent Film Producer

**How many years of work experience did you have prior to the MBA:**
Six years.

**What was your greatest concern applying to business school and how did you address it:**
I was concerned more about getting in and less about what I would do afterwards, as I thought I had that figured out. With regard to getting into school, I was worried that my nontraditional career path to that point would hamper my chances.

**Why did you select your MBA program:**
I had known about and liked Duke as a university for a long time (I almost went there for undergrad). So when I started

looking at business schools, Fuqua was definitely on my list. Around that time, I met another teacher who was a year ahead of me in the process. He went to Fuqua and was very pleased with the program. When I went for the campus interview, I was struck by the atmosphere of the place—it felt both serious and welcoming, both focused and warm. At that point I had a strong sense that Fuqua was the place for me.

## What was the most interesting part of your MBA program:

My classmates, hands down. They brought an amazing diversity of experiences and backgrounds to the school. At graduation, I remember feeling that there was still so much more to learn about my classmates—but the two years were up.

## What surprised you the most about your program:

What surprised me the most was how important extracurricular activities would be for me and for the bulk of students. During school, I devoted a great deal of time to video production, of all things! For many years, Fuqua has had a club called "Fuquavision" that puts together "Saturday Night Live"-style videos and shows them regularly to the entire school on Friday nights. As you can imagine, putting together a nearly hour-long program of videos every six weeks is very difficult and time-consuming (especially while trying to meet the other obligations of school), but it was also very enjoyable. Even more important, it gave me a chance to develop my skills and interests in filmmaking (since then, I have been an executive producer on a film featured at the Sundance Film Festival, and I continue to write and develop projects). This aspect of business school was ironic for me, since I had even considered going to film school instead of business school.

## How did you find the academic part of your program:

Both practical and interesting. I really enjoyed learning all sorts of material I had never studied before, both for its own sake and for its real-world utility, which was generally obvious. I found most of the professors not only excellent thinkers but also inspiring teachers. True, there were a few who were less than scintillating in the classroom (I imagine that's true at every school), but I was very happy to see that the administration took student concerns very seriously. As our class's representative to the Curriculum Committee, I was pleased to be part of the school's efforts to make the curriculum and teaching even better.

### How did you find the social part of your program:

Outstanding. The dean when I was there, Rex Adams, used to put it this way: "No jerks and no weenies." Don't get me wrong—I probably qualify as a weenie, or at least a geek or a nerd. That said, what Rex was getting at was the collaborative culture, the "team Fuqua" ethos that really does pervade the school. I'm sure every major business school is fun and has its share of happy hours, etc. But one thing I loved about Fuqua that I think is unique or at least rare is that the single biggest social convener is a year-long charity effort on behalf of North Carolina Special Olympics—and not just raising money for them, but interacting with the athletes and building bridges to and within the surrounding community. That's pretty cool.

### What was your job search like:

I came in focused on management consulting as an initial career step into business. As a consultant friend had put it to me, a few years as a consultant can act as a kind of "residency" after business school (as if after medical school). There were many other aspects of the consulting path that appealed to me as well. With the immense help of Fuqua's Career Services Office and many second-years (including my teacher friend), I got summer offers from McKinsey, BCG, and Bain and spent the summer with McKinsey. At the end of the summer, McKinsey made me a full-time offer, which I accepted.

## How did the MBA prepare you for your career:

It helped me in several ways:

1. Developing leadership. As a high-school teacher, I was used to directing the activities of students. However, I had only limited opportunities to exercise leadership among my peers. Fuqua gave me a chance to do just that.
2. Developing discipline among chaos. Since business school is so intense and "multifarious," so to speak, it is a great lab in which to figure out how to prioritize a multitude of commitments of differing types.
3. Developing specific knowledge/skills. As a consultant, a film producer, and an executive at a small, growing company, I have frequently drawn on specific ideas and techniques I learned or exercised in business school, from Excel modeling to negotiating contracts.

## What advice do you have for applicants to maximize their application:

Tough one! I think it's very important to figure out WHY you want to go to business school. It's not like, say, dental school: for one thing, you don't need a license to practice business, and also every business-school class contains a variety of folks with different dreams and goals for their career. So you must go into the application process with a strong sense of what you want to go and do.

# Kellogg MBA Perspective

## RACHEL ZLOTOFF (KELLOGG, 2007)

### Prior to MBA Career Experience:
I was a Coordinator at Nickelodeon Consumer Product Dept for three years (first in the apparel/home furnishing division and later in the packaged goods department). I was promoted to a manager position and had the responsibility of managing one person.

### Post-MBA Career Experience:
I did an internship at a consumer goods company in New York after my first year. I then concentrated on the Big Three consumer product companies and fortunately landed a job with one of them, Kraft.

### How many years of work experience did you have prior to the MBA:
Two and a half years.

### What was your greatest concern when applying to business school:
As an early career applicant, I worried that I may not be admitted due to limited work experience. Therefore, I applied to more schools than most (seven programs) to increase my

odds of being admitted. But despite that, I set a realistic expectation for myself: if I didn't get admitted, I had plans to reapply the following year. My application strategy was to show that my career experience was substantive despite working only a few years. It worked since I was admitted to five of the seven schools, including my first choice, Kellogg.

## Why did you select the MBA programs you applied to:

I selected my programs based on their reputation as top schools, plus I focused on programs that had a collaborative environment. The culture of the program was a huge deciding factor for me.

## What was the most interesting part of your MBA program:

I was most impressed by the opportunities offered at my program and the people that I met. They were the most interesting people I have had the fortune to work with. Their backgrounds, intelligence, and incredible achievements were all inspiring. I was constantly challenged each day.

## What surprised you the most about your program:

My greatest surprise was how truly collaborative my classmates were. For example, not having a banking or accounting background, finance and accounting were not easy subjects for me. Classmates from these industries would sit with me and dedicate time to teach me these subjects outside of classes and they wouldn't leave till I got it. Their dedication was unprecedented. Even the professors were accessible and easily approachable. They felt like friends and many of them came to our TG happy hour events.

## How did you find the social part of your program:

I found the overall Kellogg community to be very close and there is more than enough opportunity to connect with your classmates. The real challenge is learning how to balance all the social activities with the academic demands.

## How was your job search at Kellogg:

Kellogg attracted top marketing companies and I had a lot of options when it came to recruiting. I interviewed with different marketing companies and focused my search geographically to Chicago and NYC. I chose Kraft for its marketing quality and general management scope plus its exceptional, best in class training. I was looking for a position that would give me solid training and enable me to build skills that are transferable outside of Marketing. I also found the Career Management Center to be excellent. The career counselors were accessible and highly supportive. So was the Kellogg Career Network which gave students access to hundreds of companies. Everyone I knew graduated with a job, most with multiple offers. Kellogg career opportunities were vast. If you wanted a job in nonprofit, banking, or consulting, you were able to find companies from these different sectors/industries recruiting.

## How did you find the academic part of your MBA and how did the MBA prepare you for your career:

One of the main reasons I wanted an MBA was to build up my analytical abilities especially in terms of using data to drive strategic decision. Today, in my new job, I am working on several strategic projects and am able to draw directly from my business education to come up with new ideas. I also have reached out to my former professors to discuss business issues, even my marketing binders have been great reference points.

## What advice do you have for applicants to maximize their application:

Because networking is so important, make sure the MBA program is a good fit for you. Talk to as many people as possible to learn about their experiences; do not simply use school rankings to select an MBA program.

# GMAT Perspective

## ANDREW YANG (MANAGING DIRECTOR, MANHATTANGMAT)

### What is ManhattanGMAT's unique approach:

ManhattanGMAT pays its instructors four times more than Kaplan or Princeton Review ($100/hr vs. $20–$25/hr), and requires a 99th percentile score (760+, as opposed to a 680) as well as prior teaching experience. By hiring and retaining superior instructors, we are able to offer a more aggressive, ambitious curriculum that focuses on the actual content of the GMAT rather than test-taking methodologies.

### Are you limited to New York or do you offer your services outside of New York:

We have centers in New York, Boston, Chicago, San Francisco/ Bay Area, Los Angeles/Orange County, and Washington DC, and our online courses are available worldwide.

### What advice do you have for applicants who are planning to take the GMAT:

The GMAT is a skill test that presumes your ability to recognize what is being tested. Your skill level will rise with practice and exposure, as will your familiarity with the tested concepts. Be ready to work hard and immerse yourself in the ideas and language of the GMAT, and you'll get better.

## When do you recommend taking a GMAT prep course:
Several months before you plan on taking the test, which would ideally be several months before you intend to apply to business school.

## When are tutors helpful:
Tutors are helpful if you have very specific testing issues that require personalized attention, or if there's a particular type of problem that you can't untangle on your own.

## How much time do you recommend for applicants to invest in preparing for the GMAT:
Three months is a sufficient time frame for most people to re-remember the math and grammar that they've forgotten and simultaneously raise their skill level and familiarity with the GMAT.

## What are the 3 biggest GMAT mistakes that you have seen:

1. Focusing on results, not process. Many students think that they understand a problem because they got the right answer, but they aren't actually able to solve a similar problem or a harder one that tests the same concepts in a different way.
2. Focusing on quantity, not quality. This is a similar point, but many students feel that more is better—i.e. the more problems that they do or practice tests that they take, the better off they'll be. It's much more helpful to your score to dissect and understand a handful of Official Guide problems than to do a large number of them without truly developing your understanding.

3. Underestimating the stress of the testing experience. The GMAT is more stressful than most people anticipate because of the nature of the testing environment and imposed time constraints (most students struggle to finish on time). The best way to alleviate this is to occasionally simulate the stress of the testing environment when one practices, and to build up a sensitivity to solving groups of problems within time limits (i.e. learn what completing 37 or 41 questions in 75 minutes "feels" like and you'll be less affected by the stress).

## How many times do you recommend taking the GMAT:

Ideally, once would be enough! But most people should expect to take it twice, particularly as there's no downside to doing so.

## If I have a GMAT score of 500 is there still hope for me to bring my score up:

Of course! The GMAT is definitely a test that one can improve on, often quite dramatically, with diligence and the right approach.

# MBA RESOURCES

A COLLECTION OF RESOURCES HAS been compiled to help answer additional questions you may have about the business school application.

## COMMUNITY LEADERSHIP

Here are some great websites to link up with socially responsible organizations and explore ways to contribute your leadership in your community:

**VolunteerMatch (www.volunteermatch.org)**
**BoardNetUSA (www.boardnetusa.org)**
**Smart Volunteer (www.smartvolunteer.org)**
**Idealist.org (www.idealist.org)**
**Change.org (www.change.org)**

## WOMEN AND MINORITIES

**Forté Foundation** (www.fortefoundation.org) is an organization that promotes women in business. It provides a variety of resources to women considering a business career and education. Female applicants to business school who are members of the organization receive mentorship support, career advice, and access to women business leaders, and they attend admissions events where they can meet board members and receive scholarships to fund their MBA.

**The National Association of Women MBAs** (www.mbawomen.org) is dedicated to empowering women MBAs and helping them to take on leadership positions in corporate America and to enhance the diversity of the nation's workforce.

**The National Society of Hispanic MBAs** (www.nshmba.org) is an organization that fosters Hispanic leadership through graduate management education and professional development. NSHMBA works to prepare Hispanics for leadership positions throughout the United States so that they can provide the cultural awareness and sensitivity vital in the management of the nation's diverse workforce.

**The National Black MBA Association** (www.nbmbaa.org) is an association that is dedicated to developing partnerships that result in the creation of intellectual and economic wealth in the black community. In partnership with more than 400 of the country's top business organizations, the association has inroads into a wide range of industries as well as the public and private sector.

## GENERAL MBA SITES

**MBA.com** (www.mba.com) is a great website that every applicant to business school ought to visit. It includes information about assessing the value of the MBA to deciding which schools are the best fit for you. It also provides information about the GMAT, including the registration process, sample GMAT exams, and business school resource information.

**BUSINESSWEEK.com** (www.businessweek.com) provides an online community for applicants applying to business school. Applicants are able to read interview transcripts from Admissions Board members at leading MBA programs as well as participate in virtual chats where they can ask questions directly to the board members. Another major draw for applicants is that they can interact with each other through forums and discussion boards. Current MBA students also write about their MBA experiences.

**MBA Podcaster** (www.mbapodcaster.com) has expanded the way information is communicated to prospective MBA candidates. Instead of the traditional online chats, MBA Podcaster uses audio and video services to bring the most current admissions information to business school applicants. MBA Podcaster includes interviews and discussions with authorities in the MBA arena, including business school deans, admissions directors, admissions consultants, corporate recruiters, current students, and alumni. Topics include everything from a behind-the-scenes view of the admission process to post-MBA job opportunities and current market trends. Each in-depth show discusses a particular topic of interest to an MBA applicant and interviews relevant experts to help make the application process more efficient and successful. The moderator/host leads the discussion and draws conclusions to help the listening audience plan effectively for their pursuit of an MBA. The company was founded in January 2006 by Leila Pirnia, an entertainment executive and graduate from Massachusetts Institute of Technology. MBA Podcaster is dedicated to providing listeners with accurate and unbiased information.

**MBA Zone** (www.mbazone.com) was founded by Brenda Mizgorski, a Wharton MBA, nearly ten years ago. This site was one of the first online communities for MBA applicants with information covering the application process, life as an MBA student, and life after business school.

**Vault** (www.vault.com) was started by MBAs who saw a market opportunity that wasn't being filled and jumped on it. They have successfully built an online community and an extensive collection of information, books, and other products covering a variety of careers and universities. This site is helpful for applicants who want to learn more about different careers and what a typical day is like in that industry. Vault also offers a database of available jobs for its members.

**The MBA Tour** (www.thembatour.com) is an independent and high-quality information source regarding MBA admissions. Its events emphasize personal interaction between prospective MBA students, business school admissions representatives, alumni, and other like-minded education enthusiasts. Established in 1993, it has built a strong reputation based on representing top business schools from North America, Europe, Asia, and South America.

## INTERNATIONAL STUDENTS

**InternationalStudent.com** (www.internationalstudents.com) covers information on getting visas, securing financing for an education as an international student, and other international related topics.

**EducationUSA** (www.educationusa.com) is a global network of more than 450 advising centers supported by the Bureau of Educational and Cultural Affairs at the U.S. Department of State.

## SCHOLARSHIPS AND FELLOWSHIPS

**The Consortium Fellowship** (www.cgsm.org) provides financial funding to minority candidates from MBA programs that are members of the consortium organization.

**The Robert Toigo Foundation Fellowship** (www.toigo-foundation.org) provides financial funding, mentorship, and support to minority MBA candidates interested in a career in the financial services industry.

## LOAN RESOURCES

GradLoans.com (www.gradloans.com)
Gate (www.gateloan.com)
CitiAssist (www.citiassist.com)
FastWeb (www.fastweb.com)

# GMAT PREP PROGRAMS

The Graduate Management Admissions Test (GMAT) is a required exam that all top business schools use to assess candidates' academic aptitude. Following is a list of the different GMAT prep companies. You should research each of them to determine the ideal program to help you prepare for this important exam.

**ManhattanGMAT (www.manhattangmat.com)**
**The Princeton Review (www.princetonreview.com)**
**Kaplan (www.kaplan.com)**
**BellCurves (www.bellcurves.com)**
**Manhattan Review (www.manhattanreview.com)**

In addition, the **GMAT Club** (www.GMATclub.com) is an online community for aspiring MBAs to improve their GMAT scores, access admissions experts through online chats, and receive tips on the application through blogs and other resources.

# INDEX

# ABOUT THE AUTHOR

 Chioma Isiadinso is the founder and CEO of EXPARTUS (www.expartus.com), a global admissions consulting and personal branding company that prepares applicants to gain admission to elite schools. Chioma has more than ten years of admissions experience and is a former Admissions Board member at Harvard Business School and former Director of Admissions at Carnegie Mellon University School of Public Policy and Management.

Chioma is a national speaker on the subject of admissions and personal branding. Chioma has been interviewed on CNBC's *Power Lunch* and featured in the *New York Times*, *Black Enterprise*, and *Investor's Business Daily*. She has also published admissions articles for magazines like *Hispanic Magazine* and *Professional Women's Magazine*. She is the recipient of The Network Journal's 2007 40 Under 40 leadership award.

Chioma earned her Master of Education degree from the University of Pittsburgh and graduated from Hobart and William Smith Colleges with a degree in Psychology. Chioma lives in New York City with her husband and son.